Serious Delinquency

An Anthology

Thomas J. Bernard
Pennsylvania State University

Roxbury Publishing Company
Los Angeles, California

Library of Congress Cataloging-in-Publication Data

Serious delinquency : an anthology / Thomas J. Bernard.
p. cm.
Includes bibliographical references.
ISBN 1-933220-37-6 (alk. paper)
1. Juvenile justice, Administration of—United States. 2. Juvenile
delinquency—United States. 3. Juvenile delinquency—United
States—Prevention. I. Bernard, Thomas J.
HV9104.S424 2006
364.360973—dc22   2006017411
                                                        CIP

Serious Delinquency: An Anthology

Publisher: Claude Teweles
Copy Editor: Christy Graunke
Production Editor: Sacha A. Howells
Typography: Pegasus Type, Inc.
Cover Design: Marnie Kenney

Printed on acid-free paper in the United States of America. This
book meets the standards of recycling of the Environmental Protection Agency.

ISBN 1-933220-37-6

ROXBURY PUBLISHING COMPANY
P.O. Box 491044
Los Angeles, California 90049-9044
Voice: (310) 473-3312 • Fax: (310) 473-4490
Website: www.roxbury.net

Contents

Part I

Historical Background

Juvenile justice is an American invention—the first juvenile institution was founded in New York City in 1825 and the first juvenile court was established in Chicago in 1899. Prior to that time, juvenile offenders were tried in the same criminal courts as adults and received the same punishments as adults. The main difference was that, because of their age, juveniles usually received less punishment than adults who committed the same offenses.

There were several differences between the original juvenile court and the criminal courts they replaced. The juvenile court focused more on the *juveniles themselves*, whereas criminal courts focused more on the juveniles' *offenses*. The founders of the juvenile court believed that all children needed the firm but loving control of competent adults, and that delinquency indicated that a child lacked this control. The original juvenile court was to provide the firm but loving control that delinquents, for whatever reason, were not receiving from their own parents.

As it is for any firm but loving parent, the original juvenile court was guided by *the long-term best interests of the child*. Punishment was one option available to achieve this goal—it often is best for children to be punished for their behavior. But other options were also available. What was best for the child determined the actions of the original juvenile court, not the nature of the offense.

The first chapter in Part I provides a brief history of juvenile justice in the United States in the twentieth century. The second chapter examines the larger historical context of juvenile justice by discussing aspects of delinquency and the responses to it that have tended to remain the same since the beginning of recorded time. ✦

Chapter 1

Juvenile Justice
A Century of Change

Office of Juvenile Justice and Delinquency Prevention

Editor's Introduction

Chapter 1 presents an overview of the origin and development of juvenile justice in the United States. It focuses particularly on the origin and development of the juvenile court at the beginning of the twentieth century, including its original "parental" focus on the "best interests" of the child. It then discusses recent changes, mostly implemented since about 1990, that make the juvenile court more like a criminal court. Instead of focusing on the "best interests" of the child, the focus now is much more on providing proportional punishments for offenses.

As the juvenile court has become more like the criminal court, the ways to transfer juveniles into criminal court have expanded. The final part of Chapter 1 describes the three basic mechanisms by which juveniles may be transferred to criminal court. These are best understood by thinking about who makes the decision.

In "judicial waiver," *the juvenile court judge is the decision maker* (the term "judicial" refers to the judge). In these cases, the juvenile court has "original jurisdiction" over the juvenile but the juvenile court judge agrees to "waive" (i.e., give up) that jurisdiction and transfer the case to criminal court. "Original jurisdiction" means that the law, as enacted by the state legislature, specifies that this case is to be handled in juvenile court.

The state legislature also can pass laws that specify that juveniles who commit certain offenses are excluded from the jurisdiction of the juvenile court. If this is done, then "original jurisdiction" for these offenses lies in criminal court, even though the offender is underage. This is called "statutory exclusion." In

Adapted from Office of Juvenile Justice and Delinquency Prevention, "Juvenile Justice: A Century of Change," *1999 National Report Series, Juvenile Justice Bulletin*. Washington, DC: U.S. Department of Justice, 1999. Copyright is not claimed in this article, a publication of the United States government.

this case, *the state legislators are the decision makers* since they decide which offenses shall and shall not be handled in juvenile court. With statutory exclusion, the juvenile court does not "waive" jurisdiction because it did not have jurisdiction to begin with.

A third type of transfer is called "concurrent jurisdiction." In this case, the state legislators decide that some offenses are under the jurisdiction of both the criminal and juvenile courts (the word "concurrent" means "at the same time"). In this case, *the prosecutor is the decision maker* because the prosecutor chooses which court to file the case in. If the prosecutor files in criminal court, then the case is tried there and the juvenile court judge has no say over the matter.

Besides these three transfer mechanisms, many states now have so-called "blended sentences," all of which cross the boundary between juvenile and criminal courts. The most common type of blended sentence allows a juvenile court judge to sentence a juvenile offender to adult time. Another type of blended sentence allows a criminal court judge to sentence defendants who are under the age of 18 to time in the juvenile system, even though they have been legally defined as adults.

All of these mechanisms reflect the many ways in which the juvenile system is moving towards the adult. What formerly was a fairly rigid barrier between the juvenile and adult justice systems has now become quite permeable.

✦ ✦ ✦

Early in U.S. History, Children Who Broke the Law Were Treated the Same as Adult Criminals

Throughout the late 18th century, "infants" below the age of reason (traditionally age 7) were presumed to be incapable of criminal intent and were, therefore, exempt from prosecution and punishment. Children as young as 7, however, could stand trial in criminal court for offenses committed and, if found guilty, could be sentenced to prison or even to death.

The 19th-century movement that led to the establishment of the juvenile court in the U.S. had its roots in 16th-century European educational reform movements. These earlier reform movements changed the perception of children from one of miniature adults to one of persons with less than fully developed moral and cognitive capacities.

As early as 1825, the Society for the Prevention of Juvenile Delinquency was advocating the separation of juvenile and adult offenders. Soon, facilities exclusively for juveniles were established in most major cities. By mid-century, these privately operated youth "prisons" were under criticism for various abuses. Many States then took on the responsibility of operating juvenile facilities.

The First Juvenile Court in This Country Was Established in Cook County, Illinois, in 1899

Illinois passed the Juvenile Court Act of 1899, which established the Nation's first juvenile court. The British doctrine of *parens patriae* (the State as parent) was the rationale for the right of the State to intervene in the lives of children in a manner different from the way it intervenes in the lives of adults. The doctrine was interpreted to mean that, because children were not of full legal capacity, the State had the inherent power and responsibility to provide protection for children whose natural parents were not providing appropriate care or supervision. A key element was the focus on the welfare of the child. Thus, the delinquent child was also seen as in need of the court's benevolent intervention.

Juvenile Courts Flourished for the First Half of the 20th Century

By 1910, 32 States had established juvenile courts and/or probation services. By 1925, all but two States had followed suit. Rather than merely punishing delinquents for their crimes, juvenile courts sought to turn delinquents into productive citizens—through treatment.

The mission to help children in trouble was stated clearly in the laws that established juvenile courts. This benevolent mission led to procedural and substantive differences between the juvenile and criminal justice systems.

During the next 50 years, most juvenile courts had exclusive original jurisdiction over all youth under age 18 who were charged with violating criminal laws. Only if the juvenile court waived its jurisdiction in a case could a child be transferred to criminal court and tried as an adult. Transfer decisions were made on a case-by-case basis using a "best interests of the child and public" standard, and were thus within the realm of individualized justice.

The Focus on Offenders and Not Offenses, on Rehabilitation and Not Punishment, Had Substantial Procedural Impact

Unlike the criminal justice system, where district attorneys select cases for trial, the juvenile court controlled its own intake. And unlike criminal prosecutors, juvenile court intake considered extra-legal as well as legal factors in deciding how to handle cases. Juvenile court intake also had discretion to handle cases informally, bypassing judicial action.

In the courtroom, juvenile court hearings were much less formal than criminal court proceedings. In this benevolent court—with the express purpose of protecting children—due process protections afforded criminal defendants were deemed unnecessary. In the early juvenile courts, and even in some to this day, attorneys for the State and the youth are not considered essential to the operation of the system, especially in less serious cases.

A range of dispositional options was available to a judge wanting to help rehabilitate a child. Regardless of offense, outcomes ranging from warnings to probation supervision to training school confinement could be part of the treatment plan. Dispositions were tailored to "the best interests of the child." Treatment lasted until the child was "cured" or became an adult (age 21), whichever came first.

As Public Confidence in the Treatment Model Waned, Due Process Protections Were Introduced

In the 1950's and 1960's, many came to question the ability of the juvenile court to succeed in rehabilitating delinquent youth. The treatment techniques available to juvenile justice professionals never reached the desired levels of effectiveness. Although the goal of rehabilitation through individualized justice—the basic philosophy of the juvenile justice system—was not in question, professionals were concerned about the growing number of juveniles institutionalized indefinitely in the name of treatment.

In a series of decisions beginning in the 1960's, the U.S. Supreme Court required that juvenile courts become more formal—more like criminal courts. Formal hearings were now required in waiver situations, and delinquents facing possible confinement were given protection against self-incrimination and rights to receive notice of the charges against them, to present witnesses, to question witnesses, and to have an attorney. Proof "beyond a reasonable doubt" rather than merely "a preponderance of evidence" was now required for an adjudication. The Supreme Court, however, still held that there were enough "differences of substance between the criminal and juvenile courts . . . to hold that a jury is not required in the latter. . . ."

In the 1980's, the Pendulum Began to Swing Toward Law and Order

During the 1980's, the public perceived that serious juvenile crime was increasing and that the system was too lenient with offenders. Although there was substantial misperception regarding increases in juvenile crime, many States responded by passing more punitive laws. Some laws removed certain classes of offenders from the juvenile justice system and handled them as adult criminals in criminal court. Others required the juvenile justice system to be more like the criminal justice system and to treat certain classes of juvenile offenders as criminals but in juvenile court. . . .

The 1990's Have Been a Time of Unprecedented Change as State Legislatures Crack Down on Juvenile Crime

Five areas of change have emerged as States passed laws designed to crack down on juvenile crime. These laws generally involve expanded eligibility for criminal court processing and adult correctional sanctioning and reduced confidentiality protections for a subset of juvenile offenders. Between 1992 and 1997, all but three States changed laws in one or more of the following areas:

- Transfer provisions—Laws made it easier to transfer juvenile offenders from the juvenile justice system to the criminal justice system (45 States).

- Sentencing authority—Laws gave criminal and juvenile courts expanded sentencing options (31 States).

- Confidentiality—Laws modified or removed traditional juvenile court confidentiality provisions by making records and proceedings more open (47 States).

In addition to these areas, there was change relating to:

- Victims rights—Laws increased the role of victims of juvenile crime in the juvenile justice process (22 States).

- Correctional programming—As a result of new transfer and sentencing laws, adult and juvenile correctional administrators developed new programs.

The 1980's and 1990's have seen significant change in terms of treating more juvenile offenders as criminals. Recently, States have been attempting to strike a balance in their juvenile justice systems among system and offender accountability, offender competency development, and community protection. Juvenile code purpose clauses also incorporate restorative justice language (offenders repair the harm done to victims and communities and accept responsibility for their criminal actions). Many States have added to the purpose clauses of their juvenile codes phrases such as:

- Hold juveniles accountable for criminal behavior.

- Provide effective deterrents.

- Protect the public from criminal activity.

- Balance attention to offenders, victims, and the community.

- Impose punishment consistent with the seriousness of the crime. . . .

All States Allow Juveniles to Be Tried as Adults in Criminal Court Under Certain Circumstances

Transferring Juveniles to Criminal Court Is Not a New Phenomenon

In some States, provisions that enabled transfer of certain juveniles to criminal court were in place before the 1920's. Other States have permitted transfers since at least the 1940's. For many years, all States have had at least one provision for trying certain youth of juvenile age as adults in criminal court. Such provisions are typically limited by age and offense criteria. Transfer mechanisms vary regarding where the responsibility for transfer decisionmaking lies.

Transfer provisions fall into three general categories:

Judicial waiver: The juvenile court judge has the authority to waive juvenile court jurisdiction and transfer the case to criminal court. States may use terms other than judicial waiver. Some call the process *certification, remand,* or *bind over* for criminal prosecution. Others *transfer* or *decline* rather than waive jurisdiction.

Concurrent jurisdiction: Original jurisdiction for certain cases is shared by both criminal and juvenile courts, and the prosecutor has discretion to file such cases in either court. Transfer under concurrent jurisdiction provisions is also known as *prosecutorial waiver, prosecutor discretion,* or *direct file.*

Statutory exclusion: State statute excludes certain juvenile offenders from juvenile court jurisdiction. Under statutory exclusion provisions, cases originate in criminal rather than juvenile court. Statutory exclusion is also known as *legislative exclusion.*

Many States Have Changed the Boundaries of Juvenile Court Jurisdiction

Traditionally, discretionary judicial waiver was the transfer mechanism on which most States relied. Beginning in the 1970's and continuing through the present, however, State legislatures have increasingly moved juvenile offenders into criminal court based on age and/or offense seriousness, without the case-specific consideration offered by the discretionary juvenile court judicial waiver process.

State transfer provisions changed extensively in the 1990's. From 1992 through 1997, all but six States enacted or expanded transfer provisions. An increasing number of State legislatures have enacted mandatory waiver or exclusion statutes. Less common, then and now, are concurrent jurisdiction provisions.

In Most States, Juveniles Convicted in Criminal Court Cannot Be Tried in Juvenile Court for Subsequent Offenses

In 31 States, juveniles who have been tried as adults must be prosecuted in criminal court for any subsequent offenses. Nearly all of these "once an adult/always an adult" provisions require that the youth must have been convicted of the offenses that triggered the initial criminal prosecution.

Judicial Waiver Is the Most Common Transfer Provision

In all States except Nebraska, New Mexico, and New York, juvenile court judges may waive jurisdiction over certain cases and transfer them to criminal court. Such action is usually in response to a request by the prosecutor; in several States, however, juveniles or their parents may request judicial waiver. In most States, statutes limit waiver by age and offense.

Waiver provisions vary in terms of the degree of decisionmaking flexibility allowed. Under some waiver provisions, the decision is entirely *discretionary*. Under others, there is a rebuttable *presumption* in favor of waiver. Under others, waiver is *mandatory* once the juvenile court judge determines that certain statutory criteria have been met. Mandatory waiver provisions are distinguished from statutory exclusion provisions in that the case originates in juvenile rather than criminal court.

Statutes Establish Waiver Criteria Other Than Age and Offense

In some States, waiver provisions target youth charged with offenses involving firearms or other weapons. Most State statutes also limit judicial waiver to juveniles who are "no longer amenable to treatment." The specific factors that determine lack of amenability vary, but typically include the juvenile's offense history and previous dispositional outcomes. Such amenability criteria are generally not included in statutory exclusion or concurrent jurisdiction provisions.

Many statutes instruct juvenile courts to consider other factors when making waiver decisions, such as the availability of dispositional alternatives for treating the juvenile, the time available for sanctions, public safety, and the best interests of the child. The waiver process must also adhere to certain constitutional principles of fairness. . . .

Few States Allow Prosecutorial Discretion, but Many Juveniles Are Tried as Adults in This Way

As of the end of the 1997 legislative session, 15 States had concurrent jurisdiction provisions, which gave both juvenile court and criminal court original jurisdiction in certain cases. Thus, prosecutors have discretion to file such cases in either court.

State appellate courts have taken the view that prosecutor discretion is equivalent to the routine charging decisions made in criminal cases. Thus, prosecutorial transfer is considered an "executive function," which is not subject to judicial review and is not required to meet the due process standards established in *Kent*. Some States, however, have written prosecutorial transfer guidelines.

Concurrent jurisdiction is typically limited by age and offense criteria. Often concurrent jurisdiction is limited to cases involving serious, violent, or repeat crimes or offenses involving firearms or other weapons. Juvenile and criminal courts often also share jurisdiction over minor offenses such as traffic, watercraft, or local ordinance violations.

There are no national data at the present time on the number of juvenile cases tried in criminal court under concurrent jurisdiction provisions. Florida alone reports an average of nearly 5,000 such transfers per year.

Statutory Exclusion Accounts for the Largest Number of Juveniles Tried as Adults in Criminal Court

Legislatures "transfer" large numbers of young offenders to criminal court by enacting statutes that exclude certain cases from juvenile court jurisdiction. As of the end of the 1997 legislative session, 28 States had statutory exclusions. Although not typically thought of as transfers, large numbers of youth under age 18 are tried as adults in the 13 States where the upper age of juvenile court jurisdiction is 15 or 16. If the 1.8 million 16- and 17-year-olds in these 13 States are referred to criminal court at the same rate that 16- and 17-year-olds are referred to juvenile court in other States, then as many as 218,000 cases involving youth under the age of 18 could have faced trial in criminal court in 1996 because the offenders were defined as adults under State laws.

Many States exclude certain serious offenses from juvenile court jurisdiction. State laws typically also set age limits for excluded offenses. The offenses most often excluded are capital crimes and murders, and other serious offenses against persons. Some States exclude juveniles charged with felonies if they have prior felony adjudications or convictions. Minor offenses, such as traffic, watercraft, fish, or game violations, are often excluded from juvenile court jurisdiction in States where they are not covered by concurrent jurisdiction provisions.

Criminal Courts May Transfer Cases to Juvenile Court or Order Juvenile Sanctions

Of the 35 States with statutory exclusion or concurrent jurisdiction provisions, 20 also have provisions for transferring "excluded" or "direct filed" cases from criminal court to juvenile court under certain circumstances. This procedure is sometimes referred to as "reverse" waiver or transfer. In some States, juveniles tried as adults in criminal court may be transferred to juvenile court for disposition. Some States allow juveniles tried as adults in criminal court to receive dispositions involving either criminal or juvenile court sanctions, under what have come to be known as "blended sentencing" provisions. . . .

New Laws Have Had a Dramatic Impact on Sentencing for Serious or Violent Juvenile Offenders

A Trend Away From Traditional Juvenile Dispositions Is Emerging

Juvenile court dispositions were traditionally based on the offender's individual characteristics and situation. Dispositions were frequently indeterminate and generally had rehabilitation as a primary goal. As many States have shifted the purpose of juvenile court away from rehabilitation and toward punishment, accountability, and public safety, the emerging trend is toward dispositions based more on the offense than the offender. Offense-based dispositions tend to be determinate and proportional to the offense; retribution and deterrence replace rehabilitation as the primary goal.

Many State Legislatures Have Changed Disposition and Sentencing Options

From 1992 through 1997, statutes requiring mandatory minimum periods of incarceration for certain violent or serious offenders were added or modified in 16 States.

States have also raised the maximum age of the juvenile court's continuing jurisdiction over juvenile offenders. Such laws allow juvenile courts to order dispositions that extend beyond the upper age of original jurisdiction, most often to age 21. From 1992 through 1997, 17 States extended their age limit for delinquency dispositions.

Perhaps the most dramatic change will result from "blended sentences." Blended sentencing statutes, which allow courts to impose juvenile and/or adult correctional sanctions on certain young offenders, were in place in 20 States at the end of 1997. . . .

Blended sentencing options create a "middle ground" between traditional juvenile sanctions and adult sanctions. . . .

Juvenile-exclusive blend: The juvenile court may impose a sanction involving either the juvenile or adult correctional systems. . . .

Juvenile-inclusive blend: The juvenile court may impose both juvenile and adult correctional sanctions. The adult sanction is suspended pending a violation and revocation. . . .

Juvenile-contiguous blend: The juvenile court may impose a juvenile correctional sanction that may remain in force after the offender is beyond the age of the court's extended jurisdiction, at which point the offender may be transferred to the adult correctional system. . . .

Criminal-exclusive blend: The criminal court may impose a sanction involving either the juvenile or adult correctional systems. . . .

Criminal-inclusive blend: The criminal court may impose both juvenile and adult correctional sanctions. The adult sanction is suspended, but is reinstated if the terms of the juvenile sanction are violated and revoked. . . . ✦

Chapter 2

The Cycle of Juvenile Justice

Thomas J. Bernard

Editor's Introduction

Chapter 2 places our present juvenile justice system in a larger historical context. It argues that there is a cyclical pattern to handling juvenile offenders that repeats itself over the long span of history. This pattern is driven by the tendency of adults to always be dissatisfied with kids and their behavior. No matter what kids are actually like, adults always seem to believe that "kids today are no good."

The continual dissatisfaction with kids generates continual dissatisfaction with the juvenile justice system. No matter what the system is like, people tend to blame it, at least in part, for the fact that "kids today are no good." So there is a continual drive to reform the system, with the result that the system itself tends to alternate between harshness and leniency.

For example, the chapter states that young males have always been a high crime rate group, and it argues that they always will be. But people really don't like this and they want something done about it. At least in part, they blame whatever juvenile justice policy is in effect at the time, and they then reform that policy.

If this chapter is correct, then young males will continue to be a high crime rate group in the future, and the public will eventually start to blame the "get tough" policies described in Chapter 1. Then there will be another round of reforms and the "get tough" policies will be replaced.

❖ ❖ ❖

Five aspects of juvenile delinquency and juvenile justice have stayed the same for at least two hundred years:

Adapted from *The Cycle of Juvenile Justice* by Thomas J. Bernard, pp. 21–41. Copyright © 1992 by Oxford University Press, Inc. Used by permission of Oxford University Press, Inc.

1. Juveniles, especially young males, commit more crime than other groups.

2. There are special laws that only juveniles are required to obey.

3. Juveniles are punished less severely than adults who commit the same offenses.

4. Many people believe that the current group of juveniles commits more frequent and serious crime than juveniles in the past; that is, there is a "juvenile crime wave" at the present time.

5. Many people blame juvenile justice policies for the supposed "juvenile crime wave," arguing that they are too lenient (serious offenders laugh at "kiddie court") or that they are too harsh (minor offenders are embittered and channeled into a life of crime). . . .

The Behavior of Youth, Especially Young Males

Regardless of whether crime is high or low at a particular time or place, young people (and especially young males) commit a greater proportion of the crime than would be expected from their proportion in the population. . . .[1]

Even when juvenile arrest rates were what we now consider low, people were concerned about how much crime juveniles committed. For example, in 1938, England was alarmed by a report that found that convictions of males peaked at age 13, and that the probability of conviction was greater from ages 11 to 17 than at any other age.[2] In the United States, a report in 1940 pointed out that "young people between 15 and 21 constitute only 13% of the population above 15, but their share in the total volume of serious crime committed far exceeds their proportionate representation."[3] Extensive publicity about the "juvenile crime wave" followed in 1941 and 1942.[4] The FBI supported this publicity with statistics that showed big increases in delinquency, but the Children's Bureau, a government agency that also monitored delinquency, said that the increases were due to changes in reporting practices by police and court agencies.

These concerns are not confined to our century. In the middle of the 1800s, many young men roamed around the "Wild West" with guns strapped to their hips looking for trouble. Although stories about people like Billy the Kid were exaggerated into legends, it was still an exceptionally violent period. . . .[5]

Gang fights are often viewed as a modern phenomenon, but Shakespeare's play *Romeo and Juliet*, set in fifteenth-century Italy, revolves around what we would now call a gang fight. The young men of the

Montague family, which included Romeo, had been in running battle with the young men of the Capulet family, which included Juliet. On a hot summer day with "the mad blood stirring," the two groups happened to run into each other on the street. In the initial exchange, a polite greeting ("Gentlemen, good day: a word with one of you") was answered by a challenge to fight ("And but one word with one of us? Couple it with something: make it a word and a blow"). After a few more exchanges, the fight began and two youths, both about 16 years old, were killed. . . .

We could continue this tale back to the first crime recorded in the Bible, in which Cain (the eldest son of Adam and Eve) killed his younger brother Abel. Ever since then, young people in general, and young men in particular, have been committing crimes at a greater rate than other people. We are always aware of this phenomenon but tend to lose track of the fact that it has always been this way. . . .

Special Laws for Juveniles

A second aspect that has stayed the same for at least two hundred years (and seems to have remained constant over recorded history) is that certain offenses apply only to youths, not adults. At the present, these are called *status offenses*, since they only apply to people with the status of being a juvenile. The most common of these laws today are laws against running away from home, refusing to attend school (truancy), and refusing to obey parents (incorrigibility). . . .

Originally, offenses that applied solely to youths focused on the duties that people held for their parents. In the Code of Moses in the Bible, for example, there were severe penalties including death for striking or cursing your parents,[6] although these severe punishments were rarely carried out in practice.

The Puritans made these Biblical passages the basis for a "stubborn child" law in 1646.[7] That law "served as a direct or indirect model for legislation enacted by every American state making children's misbehavior a punishable offense." It was substantially modified through the years but remained in force in Massachusetts until 1973. Since the days of the Puritans, there has been a continual expansion of attempts to control the non-criminal but "offensive" behavior of children through legal means. . . .

Mitigation of Punishments for Juveniles

A third aspect that has stayed the same for at least two hundred years (and indeed over history) is that juveniles are treated more leniently than adults when they commit the same offenses. . . .

The Code of Hammurabi, written over 4,000 years ago, indicated that juveniles were to be treated more leniently than adults. In ancient Jewish law, the Talmud specified the conditions under which immaturity was to be considered for more lenient punishment. Under these provisions, there was no corporal punishment before the age of puberty, which was set at 12 for females and 13 for males, and no capital punishment before the age of 20. Similar leniency was found among the Moslems, where children under the age of 17 were generally exempt from retaliation and the death penalty, although they could be corrected.

Roman law also included a lengthy history of mitigated punishments for children. As early as the Twelve Tables (about 450 B.C.), there was absolute immunity from punishment for children below a certain age. Originally, immunity applied only to children who were incapable of speech, but eventually it was applied to all children below the age of 7. In addition, children below puberty have been given reduced punishment under Roman Law since around the year 500 A.D. Justinian, for example, established puberty at 14 for boys and 12 for girls. In between age 7 and puberty, criminal responsibility was made dependent on age, nature of offense, and mental capacity.

Under ancient Saxon law, a child below the age of 12 could not be found guilty of any felony, and a child between 12 and 14 might be acquitted or convicted on the basis of natural capacity. After 14 there was no mitigation.

English common law had acquired its modern form by about the middle of the 1300s, and was summarized by Blackstone in 1769.[8] In general, the law at that time was based on the following framework for mitigating punishments:

> Below the age of seven, juveniles have no responsibility for their actions and therefore cannot be punished for any crimes they commit.

> From seven to 14, juveniles are presumed to lack responsibility for their actions, but the prosecution can argue that they should be punished in spite of their youth.

> From 14 to 21, juveniles are presumed to be responsible for their actions, but the defense can argue that they should not be punished, despite their age.

> After the age of 21, everyone is responsible for their actions and therefore is punished to the full extent of the law. . . .

Views of Adults About the Behavior of Youth

According to Donovan, "every generation since the dawn of time has denounced the rising generation as being inferior in terms of manners and morals, ethics and honesty."[9] The view that adults have of juveniles is separate from how juveniles actually behave. This view goes as far back as history records, so it probably will remain the same into the future. . . .

For example, in 1989, *Time Magazine* described "the beast that has broken loose in some of America's young people"[10]. . . .

> . . . Juvenile crime appears to be more widespread and vicious than ever before. . . . Adolescents have always been violence prone, but there are horrendous crimes being committed by even younger children. . . . The offenders are overwhelmingly male, but girls too are capable of vicious crimes. . . . What is chilling about many of the young criminals is that they show no remorse or conscience, at least initially. Youths brag about their exploits and shrug off victims' pain.

The author suggested that this recent "upsurge in the most violent types of crimes by teens" began in 1983.

However, five years before this juvenile crime wave apparently began, *Time Magazine* seemed to be just as alarmed about the juvenile crime problem:

> Across the U.S., a pattern of crime has emerged that is both perplexing and appalling. Many youngsters appear to be robbing and raping, maiming and murdering as casually as they go to a movie or join a pickup baseball game. A new, remorseless, mutant juvenile seems to have been born, and there is no more terrifying figure in America today.[11]

The author of the 1989 article must have neglected to read this 1978 article. How could the wave of juvenile violence start in 1983 if *Time* had already carried an article about it in 1978?

. . . [I]n 1964, the long-time head of the FBI J. Edgar Hoover was similarly convinced that things had changed:

> In the Twenties and Thirties, juvenile delinquency, in general, meant such things as truancy, minor vandalism and petty theft. Today, the term includes armed robbery, assault and even murder. . . . We should not permit actual crimes to be thought of in terms of the delinquencies of a past era. I am not speaking of the relatively minor misdemeanors usually associated with the process of growing up. It is the killings, the rapes and robberies of innocent people by youthful criminals that concern me.[12]

Ten years earlier, in 1954, a New York City judge made a similar statement in *Newsweek*, except that he described the low juvenile crime as being in the 1900s and 1910s, rather than in the 1920s and 1930s:

> Back before the First World War, it was a rare day when you saw a man under 25 up for a felony. Today it's the rule. And today when one of these kids robs a bank he doesn't rush for a businesslike getaway. He stays

around and shoots up a couple of clerks. Not long ago I asked such a boy why, and he said: "I get a kick out of it when I see blood running."[13]

. . . Similar alarms were raised in the 1940s, 1930s, and 1920s.[14] At those times, people believed (as they do today) that the country was being overwhelmed in a rising tide of juvenile delinquency and crime, and that it had not been a serious problem only forty or fifty years ago. Juvenile crime itself seems to go up and down, but the quotations about how terrible juveniles are seem to stay the same. Whether juvenile crime is high or low, many people believe that it is worse today than ever before.

Belief That Juvenile Justice Policy Increases Crime

. . . Presently, widespread concern exists that lenient treatment increases juvenile crime. But that concern tends to alternate in history with the opposite concern: that harsh punishment increases juvenile crime. Let us look at these two concerns historically. . . .

Before the establishment of the first juvenile institution in New York City in 1825, only adult prisons were available for punishing juveniles. These were viewed as very harsh places that would increase the likelihood that juveniles would commit more crime. Prosecutors, judges, and juries in the criminal courts all naturally tried to avoid sending juvenile offenders to these institutions, with the result that many were freed with no punishment at all.[15]

The chief judge in New York was concerned that freeing these juveniles without any punishment encouraged them to commit further crime. He helped establish the first juvenile institution to receive these youngsters who otherwise would get off scot-free. One year after the establishment of the institution, the New York City District Attorney stated that the new institution had solved the problem.[16]

Around that same time, a "Report of the Committee for Investigating the Causes of the Alarming Increase of Juvenile Delinquency in the Metropolis" was issued in London that expressed similar concerns.[17] The problem, as it existed in both London and New York, was that only harsh punishments were available in the adult system, but that the natural tendency to provide more lenient treatments to juveniles resulted in many of them being let off without any punishment whatsoever. The juvenile justice system was originally invented to correct this problem: its goal was to provide some punishments for those who were receiving no punishments at all from the adult system. . . .

. . . The judge in New York City in the early 1820s was . . . concerned that letting juveniles off scot-free would encourage them to

commit crime. That same judge was also concerned that sending juveniles to the prisons and jails would be "a fruitful source of pauper-
ism, a nursery of new vices and crimes, and a college for the
perfection of adepts in guilt."[18] That is, this judge had to choose between providing harsh punishments or doing nothing at all, and he
believed that both choices increased crime among juveniles.

A similar concern about harshness later provided the motivation
for establishing the first juvenile court in Chicago in 1899. . . . Because of an Illinois Supreme Court decision in 1870, lenient handling
of juvenile offenders was severely restricted. This meant that juvenile
justice officials faced the same dilemma as the earlier officials in New
York City: they either had to provide harsh punishments to juvenile
offenders or they could do nothing at all. Like the New York City
judge, they believed that both choices increased crime among juveniles. The juvenile court was invented partly to provide lenient treatments for juveniles who were being harshly punished in Chicago's
jails and poorhouses, and partly to provide lenient treatments for
juveniles for whom nothing was being done at all in the adult
courts. . . .

If you think about the problem faced by officials in New York and
London in the early 1800s and in Chicago in the late 1800s, then it becomes apparent that the concern that leniency causes juvenile crime
and that harshness causes juvenile crime are really two sides of the
same coin. . . . If juvenile justice policies provide harsh punishments,
then some juveniles will receive those punishments but others will receive no punishment at all because the punishments seem inappropriate and counterproductive. Concern about the effectiveness of
these policies arises because both of these two choices are thought to
increase crime.

But if the policies provide lenient treatments, then many juveniles
receive the treatments but some laugh and feel free to commit serious
crime with impunity. Concern about the effectiveness of these policies arises because people believe that if we had only "gotten tough"
with these juveniles earlier, then the serious crimes would never have
occurred.

The Cycle of Juvenile Justice

. . . The "cycle of juvenile justice" arises from the fact that juvenile
crime rates remain high, regardless of justice policies that are in effect at the time. But many people are always convinced that these
high rates only occurred recently, that back in the "good old days" juvenile crime was low, and that juvenile crime would be low again if
only we had the proper justice policies in effect. These people then

generate continual pressure to abandon whatever justice policies are in effect at the time and replace them with new policies. Because only a limited number of policies are possible to begin with, the result is that the juvenile justice system tends to cycle back and forth between harshness and leniency.

Notes

1. Travis Hirschi and Michael Gottfredson, "Age and the Explanation of Crime," *American Journal of Sociology*, 89:552–84 (1983). See also Frank R. Donovan, *Wild Kids*, Stackpole, Harrisburg, 1967 and Wiley B. Sanders, ed., *Juvenile Offenders for a Thousand Years*, University of North Carolina Press, Chapel Hill, 1970.

2. Christopher Hibbert, *The Roots of Evil: A Social History of Crime and Punishment*, Little Brown, Boston, 1963, p. 433.

3. Quoted in Negley K. Teeters and David Matza, "The Extent of Delinquency in the United States," pp. 2–15 in Ruth Shonle Cavan, ed., *Readings in Juvenile Delinquency*, Lippincott, Philadephia, 1964, p. 4.

4. James Gilbert, *A Cycle of Outrage*, Oxford, New York, 1986, pp. 24–26.

5. James A. Inciardi, Alan A. Block, and Lyle A. Hallowell, *Historical Approaches to Crime*, Sage, Beverly Hills, 1977, pp. 59–89.

6. Exodus 21:15; Leviticus 20:9.

7. John R. Sutton, *Stubborn Children*, University of California Press, Berkeley, 1988, p. 11. See also Lee E. Teitelbaum and Leslie J. Harris, "Some Historical Perspectives on Governmental Regulation of Children and Parents," in Teitelbaum and Aiden R. Gough, eds., *Beyond Control: Status Offenders in the Juvenile Court*, Ballinger, Cambridge, MA, 1977, pp. 1–44.

8. Sir William Blackstone, *Commentaries on the Laws of England, IV*, London, 1795, p. 23.

9. Donovan, op. cit., p. 11.

10. Anastasia Toufexis, "Our Violent Kids," *Time Magazine*, June 12, 1989, pp. 52–58. See also the editorial "Meltdown in Our Cities," in *U.S. News and World Report*, May 29, 1989, for similar arguments.

11. "The Youth Crime Plague," *Time Magazine*, July 11, 1977, pp. 18–28.

12. John Edgar Hoover, "Juvenile Delinquency or Youthful Criminality?" *Syracuse Law Review* 15(4): 660–68, Summer, 1964. For a similar article written one year earlier, see Judith Viorst, "Delinquency! National Crisis," *Science News Letter*, 84:202–3 (September 28, 1963).

13. "Our Vicious Young Hoodlums: Is There Any Hope?" *Newsweek Magazine* 44:43–44 (September 6, 1954).

14. E.g., J. Edgar Hoover, "The Crime Wave We Now Face," *The New York Times Magazine*, April 21, 1946, pp. 26–27; "Children Without Morals,"

Time Magazine 40:24 (October 5, 1942); Leonard V. Harrison and Pryor M. Grant, *Youth in the Toils*, Macmillan, New York, 1939; Clyde A. Tolson, "Youth and Crime," *Vital Speeches* 2:468–72 (April 20, 1936); and "Youth Leads the Criminal Parade," *The Literary Digest*, 113:20 (April 23, 1932). For alarms raised in even earlier times, see Archer Butler Hulbert, "The Habit of Going to the Devil," *Atlantic Monthly* 138:804–6 (December, 1926).

15. Robert M. Mennel, *Thorns and Thistles*, University Press of New England, Hanover, NH, 1973, pp. xxv–xxvi.

16. Bradford Kinney Peirce, *A Half Century with Juvenile Delinquents*, Patterson-Smith, Montclair, 1969, p. 79.

17. Sanders, op. cit., p. 111.

18. Quoted in Peirce, op. cit., 41–42. ✦

The Nature and Extent of Juvenile Offending

People usually believe that juvenile crime is higher than ever before, regardless of whether juvenile crime itself is high or low. Part II examines whether that common public perception is true at the moment.

The first chapter relies on the FBI's Uniform Crime Reporting (UCR) program. This report has been published annually since 1929, and is the most commonly cited source of information about crime rates. It analyzes data collected by 17,000 law enforcement agencies nationwide, representing over 94 percent of the population of the United States.

The second chapter relies on data from the National Crime Victimization Survey (NCVS), which is conducted each year by the Bureau of Justice Statistics, an agency in the U.S. Department of Justice. Data are obtained from a nationally representative sample of 42,000 households, with a total of nearly 76,000 persons. The people are asked to report on any criminal victimization they have experienced in the preceding year. Using this data, the Bureau of Justice Statistics estimates the national rates of victimization for crimes such as rape, sexual assault, robbery, assault, theft, household burglary, and motor vehicle theft, both for the population as a whole as well as for specific subgroups of the population such as women, the elderly, members of minority groups, and juveniles. They also can estimate the rates of offending for the population as a whole and for various subgroups, including juveniles.

Between these two chapters, you should be able to get a fairly comprehensive look at the nature and extent of juvenile offending. Thus, it can shed light on the issue of whether "kids today are no good." ✦

Chapter 3

Juvenile Arrests 2002

Howard N. Snyder

Editor's Introduction

Chapter 3 focuses on changes in juvenile crime between 1980 and 2002. The chapter uses two types of data from the FBI's Uniform Crime Reports: the number of arrests involving people under age 18,[1] and the number of crimes reported to police that are "cleared" (or solved) by the arrest of one or more persons where none of them are age 18 or older.

These two measures provide somewhat different assessments of the extent of juvenile crime.[2] The reason is that *arrests count the number of offenders, while clearances count the number of offenses.* Juveniles are more likely to commit crimes in groups, so that one crime may result in several arrests of juveniles. At the same time, adults are more likely to be "professional" criminals, so that one arrest of an adult can clear multiple crimes. Thus, arrest statistics tend to over-represent the contribution of juveniles to the crime problem. Clearances are more useful for gauging the extent to which juveniles are responsible for crime in America. Nevertheless, both sets of figures are useful in gauging the extent of juvenile crime. The picture is actually fairly optimistic. In general, property crime by juveniles declined over that period. There was an increase in violent crime until the early 1990s, after which there have been steep declines.

This chapter is intended to give a sense of how juvenile crime has changed over the past few decades, but you can also look at changes over the longer run. The general pattern is that juvenile crime has been declining at least since 1975.[3] For example, in 2004 the UCR reported that arrests of juveniles accounted for 17.3 percent of all arrests. But in 1970 the UCR reported that arrests of juveniles accounted for about 45 percent of all arrests.[4] Obviously, there has been a very large decrease in the *proportion* of crime committed by juveniles.

Adapted from Howard N. Snyder, "Juvenile Arrests 2002," *Juvenile Justice Bulletin.* Washington, DC: Office of Juvenile Justice and Delinquency Prevention, 2004. Copyright is not claimed in this article, a publication of the United States government.

But there has also been a fairly large decline in the total amount of crime, at least since around 1990. For example, in 2004 the UCR estimated that the total amount of violent crime had declined 24 percent since 1995. The National Crime Victimization Survey (NCVS) reports that the crime drop has been even larger—it estimates that violent crime dropped 57 percent from 1993 to 2004.[5] In other words, at least since about 1990, all crime has decreased significantly, and at the same time the portion of crime committed by juveniles has also been going down.

Within this overall decline in juvenile crime, there are various more specific patterns. For example, clearance rates, particularly of violent crimes, have been more stable. Since 1980, arrests of juveniles cleared between 9 and 14 percent of violent crimes, and was at 12 percent in 2004. In 1972, this figure was almost identical to what it was in 2004. But among violent crimes, the biggest decreases have been in arrests and clearances for murder.

Notes

1.   Some states extend the legal status of "juvenile" only through age 15 (CT, NC, and NY). Others extend it only through age 16 (GA, IL, LA, MA, MI, MO, NH, SC, TX, and WI). In general, FBI reports do not distinguish between legal juveniles and youths under age 18.

2.   For descriptions of the proper role of UCR data in measuring juvenile crime, see Howard Snyder, *Juvenile Arrests 1998,* Juvenile Justice Bulletin, Office of Juvenile Justice and Delinquency Prevention, U.S. Department of Justice, Washington, DC, 1999, p. 2, see http://www.ncjrs.org/html/ojjdp/9912_3/contents.html; and Howard Snyder and Melissa Sickmund, *Juvenile Offenders and Victims: 1999 National Report,* Office of Juvenile Justice and Delinquency Prevention, U.S. Department of Justice, Washington, DC, 1999, pp. 112–114. See http://www.ncjrs.org/html/ojjdp/nationalreport99/index.html.

3.   Thomas J. Bernard, "Juvenile Crime and the Transformation of Juvenile Justice: Is There a Juvenile Crime Wave?" *Justice Quarterly* 16(2): 337–56, June, 1999.

4.   *Crime in the United States,* Federal Bureau of Investigation, U.S. Department of Justice, Washington, DC: U.S. Government Printing Office, 1970.

5.   Bureau of Justice Statistics, *Criminal Victimization 2004,* U.S. Department of Justice, Washington, DC, September, 2005.

✦ ✦ ✦

Introduction

In 2002, law enforcement agencies in the United States made an estimated 2.3 million arrests of persons under age 18. According to the Federal Bureau of Investigation (FBI), juveniles accounted for 17% of all arrests and 15% of all violent crime arrests in 2002. The substantial growth in juvenile violent crime arrests that began in the late 1980s peaked in 1994. In 2002, for the eighth consecutive year, the rate of juvenile arrests for Violent Crime Index offenses—murder, forcible rape, robbery, and aggravated assault—declined. Specifically, between 1994 and 2002, the juvenile arrest rate for Violent Crime Index offenses fell 47%. As a result, the juvenile Violent Crime Index arrest rate in 2002 was at the lowest level since at least 1980. From its peak in 1993 to 2002, the juvenile arrest rate for murder fell 72%.

These findings are derived from data reported annually by local law enforcement agencies across the country to the FBI's Uniform Crime Reporting (UCR) Program. Based on these data, the FBI prepares its annual *Crime in the United States* report, which summarizes crimes known to the police and arrests made during the reporting calendar year. This information is used to characterize the extent and nature of juvenile crime that comes to the attention of the justice system. Other recent findings from the UCR Program include the following:

- Of the nearly 1,600 juveniles murdered in 2002, 38% were under 5 years of age, 64% were male, 51% were white, and 48% were killed with a firearm.

- Arrests of juveniles accounted for 12% of all violent crimes cleared by arrest in 2002—specifically, 5% of murders, 12% of forcible rapes, 14% of robberies, and 12% of aggravated assaults.

- In the peak year of 1993, there were about 3,840 juvenile arrests for murder. Between 1993 and 2002, juvenile arrests for murder declined, with the number of arrests in 2002 (1,360) about one-third that in 1993.

- The juvenile violent crime arrest rate in 2002 was lower that it had been since at least 1980, and nearly half of what it was in 1994.

- Juvenile male arrest rates for aggravated assault and simple assault fell from the mid-1990s through 2002, while female rates remained near their highest level.

- The disparity in violent crime arrest rates for black juveniles and white juveniles declined substantially between 1980 and 2002.

- In 2002, the juvenile arrest rate for Property Crime Index offenses reached its lowest level since at least the 1960s.

- Between 1993 and 2002, juvenile arrests for driving under the influence increased 46%, with the increase far greater for females (94%) than males (37%). . . .

The Juvenile Share of Crime Has Declined

The relative responsibility of juveniles and adults for crime is hard to determine. Research has shown that crimes committed by juveniles are more likely to be cleared by law enforcement than are crimes committed by adults. Therefore, drawing a picture of crime from law enforcement records is likely to give a high estimate of the juvenile responsibility for crime.

The clearance data in the *Crime in the United States* series show that the proportion of violent crimes attributed to juveniles by law enforcement has declined in recent years. The proportion of violent crimes cleared by juvenile arrests grew from about 9% in the late 1980s to 14% in 1994 and then declined to 12% in 2002.

In the period since 1980, the proportion of murders cleared by juvenile arrests peaked in 1994 at 10% then dropped to 5% in 2002—the lowest level since 1987 but still above the levels of the mid-1980s. The juvenile proportion of cleared forcible rapes peaked in 1995 (15%) and then fell; however, the 2002 proportion (12%) was still above the levels of the late 1980s (9%). The juvenile proportion of robbery clearances also peaked in 1995 (20%); it fell substantially by 2002 (14%) but was still above the levels of the late 1980s (10%). The juvenile proportion of aggravated assault clearances in 2002 (12%) was slightly below its peak in 1994 (13%) and substantially above the levels of the late 1980s (8%). The proportion of Property Crime Index offenses cleared by juvenile arrests in 2002 (20%) was at its lowest level since at least 1980. . . .

Juvenile Arrests for Violence in 2002 Were the Lowest Since 1987

The FBI assesses trends in the volume of violent crimes by monitoring four offenses that are consistently reported by law enforcement agencies nationwide and are pervasive in all geographical areas of the country. These four crimes—murder and nonnegligent manslaughter, forcible rape, robbery, and aggravated assault—together form the Violent Crime Index.

After years of relative stability in the number of juvenile Violent Crime Index arrests, the increase in these arrests between 1988 and 1994 focused national attention on the problem of juvenile violence. After peaking in 1994, these arrests dropped each year from 1995 through 2002. For all Violent Crime Index offenses combined, the number of juvenile arrests in 2002 was the lowest since 1987. The number of juvenile aggravated assault arrests in 2002 was lower than in any year since 1989. With the exception of 2000, the number of juvenile arrests in 2002 for murder was lower than in any year since 1984. The number of juvenile arrests in 2002 for forcible rape was at the low levels of the early 1980s. Finally, the number of juvenile arrests for robbery was lower in 2002 than in any year since at least the early 1970s.

In the 10 years between 1993 and 2002, the decline in the number of violent crime arrests was greater for juveniles than adults:

	Percent Change in Arrests 1993–2002	
Most Serious Offense	Juvenile	Adult
Violent Crime Index	–29%	–10%
Murder	–64	–36
Forcible Rape	–27	–26
Robbery	–38	–25
Aggravated assault	–23	–4

Data source: *Crime in the United States 2002*, table 32.

Few Juveniles Were Arrested for Violent Crime

In 2002, there were 276 arrests for Violent Crime Index offenses for every 100,000 youth between 10 and 17 years of age. If each of these arrests involved a different juvenile (which is unlikely), then no more than 1 in every 360 persons ages 10–17 was arrested for a Violent Crime Index offense in 2002, or about one-third of 1% of all juveniles ages 10–17 living in the U.S.

Juvenile Arrests for Property Crimes in 2002 Were the Lowest in at Least Three Decades

As with violent crime, the FBI assesses trends in the volume of property crimes by monitoring four offenses that are consistently reported by law enforcement agencies nationwide and are pervasive in all geographical areas of the country. These four crimes, which form the Property Crime Index, are burglary, larceny-theft, motor vehicle theft, and arson.

For the period from 1988 through 1994, during which juvenile violent crime arrests increased substantially, juvenile property crime arrest rates remained relatively constant. After this long period of relative stability, juvenile property crime arrests began to fall. Between 1994 and 2002, the juvenile Property Crime Index arrest rate dropped 43%, to its lowest level since at least the 1960s. More specifically, juvenile burglary arrest rates have been declining since at least the early 1980s. In 2002, the juvenile larceny-theft arrest rate and the juvenile motor vehicle theft arrest rate were at their lowest levels since at least 1980. . . .

The Juvenile Violent Crime Index Arrest Rate in 2002 Was Lower Than in Any Year Since at Least 1980 and 47% Below the Peak Year of 1994

- In comparison with the juvenile Violent Crime Index arrest rate, the rate for young adults (persons ages 18–24) that peaked in 1992 had fallen only 28% by 2002, remaining above the rates of the early 1980s.

After Years of Relative Stability, the Juvenile Property Crime Index Arrest Rate Began a Decline in the Mid-1990s That Continued Through 2002

- The juvenile arrest rate for Property Crime Index offenses in 2002 was nearly 40% below its levels in the early 1980s. . . . ✦

Chapter 4

Victims of Violent
Juvenile Crime

Carl McCurley and Howard N. Snyder

Editor's Introduction

Juvenile offenders, acting either alone or with others, commit about one in five nonfatal violent victimizations. One interesting fact is that nearly all victims of juvenile violence know the offenders. Another interesting fact is that most victims of juvenile violence are other juveniles, including 95 percent of the victims of sexual assaults. When a juvenile does assault an adult, it most often is a member of his or her own family.

This suggests that, on the whole, juveniles engage in violence in the context of conflicts with other juveniles about their own age. There are certain exceptions to this pattern. For example, with sexual offenses there is an unusually large portion of significantly younger victims. And with robbery, an unusually large portion of the victims are adult strangers—about two-thirds.

It is interesting to note that when juveniles themselves are victims of violent crime, they usually are victimized by adults rather than by other juveniles.[1] The largest portion of these adult offenders are members of the juveniles' own family. This suggests that, in general, juveniles are more likely to be the victims of adult violence than adults are to be the victims of juvenile violence. And it also suggests that, when there are conflicts between juveniles and adults within a family, the adults in that family are more likely to victimize the juveniles rather than vice versa.

Adapted from Carl McCurley and Howard N. Snyder, "Victims of Violent Juvenile Crime," *Juvenile Justice Bulletin*. Washington, DC: Office of Juvenile Justice and Delinquency Prevention, 2004. Data source: Federal Bureau of Investigation, *National Incident-Based Reporting System Master Files* for the years 1997 and 1998. Washington, DC: U.S. Department of Justice, Federal Bureau of Investigation, 2000. Copyright is not claimed in this article, a publication of the United States government.

Note

1.   David Finkelhor and Richard Ormrod, "Characteristics of Crimes Against Juveniles," *Juvenile Justice Bulletin*, Office of Juvenile Justice and Delinquency Prevention, Washington, DC, June, 2000.

✦ ✦ ✦

Most Victims of Juvenile Violence Were Juveniles

The victims of juvenile offenders were most likely to be about the same age as the offender: 38% of the victims of juvenile violence were no more than 1 year older or younger than the offender, and the age difference was 2 years or less for 50% of victims, 5 years or less for 65% of victims. Thus, victims of juvenile crime tended to be pre-teens or teens.

Older juveniles were more likely than any other age group to be the victims of violence committed by juveniles. Among juvenile victims ages 12–17, 53% were victimized by other juveniles. In contrast, only 14% of infant victims (younger than age 1) were victimized by juvenile offenders. The proportion of juvenile offenders dropped slightly (to 13%) for 1-year-old victims, then rose steadily to 64% for 12-year-old victims. A juvenile offender was involved in fewer than 1 in 10 violent victimizations of adults.

Adults constituted only 4% of the victims of sexual assault by juvenile offenders but more than half (57%) of the victims of juvenile robbers. . . .

Nearly All Victims of Juveniles Knew Their Offender

The relationships of victims to offenders can be divided into three broad categories: acquaintance, family, and stranger. In those incidents where the relationship was known, the majority (65%) of the victims of juvenile violence were acquaintances of the offender, 23% were family members, and 12% were strangers. Victims who did not know the juvenile offender were about evenly divided between adults (7%) and juveniles (5%). Thus, about 1 in 15 victims of juvenile violence was an adult who was a stranger to the offender. . . .

Victim Relationship to Offender Varies by Victim Age

Younger victims of violent crimes committed by juvenile offenders tended to be acquaintances of the offender, whereas older victims of these crimes tended to be family members. The juvenile offender was an acquaintance for 78% of juvenile victims and 63% of victims ages 18–30 but a family member for more than half (55%) of victims older than 30.

Of all victims of juvenile violence who were acquainted with the offender, 74% were younger than 18. Of all victims of juvenile violence who were strangers to the offender, more than half (56%) were age 18 or older. Family victims were the oldest group: although 36% of family victims of juvenile offenders were younger than 18, more than half (51%) were ages 30–60.

Victim Relationship to Offender Varies by Offense

In crimes committed by juveniles, acquaintances were the majority of victims of sexual assault (69%), aggravated assault (65%), and simple assault (67%). Family members were 28% of the victims of sexual assault, 19% of the victims of aggravated assault, and 24% of the victims of simple assault. Strangers made up a small proportion of the victims of these crimes (sexual assault, 4%; aggravated assault, 16%; and simple assault, 9%).

In sharp contrast, strangers constituted about two-thirds (65%) and acquaintances about one-third (34%) of the victims of juvenile robbers. Robbery victims were very unlikely (1%) to be members of the juvenile offender's family. . . .

Many Adult Victims of Juvenile Assault Were Family Members

Parents and stepparents accounted for 9% of all victims of aggravated assaults committed by juveniles and 13% of all simple assaults by juveniles. However, among assault victims older than 30, parents and stepparents accounted for much larger shares: 37% for aggravated assault and 52% for simple assault.

Most Young Victims of Juvenile Sexual Assault Knew the Offender

Acquaintances or family members younger than 12 constituted 54% of the victims of sexual assaults committed by juvenile offenders. Of all family victims of sexual assaults by juveniles, 36% were younger than 6 and most (84%) were younger than 12. Most victims who were either acquaintances or strangers were 12 or older.

The Majority of Violent Juvenile Offenders Were Male

For 74% of the victims of juvenile violent crime, the offender was male, specifically, 92% of the sexual assault victims, 94% of the robbery victims, 78% of the aggravated assault victims, and 70% of the simple assault victims.

Among children younger than 2 who were victims of juvenile violent crime, more than one-third (34%) were victimized by female offenders. The proportion of victims of female offenders was lower for other age groups: 17% for victims ages 2–11, 27% for those ages 12–17, and 28% for adult victims. Juveniles accounted for 63% of the victims of male juvenile offenders and 58% of the victims of female juvenile offenders.

About Half of the Victims of Juvenile Violence Were Female

A majority (60%) of victims of violent crime committed by adult offenders were female. In contrast, 46% of the victims of juvenile violence were female. Three-fourths of the victims of juvenile sexual assault were female. Victims of juvenile robberies were the least likely (26%) to be female.

Most Male Victims of Juvenile Violent Crime Faced Male Offenders

For 89% of male victims of juvenile violent crime, and for 92% of male victims younger than 18, the offender was male. Among all female victims of juvenile crime, 42% were victimized by females; among female victims younger than 12, 24% were victimized by females. The proportion of female offenders rose to 52% for female victims ages 12–17, then declined to 39% for adult female victims. . . .

The Risk of Injury During Juvenile Crimes Was Greatest for Older Teens and Young Adults

In sexual assaults, robberies, and aggravated assaults committed by juveniles, 40% of the victims were injured, compared with 48% of the victims of such crimes committed by adults. By age group, the percentage of victims injured by juveniles in the commission of these crimes was 34% of victims age 15 and younger, 49% of those ages 16–24, and 43% of those age 25 and older.

Multiple Offenders Were More Likely in Juvenile Robbery Than in Other Crimes

About a third (32%) of the victims of juvenile violent crimes faced multiple offenders; 17% were victimized by two or more juveniles and 15% were victimized by juveniles acting with adults. In juvenile robberies, the share of victims who faced multiple offenders increased to 61%. . . .

Guns Were More Likely With Multiple Offenders Than Lone Offenders

By definition, guns are not present in simple assaults, but they may be present in sexual assaults, robberies, and aggravated assaults. An armed offender was encountered by 13% of the victims of juveniles committing these crimes, compared with 18% of the victims of adult offenders. Most (59%) of the victims of juvenile gun crime were age 18 or older.

In crimes committed by juveniles with a gun present, 23% of victims were injured. In contrast, 43% of victims were injured in crimes committed by juveniles with no gun present.

Victims of multiple offenders were more likely than victims of lone offenders to encounter firearms. Guns were involved in 9% of sexual assault, robbery, and aggravated assault victimizations by juvenile offenders acting alone, 17% of victimizations by two or more juveniles, and 26% of victimizations by juveniles acting with adults. In comparison, a gun was present in 16% of such victimizations committed by an adult offender acting alone and 27% of victimizations by two or more adult offenders. ✦

Causes of Delinquency and Youth Violence

S cience mirrors what we do in everyday life—we look at the world and we think about what we see. Science does this in a systematic way—this is called research. And it thinks in a systematic way about what research has seen—this is called theory.

Science involves a systematic alternation between theory and research—both require the other. Theory interprets the results of past research and charts the course of future research. Research is always based on theory and the results of research determine what theory says.

The chapters in Part III summarize some of the best theory and research on delinquency. The first chapter summarizes and organizes a fairly wide range of the theories of delinquency, while the second chapter presents the findings of one of the most important research studies on delinquency and violence. ✦

Chapter 5

Poverty, Inequality, and Youth Violence

Ronald C. Kramer

Editor's Introduction

All crime has decreased significantly since 1990, and the portion of crime committed by juveniles has also decreased significantly since that year. In fact, juvenile crime probably has been declining at least since 1975. Whenever the decline started, it is clear that juvenile crime is not as serious a problem today as it was in the recent past. Nevertheless, many people today think that that the juvenile crime problem is worse than ever before and that "kids today are no good."

Even though juvenile crime is down, it is still true that young people in general, and young males in particular, commit more than their share of offenses. Why this is true is a very large and very important question that has been the subject of an extremely large number of theories of youth crime and violence.[1] The range of answers to this question is so large that it is difficult to summarize.

Chapter 5 attempts to answer a narrower and more precise question: What explains the exceptionally high rate of juvenile violence in the United States, as compared to the rates of juvenile violence in other modern industrialized countries?

The problem of high juvenile violence is part of a larger problem of high violence in the United States. As a comparison, England and Wales have higher crime rates for virtually all serious crime except murder and rape.[2] During 1996, for example, English and Welsh police recorded twice as many burglaries and motor vehicle thefts on a per capita basis as recorded by law enforcement agencies in the United States. For murder and rape, however, the situation is re-

Adapted from Ronald C. Kramer, "Poverty, Inequality, and Youth Violence," *The Annals of the American Academy of Political and Social Science* 567: 123–39, copyright © 2000 by Sage Publications, Inc. Reprinted by permission of Sage Publications, Inc.

versed. In 1996, the murder rate in the United States was 5.7 times higher than it was in England and Wales and the rape rate was about 3 times higher. In 1981, the problem was even worse—the murder rate in the United States was 8.7 times higher and the rape rate 17 times higher than it was in England and Wales.

Juveniles, as always, are responsible for more than their share of the problem of high violence in the United States. Chapter 5 presents an explanation of this general situation. In doing so, it summarizes and organizes a fair portion of the best theory and research about delinquency and juvenile offending. So besides its particular argument, this chapter provides something of an overview of theories that address the general issue of juvenile offending.

Chapter 5 argues that the United States has higher rates of poverty than other industrialized countries. It also has more inequality—i.e., the economic distance between the richest and the poorest members in the society. Finally, it has more social exclusion—i.e., poor people in the United States are more likely to live in isolated communities where they have little or no contact with other members of the society. Most of the chapter describes the various pathways by which these three structural characteristics—poverty, inequality, and social exclusion—ultimately lead to high rates of youth violence. Basically, the argument is that these three characteristics undermine the ability of families, schools, and neighborhoods to provide the social support and informal social control that produce healthy, well-functioning children and prevent serious violent crime.

Notes

1. See, for example, Donald J. Shoemaker, *Theories of Delinquency*, 5th edition, Oxford University Press, New York, 2004. For a more general overview of theories of crime, see George B. Vold, Thomas J. Bernard, and Jeffrey B. Snipes, *Theoretical Criminology*, 5th edition, Oxford University Press, New York, 2002.

2. Patrick A. Langan and David P. Farrington, "Crime and Justice in the United States and in England and Wales, 1981–1996." Washington, DC, Bureau of Justice Statistics, 1998.

✦ ✦ ✦

This article will examine some of the more general social, economic, and cultural conditions that give rise to serious crime and violence in the United States.

Specifically, the article will explore the role of poverty, economic inequality, and social exclusion in shaping the problem of youth violence by summarizing and integrating the recent theory and research of a number of sociological criminologists, such as Elliott Currie, John Hagan, and Francis Cullen.

Poverty, Inequality, and Social Exclusion

Why does the United States have exceptionally high rates of violent crime, particularly youth homicide, compared to other industrial nations? Conservative commentators frequently assert that it is a lenient criminal justice and juvenile justice system that causes high crime rates or that crime and violence are the result of cultural decline and something called moral poverty. But the American justice system is one of the harshest in the world, and, although the cultural and moral condition of American families and communities is important to take into account in understanding crime, these conditions are strongly affected by larger social and economic forces. These larger social structural conditions are the factors that sociological criminologists point to as the roots of violence. As Currie (1998) observes, "For there is now overwhelming evidence that inequality, extreme poverty, and social exclusion matter profoundly in shaping a society's experience of violent crime. And they matter, in good part, precisely because of their impact on the close-in institutions of family and community" (114).

When we look at the research on poverty and economic inequality, we find that the United States has by far the highest poverty rate and the biggest gap between the rich and the poor of any of the developed nations (Kerbo 1996). Currie (1998) notes the findings of the Luxembourg Income Study (LIS), an international survey of poverty, inequality, and government spending in industrial countries (Rainwater and Smeeding 1995). The LIS shows that the United States, while a very wealthy society, has far more inequality and is far less committed to providing a decent life for the poor than are other developed nations. The LIS also demonstrates that, in particular, children and families in the United States are far more likely to be poor than those in other industrial democracies. Furthermore, poor American children are more likely to be extremely poor compared to children in other advanced countries.

According to the LIS and other studies, there are several reasons why poor children and families in the United States find themselves in such a plight. First, many Americans in the so-called urban underclass are trapped in a system of concentrated unemployment that results in an increasingly isolated poverty (Wilson 1996). Second, those who do work, primarily in the secondary labor market, earn very low wages compared to their counterparts in other countries. This creates the problem of the working poor. Finally, the United States provides fewer government benefits to either the underclass or the working poor to offset the problems of concentrated unemployment and poor wages. Recent changes in the welfare system are likely to aggravate the situation.

This deprivation and social exclusion are related to the high rates of violence found in the United States. Currie reviews both studies of international differences in violent crime and studies of violence within the United States and other countries to demonstrate the connection. Cross-national studies show that countries with a high degree of economic inequality have higher levels of violence (Gartner 1990). Other studies show that, even within a generally deprived population, it is the most deprived children who face the greatest risks of engaging in crime and violence (Werner and Smith 1992). Finally, Currie notes the research of Krivo and Peterson (1996), who suggest that it is the link between extreme disadvantage and violence that underlies much of the association between race and violent crime in the United States. After reviewing these and other studies, Currie (1998) concludes, the links between extreme deprivation, delinquency, and violence, then, are strong, consistent, and compelling. There is little question that growing up in extreme poverty exerts powerful pressures toward crime. The fact that those pressures are overcome by some individuals is testimony to human strength and resiliency, but does not diminish the importance of the link between social exclusion and violence. The effects are compounded by the absence of public supports to buffer economic insecurity and deprivation, and they are even more potent when racial subordination is added to the mix. And this . . . helps us begin to understand why the United States suffers more serious violent crime than other industrial democracies, and why violence has remained stubbornly high in the face of our unprecedented efforts at repressive control (131).

But how do these social and economic forces cause violence? In what specific ways do poverty, inequality, and social exclusion act to produce violent crime by young people? To help answer these questions, I suggest that we utilize the general organizing concepts of social support and informal social control. It is the absence of these two important social processes, in urban, suburban, or rural settings, that allows for the infliction of social and psychic pain on young people and the development of negative attitudes and emotions that can easily lead to violence.

The Absence of Social Support and Informal Social Control

In his presidential address to the Academy of Criminal Justice Sciences in 1994, Francis T. Cullen suggested that a lack of social support is implicated in crime. Cullen argued that social support, if approached systematically, can be an important organizing concept for criminology. He defined social support as "the perceived or actual instrumental and/or expressive provisions supplied by the community, social networks, and confiding partners" (Cullen 1994, 530). Cullen went on to develop a series of propositions, supported by criminological research, about the relationship between the lack of social support and the presence of crime at societal, community, family, and relational levels of analysis.

According to Cullen, a distinction should be made between the concepts of social support and informal social control. Informal social control involves all the sanctions and constraints used in an effort to control another individual's behavior (to make him or her conform to social norms) that fall outside of formal, legal, and bureaucratic systems. Informal social control is generally exercised by significant others, families, friends, neighbors, and community networks. The breakdown or absence of informal social control has also long been cited by criminologists as a factor in the involvement of persons in criminal behavior.

In the following sections, I will review theory and research that examine the relationship between broad structural conditions like poverty, inequality, and social exclusion; institutional-level social support and informal social control; and the problem of youth violence. First, I will consider social support as an organizing concept and then informal social control.

Social Support

One of the most significant ways in which economic deprivation and social exclusion can lead to youth violence is by inhibiting or breaking down the social supports that affect young people. Cullen (1994) reviews research that supports his proposition that "America has higher rates of serious crime than other industrial nations because it is a less supportive society" (531). He notes studies that have demonstrated the corrosive effect of America's culture of excessive individualism and pursuit of material gain without regard to means (Messner and Rosenfeld 1997). This competitive pursuit of the American Dream not only encourages individuals to obtain material goods "by any means necessary"; it also inhibits the development of a "good society" in which concern for community and mutuality of support dominate. Cullen (1994) also points out that "economic inequality can generate crime not only by exposing people to relative deprivation but also by eviscerating and inhibiting the development of social support networks" (534).

Moving down from the national level, Cullen (1994) argues that "the less social support there is in a community, the higher the crime rate will be" (534). He reviews evidence that "governmental assistance to the poor tends to lessen violent crime across ecological units," and research that reveals "that crime rates are higher in communities characterized by family disruption, weak friendship networks, and low participation in local voluntary organizations" (534–35). Finally, Cullen notes quantitative and ethnographic research on the "underclass" that documents that powerful social and economic forces have created isolated inner-city enclaves. These enclaves fray the supportive relations that once existed between adults and youths, supportive relations that previously offered protection to those youths from involvement in crime. We will return to this body of research later in a review of the work of John Hagan (1994).

Next, Cullen (1994) addresses the issue of the role of the family in offering social support. He asserts that "the more support a family provides, the less likely it is that a person will engage in crime" (538). This is the critical link between poverty, inequality, exclusion, and violence. Recall Currie's argument that these social forces matter precisely because of their impact on the close-in institutions like the family. As Cullen (1994, 538) notes, there is a considerable amount of evidence that parental expressive support diminishes children's risk of criminal involvement. He cites Loeber and Stouthamer-Loeber's (1986) comprehensive meta-analysis of family correlates of delinquency that clearly shows that indicators of a lack of parental support increase delinquent behavior. This study concludes that youth crime is related inversely to "child-parent involvement, such as the amount of intimate communication, confiding, sharing of activities, and seeking help (Loeber and Stouthamer-Loeber 1986, 42).

Both Cullen and Currie warn that any discussion of families and crime must avoid the "fallacy of autonomy—the belief that what goes on inside the family can usefully be separated from the forces that affect it from the outside: the larger social context in which families are embedded for better or for worse" (Currie 1985, 185). While any family, regardless of its socioeconomic status, can be affected, both Cullen and Currie stress the social and economic forces like poverty and inequality that have transformed and, in many cases, ripped apart families, particularly families of the underclass, in ways that have reduced their capacity to support children. The Panel on High-Risk Youth (cited in Cullen 1994, 539) states:

> Perhaps the most serious risk facing adolescents in high-risk settings is isolation from the nurturance, safety, and guidance that comes from sustained relationships with adults. Parents are the best source of support, but for many adolescents, parents are not positively involved in their lives. In some cases, parents are absent or abusive. In many more cases, parents strive to be good parents, but lack the capacity or opportunity to be so.

In his review of the research on the connections between family deprivation and violent crime, Currie (1998, 135–39) highlights four key findings: "1) extreme deprivation inhibits children's intellectual development; 2) extreme deprivation breeds violence by encouraging child abuse and neglect; 3) extreme poverty creates multiple stresses that undermine parents' ability to raise children caringly and effectively; and 4) poverty breeds crime by undermining parents' ability to monitor and supervise their children." Findings 1 through 3 provide more specific articulation about the ways in which poverty and inequality shape youth violence through the lack of social support. Stunted intellectual development that cripples children's ability to be successful in school or at work, violence and abuse that create angry and fearful children, and the lack of parental care and nurturance all contribute to the production of young people who are prone to strike out at the world through violent acts.

Social and Cultural Capital

Another important perspective on the relationship between social and economic conditions, the lack of social support, and youth crime is contained in the work of John Hagan. In presenting a "new sociology of crime and disrepute," Hagan (1994) develops the concepts of human, social, and cultural capital and capital disinvestment processes to help us understand the connections between inequality, social institutions, and violent crime. According to Hagan, the general concept of human capital refers to the skills, capabilities, and knowledge acquired by individuals through education and training that allow them to act in new ways. To this he adds the concept of social capital, which "involves the creation of capabilities through socially structured relationships between individuals in groups" (67). Social groups such as intact nuclear and extended families, well-integrated neighborhoods, stable communities, and even nation-states are the sites for the development of social capital in individuals that provides them with the resources and capacities to achieve group and individual goals. These supportive social networks can lead to the formation of cultural capital such as the credentials of higher education and involvement in high culture like the arts and their supporting institutions. As Hagan points out, "In these community and family settings, social capital is used to successfully endow children with forms of cultural capital that significantly enhance their later life changes" (69).

The ability to endow children with social and cultural capital, however, is linked to economic position. As Hagan (1994) notes, in less advantaged community and social settings, which lack abundant forms of social and cultural capital, parents are far less able to provide resources, opportunities, and supports to their children. Thus, "the children of less advantageously positioned and less-driven and controlling parents may more often drift or be driven into and along less-promising paths of social and cultural adaptation and capital formation" (70). These "less promising paths of social and cultural adaptation," of course, include embeddedness in the criminal economy of drugs and other forms of gang activity and delinquent behavior.

Hagan (1994) emphasizes that "disadvantaging social and economic processes" in the community and broader society, what he calls "capital disinvestment processes," are destructive of social and cultural capital and often produce deviant subcultural adaptations (70). The three capital disinvestment processes that "discourage societal and community level formations of conventional social capital" are residential segregation, race-linked inequality, and concentrations of poverty (70–71). Hagan describes these destructive structural conditions and the dislocations that they produce in community settings. He then reviews a considerable body of new ethnographic and quantitative research that documents and articulates the ways in which these community-level processes of capital disinvestment disrupt and destroy the social capital of families, diminishing their capacity to provide the human and cultural capital their children need to improve their life chances and become stable and productive members of the community. Thus these children are at a much greater risk of becoming embedded in the criminal economy of drugs and the violence that it often entails, as well as becoming involved in other forms of conventional criminality. As Hagan observes, "In communities that suffer from capital disinvestment and in families that have little closure of social networks and social capital to facilitate investment in their children, youths are more likely to drift into cultural adaptations that bring short-term status and material benefits, but whose longer-term consequences include diminished life-chances" (93).

Informal Social Control

As noted previously, Currie found that the lack of effective parental supervision has a strong relationship to delinquency. This raises the important issue of informal social control. The ability of adults to monitor and supervise, impose sanctions, shame, and otherwise keep young people in line through face-to-face interaction within important social institutions is an important variable in delinquency prevention. There is a considerable amount of criminological evidence that suggests that these informal mechanisms of social control, operating within families, schools, neighborhoods, workplaces, and social networks, play an important role in preventing youth crime and violence. As Minor (1993) points out, "Research has demonstrated that, during the course of childhood and adolescent socialization, the more meaningfully integrated persons become [into] those social institutions which promote informal social control, such as the family, school, and work, the lower the likelihood of delinquency" (59).

As with the lack of social support, social structural forces such as poverty and social exclusion can inhibit or erode the exercise of informal social controls within these intermediate institutions. With the erosion of these controls, the chances for young people to become involved in violent crime increases. As Minor (1993) observes,

> Through their impact on social institutions, the macro forces emanating from a society's political economic organization shape the quantity and quality of behavioral choices available to individuals. By diminishing the capacity of institutions, especially the family, to positively influence the choices made by youths and by rendering youths vulnerable to delinquent socialization in peer groups, macro forces can weaken informal mechanisms of social control. (59)

In his excellent review of the theory and research on the political and economic context of delinquency in the United States, Minor (1993) identifies three macro forces that have had important consequences for the problem of youth violence. These forces are the socially defined position of youth, the impact of market relations, and poverty and inequality.

First, compulsory education, child labor laws, and the emergence of the juvenile justice system combined to promote youth segregation, impose labor market restrictions on young people, and increase the importance of peer group socialization. Market relations led to the penetration of economic norms into all spheres of life and the fostering of a competitive individualism that undermined interpersonal cooperation and collective social welfare. Poverty and inequality had a disintegrative effect on social institutions through the lack of resources and emotional stress. According to Minor, these three forces evolved together as part of the transformation of the American economy to monopoly capitalism, and they have acted collectively to weaken informal mechanisms of social control and therefore increase youth violence.

Another perspective on the impact of cultural and structural forces on the ability of social institutions such as the family to control youth crime comes from Messner and Rosenfeld (1997). Building on Robert Merton's concept of anomie, Messner and Rosenfeld assert that the core features of the social organization of the United States—culture and institutional structure—shape the high levels of American crime. At the cultural level, they argue that the core values of the American Dream (achievement, individualism, universalism, monetary success) stimulate criminal motivations while promoting weak norms to guide the choices of means to achieve cultural goals (anomie). As Messner and Rosenfeld point out, "The American Dream does not contain within it strong injunctions against substituting more effective, illegitimate means for less effective, legitimate means in the pursuit of monetary success" (76).

At the institutional level, Messner and Rosenfeld (1997) observe that the economy tends to dominate all other social institutions and that this imbalance of institutional power fosters weak social control. There are two ways that this imbalance of power weakens social control. First, social institutions such as the family and the schools are supposed to socialize children into values, beliefs, and commitments other than those of the economic system. However, as Messner and Rosenfeld note, "as these noneconomic institutions are relatively devalued and forced to accommodate to economic considerations, as they are penetrated by economic standards, they are less able to fulfill their distinctive socialization functions successfully" (77). Thus, economic domination weakens the normative control associated with culture.

The imbalance of power also weakens the external type of social control associated with social structure. As Messner and Rosenfeld (1997, 78) point out, "External control is achieved through the active involvement of individuals in institutional roles and through the dispensation of rewards and punishments by institutions." When these noneconomic institutions are devalued and rendered impotent, then the attractiveness of the roles they offer to young people is diminished, and the incentives and penalties they can offer for prosocial behavior are limited. Messner and Rosenfeld conclude by noting that the problem of external control by major social institutions is inseparable from the problem of the internal regulation of social norms (anomie):

> Anomic societies will inevitably find it difficult and costly to exert social control over the behavior of people who feel free to use whatever means prove most effective in reaching personal goals. Hence, the very sociocultural dynamics that make American institutions weak also enable and entitle Americans to defy institutional controls. If Americans are exceptionally resistant to social control—and therefore exceptionally vulnerable to criminal temptations—it is because they live in a society that enshrines the unfettered pursuit of individual material success above all other values. In the United States, anomie is considered a virtue. (79)

Sampson and Laub's innovative reassessment (1993) of the longitudinal data gathered by Sheldon and Eleanor Glueck in the 1940s also supports the proposition that poverty and inequality undermine the ability of informal, social controls within the family and school to contain delinquent behavior. Sampson and Laub develop an age-graded theory of informal social control. Their basic thesis is that "structural context mediated by informal family and school controls explains delinquency in childhood and adolescence" (7). Their unified model of informal family social control focuses on three dimensions: discipline, supervision, and attachment. They observe that "the key to all three components of informal family social control lies in the extent to which they facilitate linking the child to family and ultimately society through emotional bonds of attachment and direct yet socially integrative forms of control, monitoring, and punishment" (68).

The second part of Sampson and Laub's theory suggests that structural background factors, such as poverty, influence youth crime largely through their effects on family process. The empirical findings support their theory. They find that negative structural forces have little direct effect on delinquency but instead are mediated by intervening sources of informal social controls in the family and the school. They offer the following summary:

> We found that the strongest and most consistent effects on both official and unofficial delinquency flow from the social processes of family, school, and peers. Low levels of parental supervision, erratic, threatening, and harsh discipline, and weak parental attachment were strongly and directly related to delinquency. . . . Negative structural conditions (such as poverty or family disruption) also affect delinquency, but largely through family and school process variables. (Sampson and Laub 1993, 247)

What Sampson and Laub find in their reassessment of the Gluecks' data on white children born in the 1920s and 1930s is supported by a more recent study of urban black children conducted by Shihadeh and Steffensmier (1994). They studied the links between economic inequality, family disruption, and urban black violence in more than 150 cities across the country. They found that as economic inequality increases, so do arrests of black youths for violent crimes. Shihadeh and Steffensmeier suggest that the link between inequality and violence, however, is indirect. Greater income inequality increases the number of black single-parent households, and the increase in single-parent households is related to the level of youth violence. Single parents, with more stress and fewer resources, have a more difficult time monitoring and supervising their children and, in general, exercising effective social control. Rutter and Giller (1983) and Larzelere and Patterson (1990) provide additional evidence on the connection between poverty and poor parenting skills. . . .

From Inequalities to Youth Violence

Even though the rates of violent crime committed by young people have declined in recent years, youth violence remains a serious social problem in the United States. While many factors must be taken into account as we search for ways to deal with youth violence in general, and school violence in particular, it is imperative to understand the broader social and economic forces that play a critical role in shaping America's experience with this problem. The theory and research that have been reviewed in this article make a compelling case for the thesis that poverty, economic inequality, and social exclusion are causal agents in the production of crime and violence by young people in the United States. Although these structural conditions do not often have a direct effect in producing violent crime, they are important because of the impact they have on social institutions like the family, the school, and the community. While families, schools, and neighborhoods in middle-class, suburban areas can also become disrupted, the evidence shows that poverty, inequality, and exclusion decisively undermine the ability of those close-in institutions to provide the social support and informal social control that produce healthy, well-functioning children and prevent serious violent crime. When these institutions, in whatever socioeconomic setting, are unable to socialize children properly, care for them appropriately, and provide them with human and social capital, violence is a possible result. When these institutions, in whatever socioeconomic setting, are unable to effectively monitor, supervise, and sanction juveniles, violent crimes can take place. . . .

References

Cullen, Francis T. 1994. Social Support as an Organizing Concept for Criminology: Presidential Address to the Academy of Criminal Justice Sciences. *Justice Quarterly* 11:527–59.

Currie, Elliott. 1985. *Confronting Crime: An American Challenge*. New York: Pantheon.

———. 1998. *Crime and Punishment in America*. New York: Metropolitan Books.

Gartner, Rosemary. 1990. The Victims of Homicide: A Temporal and Cross-National Comparison. *American Sociological Review* 55:92–106.

Hagan, John. 1994. *Crime and Disrepute*. Thousand Oaks, CA: Pine Forge Press.

Kerbo, Harold R. 1996. *Social Stratification and Inequality: Class Conflict in Historical and Comparative Perspective*. 3d ed. New York: McGraw-Hill.

Krivo, Lauren J. and Ruth D. Peterson. 1996. Extremely Disadvantaged Neighborhoods and Urban Crime. *Social Forces* 75:619–50.

Larzelere, Robert E. and Gerald R. Patterson. 1990. Parental Management: Mediator of the Effect of Socioeconomic Status on Early Delinquency. *Criminology* 28:301–23.

Loeber, Rolf and Magda Stouthamer-Loeber. 1986. Family Factors as Correlates and Predictors of Juvenile Conduct Problems and Delinquency. In *Crime and Justice: An Annual Review of Research*, ed. M. Tonry and N. Morris. Vol. 7. Chicago: University of Chicago Press.

Messner, Steven F. and Richard Rosenfeld. 1997. *Crime and the American Dream.* 2d ed. Belmont, CA: Wadsworth.

Minor, Kevin I. 1993. Juvenile Delinquency and the Transition to Monopoly Capitalism. *Journal of Sociology and Social Welfare* 20:59–80.

Rainwater, Lee and Timothy M. Smeeding. 1995. *Doing Poorly: The Real Income of American Children in a Comparative Perspective.* Syracuse, NY: Syracuse University, Maxwell School of Citizenship and Public Affairs.

Rutter, Michael and Henri Giller. 1983. *Juvenile Delinquency: Trends and Perspectives.* New York: Guilford Press.

Sampson, Robert J. and John H. Laub. 1993. *Crime in the Making: Pathways and Turning Points Through Life.* Cambridge, MA: Harvard University Press.

Shihadeh, Edward S. and Darrell J. Steffensmier. 1994. Economic Inequality, Family Disruption, and Urban Black Violence: Cities as Units of Stratification and Social Control. *Social Forces* 73:729–51.

Werner, Emily E. and Ruth S. Smith. 1992. *Overcoming the Odds: High Risk Children from Birth to Adulthood.* Ithaca, NY: Cornell University Press.

Wilson, William Julius. 1996. *When Work Disappears: The World of the New Urban Poor.* New York: Knopf. ✦

Chapter 6

The Causes and Correlates Studies

Findings and Policy Implications

Terence P. Thornberry, David Huizinga, and Rolf Loeber

Editor's Introduction

In science, one thing is said to "cause" another when there are four aspects to their relationship: *correlation, theoretical rationale, time sequence,* and the *absence of spuriousness.*

Correlation means that the two things vary together in some way. *Time sequence* means that one thing comes before the other in time. In order for one variable to cause another, the *causal* variable must be correlated with the variable that is caused, and it must come before it in time.

On the other hand, on farms around the world every day, roosters crow and then the sun comes up. These are highly correlated—they happen every single day in an enormous number of different places. And there is a consistent time sequence—roosters crow first and the sun comes up afterwards. But obviously there is no causal relationship. So inferring causation requires two additional factors: theoretical rationale and the absence of spuriousness.

Did you know that murder and the sales of ice cream are correlated with each other? Do you suppose this is because ice cream causes people to kill each other? Or is it because killers like to eat ice cream? Obviously, there is no coherent *theoretical rationale* for either of these ideas. In fact, the relationship between murder and ice cream is what we call *spurious*—i.e., both murder and ice cream sales go up in the summer when it is hot.

In general, if two things are correlated with each other and one appears in time before the other, then the first can cause the second *or* both can be caused by a third thing. With murder and ice cream, the "third thing" is the hot weather. But with a complex phenomenon like delinquency, it often is unclear whether some "third thing" exists somewhere and what it might be.

Many variables are correlated with delinquency, and many of those correlates come before delinquency in time. But it is unclear which (if any) of these correlates actually causes delinquency. Many of them probably have a "spurious" relationship to delinquency, like ice cream sales and murder.

This question is important for policy purposes. If we know the actual causes of delinquency, then we can implement policies to reduce those causes, and then we will be able to reduce delinquency. But if our policies focus on "spurious" correlates of delinquency, then it would be like trying to reduce murder rates by reducing ice cream sales.

The best way to establish which correlates are causes is with *longitudinal research*. This type of research starts at a particular point in time and follows events for a number of years into the future. Longitudinal research allows the researchers to actually observe and record events as they are happening. It tends to provide much better information about the causes of delinquency than other types of research.

Chapter 6 describes the results from three such longitudinal studies in Denver, Pittsburgh, and Rochester. This on-going research has followed about 4,000 youths for over 15 years, starting in 1987 with youths who were between 7 and 15 years old. Because serious delinquency tends to be a somewhat rare phenomenon, these studies "over-sampled" kids who were at high risk of becoming delinquent—that is, they put more of those kids into the study than you would find in a representative sample.

The studies found that physical aggression is fairly widespread in childhood, but that most children cease this behavior on their own. This is a fairly common-sense finding, but the researchers then asked a very important question: What distinguishes the kids who stop this behavior from those who continue and eventually escalate into serious and violent offending?

The researchers found that there were three "fairly orderly" developmental pathways from minor and common early aggression into more serious delinquency. They also identified two key factors that move kids more quickly along these pathways—childhood maltreatment and membership in gangs. They also found that juveniles who were arrested and incarcerated were substantially more likely to end up incarcerated as adults. Finally, they found that, despite the fact that these youths displayed many symptoms of serious future problems, most of them did not receive any social services.

In general, these researchers suggest intervening by providing services to children who are in the early stages of the developmental pathways, particularly focusing on childhood maltreatment and gang membership. You can evaluate for yourself whether these causal arguments have any practical implications in terms of controlling delinquency itself.

✦ ✦ ✦

Childhood Aggression

The vast majority of the youth in the Denver and Pittsburgh studies reported involvement in some form of physical aggression before age 13 (85 percent of the boys and 77 percent of the girls in Denver and 88 percent of the boys in Pittsburgh) (Espiritu et al., 2001). . . . As these findings indicate, aggression during childhood is quite common, although exactly how widespread depends on how aggression is defined. Involvement in aggression, however, is not necessarily extensive or long lasting. A substantial amount of delinquency, including aggression, is limited to childhood. For example, only about half (49 percent) of the Denver children involved in minor violence in which the victim was hurt or injured continued this behavior for more than 2 years. In fact, much aggressive behavior, and an even larger proportion of other delinquency, appears to be limited to childhood. However, a large proportion—about half—of aggressive children continue to be aggressive for several years into at least early adolescence. Exactly what distinguishes children who cease to be aggressive and those who continue remains to be determined.

Developmental Pathways

. . . Initial research comparing single and multiple pathways found that a model of three distinct pathways provided the best fit to the data:

- The Authority Conflict Pathway, which starts with stubborn behavior before age 12 and progresses to defiance and then to authority avoidance (e.g., truancy).

- The Covert Pathway, which starts with minor covert acts before age 15 and progresses to property damage and then to moderate and then to serious delinquency.

- The Overt Pathway starts with minor aggression and progresses to physical fighting and then to more severe violence (no minimum age is associated with this pathway). . . .

As they became older, some boys progressed on two or three pathways, indicating an increasing variety of problem behaviors over time

(Kelley et al., 1997; Loeber et al., 1993; Loeber, Keenan, and Zhang, 1997). Researchers found some evidence that development along more than one pathway was orderly. . . . Also, an early age of onset of problem behavior or delinquency was associated with escalation to more serious behaviors in all the pathways (Tolan, Gorman-Smith, and Loeber, 2000). The pathway model accounted for the majority of the most seriously delinquent boys, that is, those who self-reported high rates of offending (Loeber et al., 1993; Loeber, Keenan, and Zhang, 1997) or those who were court-reported delinquents (Loeber, Keenan, and Zhang, 1997).

The pathway model shows that the warning signs of early onset of disruptive behavior cannot necessarily be dismissed with a "this-will-soon-pass" attitude (Kelley et al., 1997). However, it is not yet possible to distinguish accurately between boys whose problem behaviors will worsen over time and those who will improve. The pathway model is a way to help identify youth at risk and optimize early interventions before problem behavior becomes entrenched and escalates.

The Overlap of Problem Behaviors

. . . Recognizing that involvement in delinquency or in other problem behaviors can be transitory or intermittent, the studies examined the level of overlap of more persistent drug use, school problems, and mental health problems[1] that lasted for at least 2 of the 3 years examined (Huizinga et al., 2000).

There was some consistency of findings for males across sites. Although a sizeable proportion of persistent and serious offenders do have other behavioral problems, more than half do not. Thus, it would be incorrect to characterize persistent and serious delinquents generally as having drug, school, or mental health problems. On the other hand, drug, school, and mental health problems are strong risk factors for involvement in persistent and serious delinquency, and more than half (55–73 percent) of the male respondents in all three sites with two or more persistent problems were also persistent and serious delinquents.

For females, the findings were different and varied by site. As with the males, fewer than half of the persistent and serious female delinquents had drug, school, or mental health problems. In contrast to males, however, these problems alone or in combination were not strong risk factors for serious delinquency. This result stems, in part, from the fact that a substantially smaller proportion of girls (5 percent) than boys (20–30 percent) was involved in persistent and serious delinquency, while their rates (within sites) of other problem behaviors were roughly similar to those of males. . . .

Thus there appears to be a concentration of offenders entering the juvenile justice system who have drug use, school, or mental health-related problems. Accordingly, the capability to identify the particular configuration of problems facing individual offenders and provide interventions to address these problems is critical to the effectiveness of the juvenile justice system.

Two Key Risk Factors for Delinquency

The Causes and Correlates studies have investigated a host of risk factors involving child behavior, family functioning, peer behavior, school performance, and neighborhood characteristics that precede and potentially lead to delinquency. Findings on just two topics—child maltreatment and gangs—are summarized here.

Child Maltreatment

Prior research indicates that child maltreatment (e.g., physical abuse, sexual abuse, neglect) that occurs at some point prior to age 18 is a risk factor for delinquency (Widom, 1989; Zingraff et al., 1993). This relationship was also observed in the Pittsburgh and Rochester studies (Smith and Thornberry, 1995; Stouthamer-Loeber et al., 2001, 2002). . . .

Of the subjects in the Rochester study, 78 percent were never maltreated and 22 percent were. Of the latter, 11 percent were maltreated in childhood only (before age 12 but not after), 8 percent were maltreated in adolescence only, and 3 percent were persistently maltreated (i.e., they had at least one substantiated case in childhood and at least one in adolescence).

The relationship to delinquency is intriguing. . . . For self-reported general delinquency that occurs from ages 16 to 18, the subjects who were maltreated during childhood only were not at significantly greater risk for delinquency (53.8 percent) than those who were never maltreated (49.6 percent). Subjects maltreated during adolescence, however, were at significantly greater risk. The delinquency level for the adolescence-only group (69.8 percent) was significantly higher than that for those who were never maltreated, and the delinquency level for those persistently maltreated—in both childhood and adolescence—was the highest (71.4 percent). The same pattern of results applies to other self-reported measures of delinquency: drug use, violent crime, and street crime (Ireland, Smith, and Thornberry, 2002). For official arrest records, 21.3 percent of youth who were never mal-

treated had arrest records and 23.5 percent of youth who were maltreated in childhood only had arrest records. In contrast, 50.7 percent
of youth maltreated in adolescence had arrest records and 50.0 percent of youth maltreated in both developmental stages had been arrested. The latter rates are significantly higher than the rate for those
never maltreated.

Gangs

The Rochester project also investigated how gang membership influences adolescent development. . . . Approximately 30 percent of
the Rochester subjects joined a gang at some point during the 4-year
period covering ages 14–18. The membership rate was virtually identical for boys (32 percent) and girls (29 percent). Gang membership
turned out to be a rather fleeting experience for most of these youth.
Half of the male gang members reported being in a gang for 1 year or
less, and only 7 percent reported being a gang member for all 4 years.
Two-thirds (66 percent) of the females were in a gang for 1 year or
less and none reported being a member for all 4 years.

Although fleeting, gang membership had a tremendous impact on
the lives of these youth. Gang members—both male and female—accounted for the lion's share of all delinquency. Although gang members were only 30 percent of the studied population, they were
involved in 63 percent of all delinquent acts (excluding gang fights),
82 percent of serious delinquencies, 70 percent of drug sales, and 54
percent of all arrests.

Two explanations for the strong association between gang membership and delinquency are frequently raised. One focuses on the individual: gangs attract antisocial adolescents who will likely get into
trouble whether or not they are in a gang. The second focuses on the
group: individual gang members are not fundamentally different
from nonmembers, but when they are in the gang, the gang facilitates
their involvement in delinquency.

If the second explanation is correct, gang members should have
higher rates of delinquency only during the period of membership,
not before or after that period. That is precisely what the Rochester
data showed. . . . This pattern is found across the 4-year period studied and is observed for various offenses, particularly violence, drug
sales, and illegal gun ownership and use.

The impact of being in a street gang is not limited to its short-term
effect on delinquent behavior. It also contributes to disorderly transi-
tions from adolescence to adulthood. As compared with individuals
who were never members of a gang, male gang members were significantly more likely to drop out of school, get a girl pregnant, become a
teenage father, cohabit with a woman without being married, and

have unstable employment. Female gang members were significantly more likely to become pregnant, become a teenage mother, and to have unstable employment.

. . . [A] fair proportion of both genders in Denver—18 percent of the males and 9 percent of the females—have been gang members. Denver findings also reveal that gang members accounted for a very disproportionate amount of crime, as do findings in the other studies (Hill et al., 1996; Huizinga and Schumann, 2001). Denver male and female gang members accounted for approximately 80 percent of all serious and violent crime (excluding gang fights) committed by the sample. Further, over a 5-year period, these individuals committed the vast majority of crimes while they were gang members (e.g., 85 percent of their serious violent offenses, 86 percent of their serious property offenses, and 80 percent of their drug sale offenses). The social processes of being an active gang member clearly facilitate or enhance involvement in delinquent behavior. . . .

Responding to Delinquency

There are various ways to respond to juvenile crime, including interventions through the juvenile justice system and the provision of general social services or specialized prevention and treatment programs. The Causes and Correlates studies have investigated these different strategies, and the longitudinal results suggest alternative strategies.

Arrest

The Denver study conducted several examinations of the impact of arrest using various analytical strategies (Esbensen, Thornberry, and Huizinga, 1991; Huizinga and Esbensen, 1992; Huizinga, Esbensen, and Weiher, 1996; Huizinga et al., 2003). The findings from these studies are quite consistent. In general, arrest has little impact on subsequent delinquent behavior, and when it does have an impact, it is most likely an increase in future delinquent behavior. These findings are in agreement with several other studies of the impact of arrest (Klein, 1986; Sherman et al., 1997). In addition, those who are arrested and incarcerated as juveniles are substantially more likely to be incarcerated as adults (Huizinga, 2000).

There are different possible explanations for these findings. For example, those arrested may be more serious offenders who are on a different life trajectory than delinquents who are not arrested. However, arrest and sanctioning do not appear to have had the desired effect on the future offending of many delinquent youth. It should be noted that arrest and sanctions need not demonstrate an ameliorative effect to justify their use because the need to protect public safety, perceived needs for retribution, and the influence of these actions on general deterrence within the population cannot be disregarded. Nevertheless, the findings do suggest that arrest and subsequent sanctions generally have not been a particularly viable strategy for the prevention of future delinquency and that other alternatives are needed. The findings also suggest that the use of the least restrictive sanctions, within the limits of public safety, and enhanced reentry assistance, monitoring, and support may reduce future delinquency. . . .

Utilization of Services

Several service-providing agencies can potentially help both youth involved in delinquency and their families. These agencies include the juvenile justice system and external agencies such as schools and social services. Are they utilized? The Pittsburgh Youth Study investigated this question by examining the extent to which the parents of delinquent boys received help for dealing with their problems (Stouthamer-Loeber, Loeber, and Thomas, 1992; Stouthamer-Loeber et al., 1995). The study considered help received from anyone (including lay people) and from professionals (especially mental health professionals). In general, seeking help for behavior problems was twice as common for the oldest boys as compared with the youngest (21 percent versus 11 percent, respectively). In 25 percent of the cases, however, seeking help resulted in only one contact with a help provider, and it is doubtful that positive results were achieved in one session.

The percentage of parents who sought any help—help for behavior problems or help from mental health professionals—increased with the seriousness of the delinquency. However, less than half of the parents of seriously delinquent boys received any help, and only one-quarter of the parents of these boys received help from a mental health professional (Stouthamer-Loeber, Loeber, and Thomas, 1992).

Help in Schools. Division of the Pittsburgh sample into four groups (nondelinquents, persistent nonserious offenders, persistent property offenders, and persistent violent offenders) showed that all three persistent offender groups were placed in special education classes for learning problems at the same rate as nondelinquents (less than 10 percent). However, more of the persistently delinquent boys, as compared with the nondelinquent boys, were placed in classes for behavior problems; this was particularly true for the violent boys (22.3 percent versus 2.8 percent of the nondelinquents). Nevertheless, three-quarters (77.7 percent) of the persistent violent offenders were never placed in a class for behavior problems, and two-thirds were never placed in any special class.

It is commonly believed that certain groups of boys receive a disproportionate share of resources from various agencies. When researchers examined persistent property and persistent violent offenders, they found that just under half did not receive any help inside or outside of school (about 48 percent), and only 15.4 percent of the persistent property offenders and persistent violent offenders received help from mental health professionals in addition to help in school.

Steps in Developmental Pathways. Stouthamer-Loeber and colleagues (1995) compared movement along the developmental pathways described above with seeking help for services. In general, the higher the advancement in multiple pathways, the higher the chances that help was sought. An early onset of disruptive behaviors, however, did not increase the frequency at which help was sought.

Court Contact. Comparison of court-involved boys with those who had not had court contact showed that the former group received more intensive help. It may be possible that court intervention brought the necessity for help to the parents' attention. Only 17 percent of the boys' parents sought help before the year in which their boys were referred to the juvenile court.

In summary, the development of disruptive and delinquent behaviors was largely left unchecked by parents and helping agencies. These findings have important implications for policymakers and planners of preventive interventions. Merely having programs available may not be adequate; outreach to the most seriously delinquent youth and their families may also be essential.

Implications for Prevention

. . . The average age at which individuals took their first step in any of the pathways was approximately 7; moderately serious problem behavior began at about age 9.5 and serious delinquency at about age 12. The average age at which youth first came into contact with the juvenile court was 14.5. Thus, approximately 7 1/2 years elapsed between the earliest emergence of disruptive behavior and the first contact with the juvenile court. It should be noted that delinquent boys who were not referred to the juvenile court also tended to have long histories of problem behaviors.

Research findings from all three Causes and Correlates projects show that youth who start their delinquency careers before age 13 are at higher risk of becoming serious and violent offenders than those who start their delinquency careers later (Huizinga, Esbensen, and Weiher, 1994; Krohn et al., 2001; Loeber and Farrington, 1998, 2001). These results imply that preventive interventions to reduce offending should be available at least from the beginning of elementary school-age onward. However, it is important to be mindful of the results of the studies' investigation of childhood offending. Many of the aggressive children did not progress to serious involvement in serious juvenile crime. This suggests that great care is needed in the design of intervention programs for aggressive children. Not all programs are benign, and some may lead to or exacerbate later problems (Dishion, McCord, and Poulin, 1999).

Further research is needed to identify those individuals whose childhood aggression leads to violent behavior later in life. Intervention programs for aggressive children must be developed, and the outcomes for the children served by these programs must be carefully evaluated. The pathways model may be particularly helpful in designing these interventions. Overall, it seems that the judicious use of early interventions known to have long-term effectiveness is warranted.

In addition, although it is "never too early" to try to prevent offending, it is also "never too late" to intervene and attempt to reduce the risk of recidivism for serious offending (Loeber and Farrington, 1998). There is a complex relationship between when individuals begin to commit offenses and how long they persist. A full range of developmentally appropriate and scientifically validated programs is needed.

The Causes and Correlates results regarding the impact of maltreatment are consistent with the importance of developmentally appropriate interventions. It does not appear that childhood-only maltreatment, as long as it does not continue into adolescence, is a risk factor for delinquency. Sources of resiliency, including, perhaps, effective services, must come into play to help children overcome this adversity. Understanding these resiliency processes is an important goal for future research, as these processes have important implications for the design of programs.

Maltreatment that occurs during adolescence, however, appears to be a substantial risk factor for later delinquency. This suggests the need for enhanced services for adolescent victims and, in particular, for services that reduce the chances of delinquent behavior. . . .

A general strategy for reducing youth crime also needs to be mindful of the sizeable impact that gang membership has on serious and violent delinquency. Working directly with gangs, however, has not yet proved successful and can even be counterproductive. It may be more productive for juvenile justice practitioners to use gang membership as a marker variable and send gang members, on an individual basis, to programs for serious delinquency that are proven effective (see Thornberry et al., 2003). . . .

Note

1. Drug use included use of marijuana, inhalants, and hard drugs. School problems included poor grades and dropping out of school. Mental health problems were indicated by scores in the top 10 percent of either an emotional problem or nondelinquent behavioral problem measure.

References

Dishion, T.J., McCord, J., and Poulin, F. 1999. When interventions harm: Peer groups and problem behavior. *American Psychologist* 54(9):755–764.

Esbensen, F.A., Thornberry, T.P., and Huizinga, D. 1991. Arrest and delinquency. In *Urban Delinquency and Substance Abuse*, edited by D. Huizinga, R. Loeber, and T.P. Thornberry. Washington, DC: U.S. Department of Justice, Office of Justice Programs, Office of Juvenile Justice and Delinquency Prevention.

Espiritu, R., Huizinga, D., Loeber, R., and Crawford, A. 2001. Epidemiology of self-reported delinquency. In *Child Delinquents*, edited by R. Loeber and D.F. Farrington. Thousand Oaks, CA: Sage Publications.

Hill, K.G., Hawkins, J.D., Catalano, R.F., Kosterman, R., Abbott, R., and Edwards, T. 1996. The role of gang membership in delinquency, substance use, and violent offending. Paper presented at the annual meeting of the American Society of Criminology, Chicago, IL.

Huizinga, D. 2000. Who goes to prison? Paper presented at the Annual Conference on Criminal Justice Research and Evaluation, Washington, DC.

Huizinga, D., and Esbensen, F.A. 1992. An arresting view of juvenile justice. *School Safety* 3:15–17.

Huizinga, D., Esbensen, F.A., and Weiher, A.W. 1994. Examining developmental trajectories in delinquency using accelerated longitudinal designs. In *Cross-National Longitudinal Research on Human Development and Criminal Behavior*, edited by H.-J. Kerner and E.G.M. Weitekamp. New York, NY: Kluwer Academic Publishers.

———. 1996. The impact of arrest on subsequent delinquent behavior. In *Annual Report of the Program of Research on the Causes and Correlates of Delinquency*, edited by R. Loeber, D. Huizinga, and T.P. Thornberry. Washington, DC: U.S. Department of Justice, Office of Justice Programs, Office of Juvenile Justice and Delinquency Prevention.

Huizinga, D., Loeber, R., Thornberry, T.P., and Cothern, L. 2000. *Co-occurrence of Delinquency and Other Problem Behaviors. Bulletin*. Washington, DC: U.S. Department of Justice, Office of Justice Programs, Office of Juvenile Justice and Delinquency Prevention.

Huizinga, D., and Schumann, K. 2001. Gang membership in Bremen and Denver: Comparative longitudinal data. In *The Eurogang Paradox*, edited by M.W. Klein, H.-J. Kerner, C.L. Maxson, and E.G.M. Weitekamp. London, England: Kluwer Academic Publishers.

Huizinga, D., Schumann, K., Ehret, B., and Elliott, A. 2003. The effect of juvenile justice system processing on subsequent delinquent behavior: A cross-national study. Unpublished report submitted to the U.S. Department of Justice, Office of Justice Programs, National Institute of Justice.

Ireland, T., Smith, C.A., and Thornberry, T.P. 2002. Developmental issues in the impact of child maltreatment on later delinquency and drug use. *Criminology* 40(2):359–399.

Kelley, B.T., Loeber, R., Keenan, K., and DeLamatre, M. 1997. *Developmental Pathways in Disruptive and Delinquent Behavior*. Bulletin. Washington, DC: U.S. Department of Justice, Office of Justice Programs, Office of Juvenile Justice and Delinquency Prevention.

Klein, M. 1986. Labeling theory and delinquency policy—An empirical test. *Criminal Justice and Behavior* 13:47–79.

Krohn, M.D., Thornberry, T.P., Rivera, C., and LeBlanc, M. 2001. Later delinquency careers. In *Child Delinquents: Development, Intervention, and Service Needs*, edited by
R. Loeber and D.P. Farrington. Thousand Oaks, CA: Sage Publications.

Loeber, R., and Farrington, D.P., eds. 1998. *Serious and Violent Juvenile Offenders: Risk
Factors and Successful Interventions*. Thousand Oaks, CA: Sage Publications.

———, eds. 2001. *Child Delinquents: Development, Intervention, and Service Needs*.
Thousand Oaks, CA: Sage Publications.

Loeber, R., Keenan, K., and Zhang, Q. 1997. Boys' experimentation and persistence in
developmental pathways toward serious delinquency. *Journal of Child and Family
Studies* 6:321–357.

Loeber, R., Wung, P., Keenan, K., Giroux, B., Stouthamer-Loeber, M., Van Kammen,
W.B., and Maughan, B. 1993. Developmental pathways in disruptive child behavior.
Development and Psychopathology 5:101–132.

Sherman, L.W., Gottfredson, D., MacKenzie, D., Eck, J., Reuter, P., Bushway, S. 1997.
Preventing Crime: What Works, What Doesn't, What's Promising. A Report to the
United States Congress. Washington, DC: U.S. Department of Justice, Office of Jus-
tice Programs, National Institute of Justice.

Smith, C.A., and Thornberry, T.P. 1995. The relationship between childhood maltreatment and adolescent involvement in delinquency. *Criminology* 33(4):451–481.

Stouthamer-Loeber, M., Loeber, R., Homish, D.L., and Wei, E. 2001. Maltreatment of
boys and the development of disruptive and delinquent behavior. *Development and
Psychopathology* 13:941–955.

Stouthamer-Loeber, M., Loeber, R., and Thomas, C. 1992. Caretakers seeking help
for boys with disruptive delinquent behavior. *Comprehensive Mental Health Care*
2:159–178.

Stouthamer-Loeber, M., Loeber, R., Van Kammen, W.B., and Zhang, Q. 1995. Uninter-
rupted delinquent careers: The timing of parental helpseeking and juvenile court
contact. *Studies on Crime and Crime Prevention* 4(2):236–251.

Stouthamer-Loeber, M., Wei, E., Homish, D.L., and Loeber, R. 2002. Which family
and demographic factors are related to both maltreatment and persistent serious
juvenile delinquency? *Children's Services: Social Policy, Research, and Practice*
5(4):261–272.

Thornberry, T.P., Krohn, M.D., Lizotte, A.J., Smith, C.A., and Tobin, K. 2003. *Gangs and
Delinquency in Developmental Perspective*. Cambridge, England: Cambridge University Press.

Tolan, P.H., Gorman-Smith, D., and Loeber, R. 2000. Developmental timing of onsets of
disruptive behaviors and later delinquency of inner-city youth. *Journal of Child and
Family Studies* 9:203–230.

Widom, C.S. 1989. The cycle of violence. *Science* 244(4901):160–166.

Zingraff, M.T., Leiter, J., Myers, K.A., and Johnsen, M.C. 1993. Child maltreatment and
youthful problem behavior. *Criminology* 31(2):173–202. ✦

Part IV

Juveniles and the Police

The police are by far the most common way that juveniles enter the justice system. Only a few juveniles enter the system by some other means, such as by complaints filed directly with the juvenile court by parents, neighbors, schools, or welfare workers.

Part IV contains two chapters about how the police deal with juveniles. The first chapter reports on an observational study of police behavior, so that it focuses on normal practices of routine policing. Most of the interactions police have with juveniles are fairly minor, and police mostly handle the juveniles in informal ways—i.e., without arresting them.

The second chapter focuses on a special kind of policing called "problem-oriented policing." Rather than simply responding to crimes by arresting criminals, police step back and try to think about how a larger problem might be confronted. In this case, the larger problem had to do with gun violence committed by gang members in Boston. ✦

Police Encounters With Juvenile Suspects

Explaining the Use of Authority and Provision of Support

Stephanie M. Myers

Editor's Introduction

Chapter 7 reports on the results of an observational study of police in St. Petersburg, Florida, and Indianapolis, Indiana. During the summers of 1996 and 1997, trained observers rode with police and systematically recorded police interactions with juveniles. In particular, the observers recorded how often police used their *authority* in these interactions, as well as how often the police provided *support* or help to the juvenile.

The study found that police exercised their authority in 95 percent of their interactions with juveniles. Most of the time, however, police did not arrest the juvenile—only 13 percent of the juveniles were arrested. The rest of the time police used their authority in other ways—for example, about half the time they interrogated the juvenile, and about 40 percent of the time they issued a command or threat that the juvenile cease a particular behavior or leave a particular area.

The police were more likely to arrest juveniles when the problem was serious, the evidence was strong, a weapon was present, and the police already knew the juvenile. The study found that the race and gender of the juvenile had little impact on the decision to arrest, although other studies have found that these characteristics do influence police decisions.[1]

Adapted from Stephanie M. Myers, "Police Encounters With Juvenile Suspects: Explaining the Use of Authority and Provision of Support, Executive Summary Report," available at http://www.ncjrs.org/pdffiles1/nij/grants/205124.pdf, 2004. Copyright is not claimed in this article, a publication of the United States government.

The study also found that youths who were disrespectful to the police were more likely to be arrested and they also were more likely to receive support or help. Several other studies also have found that disrespectful youths are more likely to be arrested, although there is some dispute about whether this reflects the disrespect itself or other things that the juvenile is doing at the same time.[2]

The finding that police only arrested 13 percent of the youths they encountered is consistent with earlier observational studies of police behavior, which found that police arrest about 15 percent of juveniles they encounter.[3] It is interesting to combine this finding with a fact reported in Chapter 3, "Juvenile Arrests 2002": police handle 20 percent of the juveniles they arrest either entirely by themselves (18 percent) or by referring the juvenile to some other police or service agency (2 percent).

Thus, about 90 percent of the juveniles that police encounter are handled entirely by the police themselves without any involvement by juvenile or criminal court. In terms of the sheer volume of juveniles, police are the backbone of the juvenile justice system.

Notes

1. Past research on these subjects is quite complex and the results difficult to evaluate. With respect to race, Rodney L. Engen, Sara Steen, and George S. Bridges ("Racial Disparities in the Punishment of Youth: A Theoretical and Empirical Assessment of the Literature," *Social Problems* 49 (2):194–220, 2002) review 65 studies and come to the conclusion that there is an effect on police decision-making if the juvenile is black. With respect to gender, see John M. MacDonald and Meda Chesney-Lind, "Gender Bias and Juvenile Justice Revisited," *Crime & Delinquency* 47(2):173–195, April 2001.

2. Suspect demeanor is hard to disentangle from behaviors that are legally relevant to arrest. See Robin Shepard Engel, James J. Sobol, and Robert E. Worden, "Further Exploration of the Demeanor Hypothesis," *Justice Quarterly* 17(2):235–58, 2000.

3. See Donald Black and Albert J. Reiss, "Police Control of Juveniles," *American Sociological Review* 35(1):63–77, 1970; Richard Lundman, Richard E. Sykes, and John P. Clark, "Police Control of Juveniles: A Replication," *Journal of Research in Crime and Delinquency* 15 (1):74–91, 1978. Studies that that rely on official police records typically find that police arrest about 30 percent of juveniles they encounter. See, for example, Marvin Wolfgang et al., *Delinquency in a Birth Cohort,* University of Chicago Press, Chicago, 1972. This probably is because police fail to make any record for about half of their interactions with juveniles, none of which result in arrest. See Thomas J. Bernard and R. Richard Ritti, "The Philadelphia Birth Cohort and Selective Incapacitation," *Journal of Research in Crime and Delinquency* 28(1):33–54, 1990.

✦ ✦ ✦

Observers ... recorded information on 443 police juvenile encounters where at least one juvenile was treated by the police as a suspect. In all, 654 juvenile suspects were involved in these encounters. Police interacted with one juvenile in 69% of encounters, with two juveniles in 20%, and three or more in only 11% of encounters.

In contrast from what research in the 1960's and 1970's show, encounters between police and juveniles are as likely to be initiated by police themselves as they are by some other source (e.g., a complainant). In addition, findings here indicate that police-juvenile interactions are more likely than not of a minor nature—but that there are times when the problem is a serious one. It is unlikely for a complainant to be present during these encounters and, when they are present, very few actually request that police take some specific action with juvenile suspects.

When police encountered these suspects they were most likely to interact with a minority male, who appeared to have a low level of wealth. A very small number of juveniles (42) showed indication of, or behaved as though, they were under the influence of alcohol or drugs. Twelve percent of juveniles were disrespectful to police. . . .

When juvenile suspects in these two cities interact with the police they are most likely to interact with a male, white officer who has some formal college education. In most encounters (almost 90%) the police officer was a regular 'run' or '911' patrol officer while in approximately ten percent of encounters the officer was a community policing officer or specialist. However, regardless of this assignment, most officers had been exposed to some training in community policing. In three-quarters of encounters the observed officer reported receiving at least one day of community policing training—and many officers had received more than one day of training. In addition, some officers had been exposed to training in mediation skills—though only 29% had received one day of training in mediation.

A total of six measures were constructed to examine officer attitudes. They include measures of officer cynicism about citizen willingness to cooperate, agreement about the importance of assisting citizens, attitudes about aggressive policing on the street and selective enforcement of the law, and role orientation. Officers were found to vary on these attitudinal measures. The influence of these attitudes on police behavior with juveniles is discussed below.

Dependent Variables: Authority and Support

For this research police outcomes are examined in terms of police use of authority and police provision of support. When police interact with juvenile suspects we can expect them to use their authority in some way. Typically, when we think of police authority we conceptualize it in terms of an arrest or some other formal police action, like a traffic ticket. Researchers often operationalize police authority by analyzing the arrest decision. Of the 654 juvenile suspects encountered by police, 84, or 13% were arrested. However, these data also indicate that *when* police officers do not make an arrest they are still doing something to remedy the current situation and/or curb the future misconduct of juvenile troublemakers. Tactics that police use, other than arrest, often go undetected by traditional data sources (i.e., official police records). The types of police authority captured here include minimally coercive behaviors (e.g., making suggestions or requests) and range to more formalized, coercive police responses like interrogating, searching, and issuing commands and threats to suspects. Only 6% of the 654 suspects were not subject to any of the forms of police authority studied for this project.

Police inquired about the nature of the problem with 45% of juvenile suspects, [and] made a suggestion or request that the suspect leave the area, cease disorderly behavior, discontinue illegal behavior, or provide some information to 33% of juvenile suspects. Police lectured 22% of the suspects they encountered.

One might expect that police begin to handle problems with juveniles by using only slightly coercive tactics—and that the authoritativeness, or coercive nature, of the response will increase only when faced with resistance from the suspect or as the situation appears to be one of a more serious nature. Indeed, police did respond in a more authoritative, coercive way with some juveniles.

Police took a report on the situation with 15% of juveniles, they interrogated 48% and police performed a search (either of the juvenile, their belongings, or the immediate area) in 20% of cases. Police threatened or commanded 38% of juveniles to leave the area, discontinue illegal behavior, or cease disorderly behavior. Only 3% of juveniles were issued a citation. Police decided to tell the parents or guardians about the suspected wrongdoing or problem with 16% of juveniles. Although this is not a formal police response (like arrest) it is a response which could have more serious consequences for a juvenile (who now must deal with their parents at home), this police response carries more weight than investigative tactics and it usually involves more effort on the part of the police.

In addition to exercising their authority, police were found to rely on a more latent (or less recognized) part of their role by frequently providing support to juvenile suspects. It was expected that while police would use supportive behaviors to solve problems with juveniles, they would not use these types of responses as often as they would exercise their authority. This is indeed what the findings indicate, that while police do employ supportive behaviors they are not used as often as authoritative behaviors. . . .

For this research police behavior labeled as supportive included complying with a juvenile's request, providing information on how to deal with a problem, and providing comfort and sympathy. Like measures of police authority, the support measures were operationalized using coded and narrative data. Very few juveniles requested that the police provide assistance or information on how to deal with a problem—but when they did make such a request police usually complied. Police were much more likely to provide information to juvenile suspects on their own initiative; almost 20% of juveniles were recipients. Fewer than 5% of juveniles were recipients of some other officer initiated support (physical assistance) and the same number were offered comfort or sympathy. Overall, about one-quarter of juvenile suspects were recipients of police support or assistance—comparatively, almost 95% of juveniles were subject to some form of police authority and over three-quarters were subject to fairly high levels of authority (ranging from investigative actions to commands and threats, and, at times, arrest).

Multivariate Analysis

To examine the extent to which police authority and support with juvenile suspects is shaped by situational and individual factors multivariate analyses were performed using several variations of the dependant variables (authority and support). Next, I will highlight some of the significant findings (statistically and substantively speaking), beginning with police authority.

Beginning with a binary measure of police authority, the decision to arrest or not, some parallels to previous research are revealed. First, the percent of juveniles arrested (13%) is consistent with previous research. Also consistent, and expected, are the findings that police are more likely to make an arrest when the problem is of a more serious nature, when they have sufficient evidence and when the juvenile is verbally or behaviorally disrespectful. Police are also more likely to arrest when there is a weapon present (this happened infrequently) or when the police know the juvenile prior to the observed encounter. With the exception of victim preference for arrest (not found to have an effect here) it seems many of the same factors shaping the arrest decision twenty and thirty years ago continue to be influential today.

In addition to testing the temporal reliability and generalizability of those hypotheses, some additional hypotheses were tested as part of this research. For example, findings indicate that police decisions to arrest are also shaped to some extent by the presence of a supervisor at the scene. As expected, police are more likely to arrest a juvenile when a supervisor is present. Departmental influences are also apparent here as police in St. Petersburg were significantly less likely to arrest juvenile suspects than officers in Indianapolis. This finding supports the stated hypothesis, as the overall policing philosophy in St. Petersburg encompassed a softer, less aggressive approach to community policing. This is also evidence to support a more general supposition; that police administrators can, and do, have some impact on police behavior.

While arrest may be considered the most coercive police action, it is not the only tool police have to restore order and solve problems with juvenile suspects. This research clearly shows through descriptive statistics that when police did not arrest juvenile suspects it is likely that police did *something* to resolve the situation. Because police authority is not only inclusive of arrest additional analyses were performed on nominal measures of police authority. These results are briefly summarized below.

Multivariate analysis of a more encompassing measure of police authority provides insight into how police decisions to arrest, issue citations or tell the juvenile's parents, issue commands and threats, and perform investigative tactics—are shaped by individual and situational factors. For this analysis police authority is a nominal measure where the *most coercive* police behavior during the encounter falls into one of five categories. From least to most coercive, these categories are: (1) released (where the juvenile was released or was simply asked to do [or not do] something); (2) investigative tactics (where police question the suspect or search the area or the juvenile); (3) issuing commands or threats (where police issues commands or threats to leave the area, discontinue behavior, etc.); (4) issuing a citation or informing the juvenile's parents; (5) making an arrest. For this discussion, the reference category is release (1). The relationship between police authority and situational and individual factors will be discussed below. The full text reveals a much deeper analysis where the reference category varies to better understand police behavior.

Several relationships are noteworthy. First, police are more likely to take any of the authoritative actions (arrest, tell parents, issue commands or threats, perform investigative tactics) rather than release the juvenile when they have evidence of wrongdoing and as the seriousness of the problem increases. This suggests that while police do not always make an arrest in these situations, they are likely to do *something* to try and curb the future problematic behavior of the suspect. Interestingly, another legal variable, apparent use of alcohol or drugs, had rather insignificant effects on police behavior. Police were more likely to issue commands and threats rather than release the suspect, though they were no more likely to make an arrest or tell the juvenile's parents when the juvenile appeared to be under the influence.

Second, there is little evidence here to support hypotheses about police use of authority being shaped by the race, sex, or level of wealth of the juvenile suspects. Unexpectedly, findings here suggest that police are more lenient with minority suspects. One extra-legal factor, whether or not the complainant is a minority, suggests that police are significantly less likely to perform investigative tactics and less likely to tell juveniles' parents than they are to simply release a suspect in this situation. *This* suggests that perhaps police accord less priority to the concerns of minority citizens—however, it might also be the case that minority complainants are lobbying for the police to do nothing more than simply talk to juvenile troublemakers about the problem.

Third, the analysis of the more comprehensive measure of police authority reveals that the influence of having a police supervisor present at the scene is more complicated than one would surmise if basing interpretations on the analysis of the binary arrest variable. The nominal analysis suggests that police are not more likely to arrest than they are to release suspects when supervisors are present—but clearly the reference category is much different in this analysis. Additional analyses reveal that police are significantly more likely to arrest than they are to investigate or tell juveniles' parents and the full text reveals other subtle relationships between supervisor presence and police use of the authority. Clearly, having a supervisor at the scene of a police juvenile encounter has some impact on the outcome of that police juvenile interaction. This might mean that police are aware of how the supervisor would expect them to handle a situation—or that perhaps they decide to play it safe and 'go by the book' when their supervisor is watching. Other organizational influences are apparent here at a more general level and findings here support hypotheses regarding organizational (department) influences on police behavior.

Fourth, there is little evidence to support hypotheses about the impact of officer characteristics and attitudes on police behavior. The race and sex of the observed officers were not significantly related to the use of police authority, and the overall impact of other characteristics was not significant. Further, while variation in police officer attitudes is documented, such variation appears unrelated to any patterned variation in police use of authority. Very few coefficients reached a level of statistical significance. With so few direct relationships between police use of authority and officer characteristics and attitudes, one might surmise that police authority with juveniles is shaped largely by the situation—or perhaps by individual factors not yet identified by researchers.

Like police use of authority, the second dependant variable examined, police provision of support, was examined two ways. First, as a dichotomous variable measured in terms of having provided some type of support or none at all. Second, as a trichotomous (nominal) variable measured, in ascending order (none to most supportive categories), where police provided no support, provided some support in the form of helpful information on how to deal with a problem, or provided support to juveniles in the form of physical assistance, comfort, or sympathy. The latter analysis will be briefly summarized as it provides a better understanding of police use of supportive behaviors in their interactions with juvenile suspects. The comparison category for the analysis consists of those juveniles who were not recipients of any police support.

The examination of police provision of support reveals several interesting fmdings. Perhaps most interesting is that unlike police use of authority with juveniles, police support is patterned more by officer characteristics than by situational factors. This is quite a divergence as police use of authority is patterned mostly by situational cues and hardly at all by officers' individual characteristics. With regard to supportive behaviors, the only legal variable significantly influencing police behavior is evidence strength. Police are more likely to offer both types of support (information and comfort) than they are to provide no support at all when there is more evidence or wrongdoing. The seriousness of the problem has no significant impact on police providing support.

Few extralegal factors are found to have a significant impact. As expected, when the encounter takes place in a more socially disadvantaged neighborhood, police are significantly more likely to provide support in the form of physical assistance or comfort than they are to release the suspect without providing any support. Perhaps, as hypothesized, police suspect that juveniles encountered in these neighborhoods do not receive much informal guidance from their families or the community and are willing to step in and provide what they might surmise is missing. Also as expected, police are more likely to provide support to female suspects rather than release them but this only holds true for the more supportive category (comfort/ sympathy/physical assistance) and not for the middle category where police provide information to help with a particular problem.

Many officer characteristics seem to influence police officers' likelihood of providing support to juvenile suspects. As hypothesized, minority officers are more likely than white officers to provide helpful information, officers with more time on the job are more likely to provide support to juveniles, and officers with more education are more likely than officers with less education to provide helpful information, and comfort and sympathy than they are to provide no support during the encounter. . . . ✦

Chapter 8

Reducing Gang Violence in Boston

Anthony A. Braga and David M. Kennedy

Editor's Introduction

Most of the time, police encounter juveniles in the routine operation of their jobs. But police can also organize themselves to confront very specific problems. Chapter 8 looks at a particular program in Boston, called "Operation Cease Fire," in which police attempted to stop a wave of gang-related gun killings in the early 1990s. Boston was similar to many other large American cities at the time in that it experienced a wave of juvenile gun homicides.[1] However, the Boston response went beyond the traditional police stance of arresting the perpetrators. Rather, their response was part of a new and much broader police strategy called "problem-oriented policing."

Traditionally, police respond to crimes by arresting the criminals. But in some situations, that seems to have little effect on the overall problem. That was the case with youth homicides in Boston—police arrested the offenders after the killings had occurred, but the killings had taken on lives of their own. Each killing generated more killings, and arresting the killers seemed to do nothing to break this self-perpetuating cycle. At some point, besides arresting the young killers, the police also started to think about how they might attack the overall problem of high juvenile homicides.

The result was the strategy that became known as "Operation Cease Fire." The strategy was created by a "Working Group" composed of officials from the Boston Police Department (BPD) and academics from Harvard University's Kennedy School of Government. After the strategy was designed, the Working Group was joined by the "Ten Point Coalition," a group of black ministers formed after gang members invaded a church during the funeral of a rival gang

Adapted from Chapter 9 in Winifred L. Reed and Scott H. Decker, eds., *Responding to Gangs: Evaluation and Research,* NIJ Research Report, July 2002. U.S. Department of Justice, National Institute of Justice. Copyright is not claimed in this article, a publication of the United States government.

member and attacked mourners with guns and knives. These ministers helped legitimize the efforts of police to aggressively address the problem of gang violence in black neighborhoods.

In Operation Cease Fire, police and other agencies attempted to deter gang violence through a strategy that combined "pulling levers" and communication.[2] Each time there was an incidence of gang violence, police and other agencies would converge on the gang and "pull every lever" to put the offenders away for as long a time as possible. For example, the Department of Youth Services (DYS) might revoke the juvenile's parole for some violation that normally would not result in a revocation. They then would spend a lot of time and effort communicating what they had done to the gang members themselves, and would promise to do the same thing again the next time there was any gang violence. They framed this communication in terms of achieving a "cease fire" in the gang war and argued that this was in the interests of the gang members themselves, since they were the ones being killed. At the same time, "Streetworkers" from a Boston social service program would offer all kinds services to help the gang "go straight" if that is what they wanted to do. Thus, the "pulling levers" approach included both the carrot and the stick—do what we want and we will do everything we can to help you out (the carrot); otherwise we will do everything we can to put you away (the stick).

The turning point came when a gang member who had been "targeted" because of participation in gang violence was sentenced to over 19 years in prison, without the possibility of parole, for the possession of a single bullet. Posters were put up in gang neighborhoods explaining what had happened and promising that it would happen again if there was any more violence.[3] After that, the gang violence dropped.

Notes

1. In general, see James C. Howell, "Youth Gang Homicides: A Literature Review," *Crime and Delinquency* 45(2):208–41, April 1999.

2. Operation Cease Fire also included an attempt to interdict the flow of illegal weapons, primarily semiautomatic guns, to the gangs. However, this attempt seemed to have little effect.

3. For a representation of the poster, see David M. Kennedy et al., *Reducing Gun Violence: The Boston Gun Project's Operation Ceasefire,* Washington, DC: National Institute of Justice, 2001, p. 38. This document contains a detailed account of the specific events involved in the "pulling levers" strategy.

✦ ✦ ✦

In the summer of 1995, Boston had 61 gangs comprising only about 1,300 gang members (Kennedy, Braga, and Piehl 1997). . . . Although it is difficult to set upper and lower bounds on the age distribution of gang members in practice, most are between 14 and 24 years of age. According to 1996 U.S. Census estimates, these 1,300 gang members represented less than 1 percent of their age group city-wide and less than 3 percent of their age group in Boston neighborhoods with gang turf (Kennedy, Braga, and Piehl 1997). . . . Project research revealed that Boston gangs were well known to authorities and streetworkers; many gang members were also well known and tended to have extensive and quite varied criminal histories (Kennedy, Piehl, and Braga 1996). . . .

Boston gangs also congregated in and defended "turf"—very small, well-defined areas within their neighborhoods. . . . The physical spaces occupied by Boston gangs were typically very small; often, the turf occupied by a particular gang was no larger than a piece of a single street block or the grounds surrounding an apartment building. The total geographic expanse of the 61 gang areas was 1.7 square miles, only 3.6 percent of Boston's 47.47 square miles (Kennedy, Braga, and Piehl 1997). Turf made up only 8.1 percent of the area of the Boston neighborhoods with gangs—Roxbury, Dorchester, Mattapan, Jamaica Plain, Hyde Park, and the South End (Kennedy, Braga, and Piehl 1997). Although these areas were small, violence was disproportionately clustered in gang turf. About 25 percent of incidents involving youth homicides, weapons offenses, simple and aggravated assaults, armed robberies, and "shots fired" calls for service occurred inside these gang areas (Kennedy, Braga, and Piehl 1997). . . .

Chronic disputes among gangs were the primary drivers of gang violence in Boston (Braga, Piehl, and Kennedy 1999). The majority of Boston youth homicides identified as gang-related were not about drugs, money, or other issues for which the violence could be considered instrumental. In fact, only 6 percent of the gang-related homicides directly involved a drug dispute (Braga, Piehl, and Kennedy 1999). Rather, Boston's gang-related youth homicides were usually personal and vendetta-like. This does not mean that vendettas might not have started over drug- or money-related issues; however, if the vendettas had such a genesis, they had taken on an independent life by the time the Boston Gun Project research was conducted. Also, the gang-related homicides largely were not "senseless" or random, at least to the participants. The incidents had a history, however absurd to observers, and the episode was part of a larger history. . . .

The Operation Ceasefire Strategy to Reduce Gang Violence in Boston

Research findings and the Working Group process led to development of the "Operation Ceasefire" intervention. [This included] an attempt to generate a strong deterrent to gang violence (Kennedy, Piehl, and Braga 1996). . . .

This approach involved deterring chronic gang offenders' violence by reaching out directly to gangs, saying explicitly that violence would no longer be tolerated, and backing that message by "pulling every lever" legally available when violence occurred (Kennedy 1997, 1998). Boston gangs were not subjected to increased law enforcement attention arbitrarily nor did the Working Group develop a "hit list" of gangs. Rather, the Working Group's enforcement actions occurred in response to outbreaks of gang violence. In other words, Boston gangs selected themselves for focused law enforcement attention by engaging in violence. When gang violence occurred, Working Group members sent a direct message to gang members that they were "under the microscope" because of their violent behavior (Braga, Kennedy, Waring, and Piehl 2001). Police officers, probation officers, and DYS caseworkers immediately flooded the targeted gang's turf and communicated to gang members that their presence was in response to the violence. Streetworkers and members of the Ten Point Coalition walked the streets and explained that they wanted the violence to stop and supported the efforts of their law enforcement counterparts to make that happen. They also offered services and opportunities to gang members, including health and social services, educational and recreational opportunities, substance and alcohol abuse intervention programs, and food and shelter.

As Operation Ceasefire unfolded, the Working Group assessed the enforcement levers available to stop violent gang activity (Kennedy 1997). Enforcement responses were tailored to particular gangs and often included a wide range of actions, such as conducting probation checks, changing community supervision conditions, serving outstanding arrest warrants, focusing special prosecutorial attention on crimes committed by violent gang members, increasing disorder enforcement, and disrupting street-level drug markets. A basic premise of the pulling levers approach was to take advantage of the chronic-offending behaviors of gang members. The Working Group recognized that gang members were vulnerable to a variety of criminal justice sanctions and that targeted enforcement actions could be used to good effect in controlling their violent behavior (Kennedy 1997). Although Operation Ceasefire implemented varying enforcement tactics on particular gang members within a group, the focus of the operation was to stop the group's violent activities.

The enforcement actions selected by the Working Group were only as harsh as necessary to stop a gang from engaging in violence. For many gangs and gang members, heightened levels of police, probation, and DYS enforcement were sufficient to end the violence. Quickly shutting down drug markets, serving warrants, enforcing probation and DYS supervision conditions, making disorder arrests, and dealing more strictly with resulting cases as they were prosecuted and adjudicated were generally powerful enough actions to stop the violence. To curb violence among some hardcore gangs and gang members, however, the enhanced enforcement capabilities of Federal authorities were needed. In these instances, ATF, DEA, and FBI investigations, prosecutions by the U.S. Attorney's Office, and the prospect of serving a substantial term in a Federal prison far from home were used to quell the violence.

While carrying out enforcement actions, Working Group members continued communicating with violent gang members. The Group believed it was crucial to demonstrate cause and effect to gang members subjected to the Operation Ceasefire intervention. The Working Group delivered a direct and explicit message to violent gangs that violent behavior would no longer be tolerated and that it would use all legally available means to stop the violence (Kennedy 1998). This message also was communicated to gangs not engaged in violence so they would understand what was happening to the violent gang and why.

In addition to talking to gang members on the street, the Working Group delivered the deterrence message through fliers explaining the enforcement actions and through forums with gang members (Kennedy 1997, 1998). Forums were usually held in a public facility, such as a courthouse or community recreational center. Gang members under criminal justice system supervision were required to attend a forum by their probation or parole officers; gang-involved juveniles under DYS community supervision were required to attend by their caseworkers. Streetworkers and members of the Ten Point Coalition were able to bring other gang members to a forum by persuading them that it was in their best interest to attend. At each forum, representatives of the law enforcement agencies involved in Operation Ceasefire explained their actions to the gang members. Streetworkers and the Ten Point clergy voiced their support of the law enforcement actions, asked the youths to stop the violence, and reiterated their offers of services and opportunities. At the end of the presentation, gang members were encouraged to ask questions on the anti-violence campaign.

The Impact of Operation Ceasefire on Youth Violence in Boston

Immediately after Operation Ceasefire was implemented in mid-1996, the annual number of Boston youth homicides fell markedly. As mentioned earlier, Boston averaged about 44 youth homicides per year between 1991 and 1995. In 1996, that number fell to 26 homicides and further decreased to 15 youth homicides in 1997, a trend that continued through 1998 (18) and 1999 (15).

Although these numbers show a sudden, large decrease in Boston youth homicides, they do not establish whether Operation Ceasefire was associated with that decrease. Thus, with the support of NIJ, researchers from Harvard University's John F. Kennedy School of Government rigorously evaluated the effects of Operation Ceasefire on youth violence in Boston (Braga, Kennedy, Waring, and Piehl 2001). Using carefully constructed time series analysis models that controlled for trends and seasonal variations, the Kennedy School evaluation team found that implementation of Operation Ceasefire was associated with the following monthly numbers for Boston: a 63-percent decrease in youth homicides, a 32-percent decrease in calls about shots fired, a 25-percent decrease in Boston gun assaults, and a 44-percent decrease in youth gun assault incidents in one high-risk district (Braga, Kennedy, Waring, and Piehl 2001).

The youth homicide and gun violence reductions associated with Operation Ceasefire could have been caused or meaningfully influenced by other causal factors. Therefore, the evaluation team added control variables to the time series analysis models, including changes in the unemployment rate, in Boston's youth population, in violent index crimes, in older homicide victimization, and in street-level drug activity as measured by BPD arrest data (Braga, Kennedy, Waring, and Piehl 2001). The addition of these control variables did not substantively change the findings. Operation Ceasefire was still associated with significant decreases in the monthly number of youth homicides and other indicators of nonfatal serious violence.

These analyses supported the conclusion that a large reduction in Boston's youth homicide and gun violence was associated with Operation Ceasefire. However, because many major cities in the United States have enjoyed noteworthy reductions in homicide and nonfatal serious violence, the Kennedy School research team also distinguished Boston's youth homicide trends from national and regional trends. Using Supplementary Homicide Report data, the team analyzed monthly numbers of homicide victims ages 24 and under for 29 major New England cities and 39 major U.S. cities. (For a complete methodological description, see Braga, Kennedy, Waring, and Piehl 2001.) Drawing on carefully constructed time series analyses, the research suggested that the significant reduction in youth homicide associated with Operation Ceasefire in Boston was distinct when compared with youth homicide trends in most major New England and U.S. cities.

The Effectiveness of Operation Ceasefire

A central hypothesis within the Working Group was that a meaningful period of substantially reduced youth violence might serve as a "firebreak" and result in a relatively long-lasting reduction in future youth violence (Kennedy et al. 1996). The idea was that youth violence in Boston had become a self-sustaining cycle among a relatively small number of youths, with objectively high levels of risk leading to nominally self-protective behavior, such as gun acquisition and use, gang formation, and tough street behavior, all of which fueled the cycle of violence (Kennedy et al. 1996). If this cycle could be interrupted, a new equilibrium at a lower level of risk and violence might be established, perhaps without the need for continued high levels of either deterrent or facilitative intervention. The impact evaluation suggests that youth violence did indeed settle at a new lower equilibrium after Operation Ceasefire was implemented. . . .

Suppression

. . . Beyond the certainty, severity, and swiftness of sanctions, effective deterrence depends on communicating threats of punishment to the public. As Zimring and Hawkins (1973) observe, "the deterrence threat may best be viewed as a form of advertising" (142). The Operation Ceasefire Working Group recognized that for the strategy to be successful, it was crucial to deliver a credible deterrence message to Boston gangs. Therefore, Operation Ceasefire only targeted those gangs engaged in violent behavior, rather than wasting resources on those that were not. Spergel (1995) suggests that problem-solving approaches to gang problems based on more limited goals, such as gang violence reduction rather than gang destruction, are more likely to be effective in controlling gang problems. Operation Ceasefire did not attempt to eliminate all gangs or eliminate all gang offending in Boston. Despite the large reductions in youth violence, Boston still has gangs that commit crimes. However, the city's gangs do not commit violent acts as frequently as they did in the past.

The pulling-levers approach attempted to prevent gang violence by making gang members choose to change their behavior to avoid consequences that would follow from their violence and gun use. A key element of this strategy was the delivery of a direct, explicit "retail deterrence" message to a relatively small target audience about the kind of behavior that would provoke a special response and what that response would be. In addition to any increases in certainty, severity, and swiftness of sanctions associated with acts of violence, the Operation Ceasefire strategy pursued deterrence through advertising its law enforcement strategy and the personalized nature of its application. It was crucial that gang youths understood the new regime that the city was imposing. Beyond the particular gangs and gang members subjected to the intervention, the deterrence message was communicated to a relatively small audience (all gang-involved youths in Boston) rather than to a general audience (all Boston youths), and it articulated explicit cause-and-effect connections between the behavior of the target population and that of the authorities. Knowledge of what happened to others in the target population was intended to prevent further acts of violence by gangs in Boston.

In communicating the deterrence message, the Working Group also wanted to reach a shared moral ground with gang members. The Group wanted gang members to understand that most victims of gang violence were other gang members, that the strategy was designed to protect both gang members and the community in which they lived, and that the Working Group had gang members' best interests in mind—even if their own actions required coercion to protect them. The Working Group also hoped that face-to-face communication with gang members would undercut any feelings of anonymity and invulnerability they might have, and that a clear demonstration of interagency solidarity would enhance offenders' sense that something new and powerful was happening.

Operation Ceasefire was also intended to provide gang youths with a way to save face when confronted with the threat of violence. Youths in inner city neighborhoods adopt street behavior that is often reinforced by their peers (Anderson 1994). Street culture dictates that young men earn respect through tough behavior. Youths may be expected by members of their groups to respond to threats and challenges in violent, expressive ways (Wilkinson and Fagan 1996). Failure to adhere to these "scripts" may result in loss of status and exposure to a greater risk of victimization or isolation from peers (Wilkinson and Fagan 1996). The Working Group recognized these dynamics in conflicts between Boston gangs. A gang that suffered violence had to respond or it would lose status and respect on the street and open itself to further victimization. Operation Ceasefire was intended to give gang youths an "out" from responding violently to these status challenges by swiftly addressing the offending group, eliminating the need for a response and providing the victimized group with a justification for inaction. Victimized gang youths could save face by asserting that the authorities had removed the offending gang youths from the street and that a violent response was unwise, given the increased attention to the current situation.

Social Intervention and Opportunity Provision

... Boston's Mayor established the Boston Community Centers' Streetworkers social service program in 1991. Streetworkers were charged with seeking out at-risk youths in Boston's neighborhoods and providing them with services such as job skills training, substance abuse counseling, and special education. Many Boston streetworkers are themselves former gang members. Gang researchers have suggested that meaningful gang crime prevention programs should recruit gang members to participate in the program as staff and consultants (Hagedorn 1988; Bursik and Grasmick 1993). Beyond their important roles as social service providers, streetworkers attempted to prevent outbreaks of violence by mediating disputes between gangs. If the streetworkers had good relations with members of two gangs in conflict, they would work to settle the dispute between them through separate meetings with each group that would culminate in a negotiation session with key members of both rival groups. Although this tactic was not explicitly used in Operation Ceasefire, Boston's streetworkers used these negotiating skills and relationships with gang youths to support law enforcement efforts to stop outbreaks of violence. Streetworkers also ran programs intended to keep gang-involved youths safely occupied and bring them into contact in ways that might breed tolerance, including a Peace League of gang-on-gang basketball games held at neutral, controlled sites.

With these resources, the Working Group was able to pair criminal justice sanctions, or the threat of sanctions, with help and services. The premise behind this strategy was straightforward: When the risk to drug-dealing gang members increases, legitimate work becomes more attractive; when legitimate work is more available, raising risks will be more effective in reducing violence. The availability of social services and opportunities was intended to increase Operation Ceasefire's preventive power by offering gang members any assistance they might want, including protection from their enemies, drug treatment, and access to education and job training programs.

Community Organization

Community organization strategies to cope with gang problems include attempts to create community solidarity, networking, education, and involvement (Spergel and Curry 1993). The Ten Point Coalition of activist black clergy played an important role in organizing Boston communities suffering from gang violence (see Winship and Berrien 1999). The Coalition formed in 1992 after gang members invaded the Morningstar Baptist Church, where a slain rival gang member was being memorialized, and attacked mourners with knives and guns. In the wake of that incident, the Ten Point Coalition decided to respond to violence in their community by reaching out to youths involved in drugs and gangs and by organizing within Boston's black community. The Ten Point clergy came to work closely with the Boston Community Centers' streetworkers program to provide at-risk youths with opportunities. Although the Coalition was initially critical of the Boston law enforcement community, it eventually forged a strong working relationship. Ten Point clergy and others involved in this faith-based organization accompanied police officers on home visits to the families of troubled youths and acted as advocates for youths in the criminal justice system. The clergy's home visits and street work were later incorporated into Operation Ceasefire's portfolio of interventions. Ten Point clergy also provided a strong moral voice at the forums held to present Operation Ceasefire's antiviolence message to gang members.

Although it was not involved in Operation Ceasefire until after the intervention strategy had been designed and implemented, the Ten Point Coalition played a crucial role in framing the discussion that made it much easier to speak directly about youth violence in Boston. Members of the Ceasefire Working Group could speak with relative safety about the painful realities of minority male offending and victimization, gangs, and chronic offenders. The Ten Point clergy also made it possible for Boston's minority community to have an ongoing conversation with the city's law enforcement agencies on legitimate and illegitimate means to control crime. The clergy supported Operation Ceasefire's tight focus on violent youths, but condemned indiscriminate, highly aggressive law enforcement sweeps that put non-violent minority youths at risk of being swept into the criminal justice system. Before the Coalition developed its role as an intermediary, Boston's black community viewed past activities of law enforcement agencies to monitor violent youths as illegitimate and suspicious. As Winship and Berrien (1999) observe, the Ten Point Coalition evolved into an institution that provides an umbrella of legitimacy for police actions. With the Coalition's approval of and involvement in Operation Ceasefire, the community supported the approach as a legitimate youth violence prevention campaign. . . .

References

Anderson, Elijah. 1994. "The Code of the Streets." *The Atlantic Monthly* May: 81–94.

Braga, Anthony A., David M. Kennedy, Elin J. Waring, and Anne M. Piehl. 2001. "Problem-Oriented Policing, Deterrence, and Youth Violence: An Evaluation of Boston's Operation Ceasefire." *Journal of Research in Crime and Delinquency* 38(3): 195–225.

Braga, Anthony A., Anne M. Piehl, and David M. Kennedy. 1999. "Youth Homicide in Boston: An Assessment of Supplementary Homicide Report Data." *Homicide Studies* 3: 277–299.

Bursik, Robert, and Harold G. Grasmick. 1993. *Neighborhoods and Crime: The Dimensions of Effective Community Control.* New York: Lexington Books.

Hagedorn, John. 1988. *People and Folks: Gangs, Crime, and the Underclass in a Rustbelt City.* Chicago: Lakeview Press.

Kennedy, David M. 1997. "Pulling Levers: Chronic Offenders, High-Crime Settings, and a Theory of Prevention." *Valparaiso University Law Review* 31: 449–484.

———. 1998. "Pulling Levers: Getting Deterrence Right." *National Institute of Justice Journal* 136 (July): 2–8.

Kennedy, David M., Anthony A. Braga, and Anne M. Piehl. 1997. "The (Un)Known Universe: Mapping Gangs and Gang Violence in Boston." In *Crime Mapping and Crime Prevention*, eds. David Weisburd and Tom McEwen. New York: Criminal Justice Press: 219–262.

Kennedy, David M., Anne M. Piehl, and Anthony A. Braga. 1996. "Youth Violence in Boston: Gun Markets, Serious Youth Offenders, and A Use-Reduction Strategy." *Law and Contemporary Problems* 59: 147–196.

Spergel, Irving A. 1995. *The Youth Gang Problem: A Community Approach.* New York and London: Oxford University Press.

Spergel, Irving A., and G. David Curry. 1993. "Strategies and Perceived Agency Effectiveness in Dealing with the Youth Gang Problem." In *Gangs in America*, ed. C. Ronald Huff. Newbury Park, CA: Sage Publications: 288–309.

Wilkinson, Deanna L., and Jeffrey Fagan. 1996. "The Role of Firearms in Violence 'Scripts': The Dynamics of Gun Events Among Adolescent Males." *Law and Contemporary Problems* 59: 55–90.

Winship, Christopher, and Jenny Berrien. 1999. "Boston Cops and Black Churches." *The Public Interest*, Summer: 52–68.

Zimring, Franklin, and Gordon Hawkins. 1973. *Deterrence: The Legal Threat in Crime Control.* Chicago: University of Chicago Press. ✦

Part V

Juvenile Courts

The original juvenile courts focused on juveniles themselves, rather than on offenses, as offenses were seen as symptoms of the larger problems that the court would attempt to treat. Because of this treatment focus, in many ways the courts were more like coercive social work agencies than criminal courts.

This difference in philosophy was reflected in differences in terminology. For example, the *adjudication hearing* is the juvenile court term for a trial in criminal court, and the *disposition hearing* is what sentencing is called in criminal court. These terms reflect the original social work philosophy: juvenile courts did not subject juveniles to "trial" and "sentencing"—instead they "adjudicated" (i.e., made judgments about) the case by deciding whether to take jurisdiction over it and then "disposed of" the case by deciding what was best for the youth under the circumstances.

Nowadays, adjudication hearings in juvenile courts look very much like criminal trials. This is because, as discussed briefly in Chapter 1, juveniles now have all the same constitutional rights of adults except the right to a jury trial. As a result of these rights, adjudication hearings now are quite formal. In the original juvenile court, adjudication hearings were quite informal, with participants (including the juveniles) typically sitting around a table and talking about what should be done.

The first chapter in Part V looks at the current trend of enacting sentencing guidelines in disposition hearings. Like the changes in adjudication hearings, these changes in disposition hearings reflect movement toward a criminal court philosophy. In particular, they reflect a focus on providing proportional punishments for offenses, rather than a focus on addressing the needs of the juvenile. But despite this trend toward sentencing guidelines, the authors of this chapter argue that there still is a substantial focus on addressing the needs of the juvenile at disposition hearings.

The second chapter in Part V looks at a new phenomenon—teen courts. With juvenile courts becoming more and more like criminal courts, teen courts are returning to the original juvenile court philosophy of informal procedures and a focus on determining what is best for the youth. These new courts are rapidly spreading as juvenile courts themselves become more like criminal courts.

These two chapters suggest that the original philosophy of the juvenile court remains alive and well in American juvenile justice, despite recent trends toward the philosophy of the criminal court. ✦

Chapter 9

Sentencing Guidelines and the Transformation of Juvenile Justice in the 21st Century

Daniel P. Mears

Editor's Introduction

As one of their goals, the founders of the original juvenile court wanted a greater focus on juveniles and their needs and problems, rather than on the specific offenses that they committed. The offenses were viewed largely as symptoms of some underlying problems that needed to be addressed by the court. So while the offenses were important, they were not the sole determining factor of the court's response.

As a result of this viewpoint, the original juvenile court gave the judges a great deal of *discretion*—i.e., they had considerable latitude for making decisions about what to do with particular juveniles. The results therefore included a considerable amount of what today we would call *disparity*—i.e., juveniles who committed similar offenses might be treated very differently in court. All this was because the founders of the original juvenile court viewed offenses as symptoms of larger problems.

The recent "get-tough" changes in juvenile justice include much greater focus on the offense rather than on the offender. Because they focus on the offense, they largely limit the discretion of judges in responding to different cases—two youths who each commit a burglary should each receive similar punishments. As a result, these changes are designed to reduce the widespread disparity that was considered beneficial in the original juvenile court. All this is appealing in today's world, but would have made no sense to the founders of the juvenile court.

Adapted from Daniel P. Mears, "Sentencing Guidelines and the Transformation of Juvenile Justice in the 21st Century," *Journal of Contemporary Criminal Justice* 18 (1):6–19, copyright © 2002 by Sage Publications, Inc. Reprinted by permission of Sage Publications, Inc.

One of the ways to achieve uniformity in sentencing is with sentencing guidelines, which are widely used in the adult criminal courts for sentencing. Typically, the guidelines specify a relatively narrow range of sentences for each type of offense, where that range is somewhat greater or somewhat smaller depending on the offender's prior record. Sentencing guidelines necessarily are offense-based, since the sentence is determined entirely by the present offense and prior offenses. As such, they limit the discretion of judges and are intended to reduce the disparity in the handling of juvenile offenders.

The author of Chapter 9 raises the question, given the implementation of sentencing guidelines in juvenile courts, whether the juvenile court should continue to exist. It would appear that both juvenile and criminal courts provide offense-based punishments and the only difference between them is mitigation—juveniles typically receive less punishment for similar offenses than adults. That is identical to the situation before the founding of the juvenile court.

However, this author argues that, even with the implementation of sentencing guidelines, there is still a distinct need for a separate juvenile court system. In particular, there remains a strong focus on the original idea of the juvenile court: "a system designed to intervene on an individualized, case-by-case basis, addressing the particular risks and needs of offenders."

$$\text{✦ ✦ ✦}$$

The early juvenile court emphasized individualized, offender-based treatment and sanctioning. Indeed, almost every justification of the juvenile court rests on the notion that the most appropriate and effective intervention for youth is one that takes into account their particular needs and resources. Ironically, despite the establishment of this view more than 100 years ago, recent research provides considerable empirical support for it—the most effective interventions are those premised on addressing the specific risk, needs, and capacities of youth (Cullen & Gendreau, 2000; Lipsey, 1999). Under the Office of Juvenile Justice and Delinquency Prevention's (OJJDP's) Comprehensive Strategy for Serious, Violent, and Chronic Juvenile Offenders (Howell, 1995; Wilson & Howell, 1993), states have been encouraged to adopt individualized sanctioning and to emphasize risk and needs assessment. Many have responded by enacting guideline systems that are modeled to a considerable extent on the Comprehensive Strategy. In some states, these guideline systems are voluntary, in others there are incentives to use them, and in still others they are required. In each instance, the guidelines typically are offense-based and outline a sequence of increasingly tougher sanctions, while at the same time emphasizing rehabilitative interventions when appropriate.

In 1995, for example, Texas enacted what it termed the Progressive Sanctions Guidelines. The Guidelines outline seven tiers of sanctioning, with each linked to the instant offense and the offender's prior record. Once the appropriate level of sanctioning is established, courts are encouraged to include additional, non-punitive interventions. Although the Guidelines are voluntary, Texas documents the extent to which county-level sanctioning deviates from the recommendations of the Guidelines (Texas Criminal Justice Policy Council, 2001). Similar approaches have been implemented in other states, including Illinois, Kansas, Nebraska, New York, Utah, Virginia, and Washington (Corriero, 1999; Demleitner, 1999; Fagan & Zimring, 2000; Lieb & Brown, 1999; National Criminal Justice Association, 1997; Torbet et al., 1996).

State guideline systems often identify their goals explicitly. In Texas, for example, the Progressive Sanction Guidelines are used to "guide" dispositional decision making in providing "appropriate" sanctions and to promote "uniformity" and "consistency" in sentencing (Dawson, 1996). At the same time, the Guidelines are seen as furthering the newly established and explicitly stated goal of the Texas Juvenile Justice Code—namely, punishment of juveniles. But they also promote rehabilitative sanctioning by encouraging appropriate treatment and interventions for each recommended sanction level. In addition, the Guidelines implicitly promote certain goals, including public safety through incapacitation of the most serious or chronic offenders and reduced crime through get-tough, deterrence-oriented sanctioning. Other states have followed similar paths. For example, Washington established sentencing guidelines aimed directly at reducing the perceived failings of a system founded on practitioner discretion (Lieb & Brown, 1999). The guidelines focus not only on offense-based considerations but also on the juvenile's age, with younger offenders receiving fewer "points" and thus more lenient sanctions. Similarly, Utah has enacted sentencing guidelines focusing on proportionate sentencing, early intervention, and progressively intensive supervision and sanctioning for more serious and chronic offenders (Utah Sentencing Commission, 1997).

Because many states increasingly are adopting sentencing guidelines and because the guidelines focus on all youth rather than simply those who may be transferred, an examination of them can help to identify underlying trends and issues emergent in juvenile justice. By contrast, a focus on transfer, typical of most research on recent reforms, provides relatively little leverage to do so. Transfer laws typically focus on "easy cases," those in which the seriousness of the offense largely vitiates, rightly or wrongly, concerns many would have about individualized or rehabilitative sanctioning. Any resulting debate therefore centers on extremes: Should we retain or eliminate the juvenile court?

But a broader issue in juvenile justice is how to balance individualized, offender-based sanctioning with proportional and consistent punishment. These issues, among several others, are a consideration in almost every case coming before the juvenile court. It is appropriate, therefore, to focus on a recent reform, such as sentencing guidelines, that typically target, in one manner or another, all youth and that reflect attempts to shape the entire juvenile justice system. For this reason, the remainder of this article uses a focus on sentencing guidelines to identify key trends and issues in the transformation of juvenile justice.

Juvenile Sentencing Guidelines: Trends and Issues in the Transformation of Juvenile Justice in the New Millennium

Balancing Multiple and Conflicting Goals

The motivation for transforming juvenile justice has come from many sources. Scholars cite a range of factors, including the desire to address violent crime, inconsistency and racial/ethnic disproportionality in sentencing, financial burdens faced by counties versus states, and public support for get tough and rehabilitative measures (Bazemore & Umbreit, 1995; Bishop, Lanza-Kaduce, & Frazier, 1998; Butts & Mitchell, 2000). As suggested by the different motivations for reform, a key trend in juvenile justice is the move toward balancing multiple and frequently competing goals, only one of which includes the punitive focus associated with transfer (Bazemore & Umbreit, 1995; Guarino-Ghezzi & Loughran,1996; Mears, 2000). Today, many juvenile justice codes and policies focus on retributive/punitive sanctioning (through get-tough sanctions generally), incapacitation, deterrence, rehabilitation, individualized as well as consistent and proportional sentencing, and restorative sanctioning.

Reduced crime is a broad goal underlying many but not all of these more specific goals. For example, get-tough sanctions are viewed as a primary mechanism to instill fear and achieve specific or general deterrence (i.e., reduced offending among sanctioned or would-be offenders) or to reduce crime through temporary incapacitation of offenders. In many instances, retribution serves as the primary focus of sanctioning, irrespective of any potential crime control impact.

Some goals, like rehabilitation, serve as steps toward enhancing the lives of juveniles, not simply reducing their offending. Others, such as restorative sanctioning, focus on reintegrating offenders into their communities while at the same time providing victims with a voice in the sanctioning and justice process. Still others, including proportional and consistent sentencing, focus primarily on fairness rather than crime control. That is, the motivation is to provide sanctions that are proportional to the crime and that are consistent within and across jurisdictions so that juveniles sanctioned by Judge X or in County X receive sanctions similar to those administered by Judge Y or in County Y.

Historically these different goals, including what might be termed intermediate goals leading to reduced crime, have overlapped considerably with those of the criminal justice system (Snyder & Sickmund, 1999, pp. 94–96). In general, though, criminal justice systems have given greater weight to punishment than rehabilitation, whereas juvenile justice systems generally have favored rehabilitation more than punishment.

In reality, the goals in each system are diverse, as are the weightings given to each goal. Indeed, the diversity of goals and their weightings can make it difficult to determine how exactly the two systems differ, especially if we focus only on new transfer laws (see, however, Bishop & Frazier, 2000). But one major difference between the two is that juvenile justice systems—as is evident in their sentencing guideline systems—are actively struggling to balance as wide a range of goals as possible. By contrast, most criminal justice systems have veered strongly toward retribution and incapacitation (Clark, Austin, & Henry, 1997).

Giving Priority to Punishment Through Offense-Based Guidelines and Changes in Discretion

Most state guideline systems use offense-based criteria for determining which types of sanctions to apply (Coolbaugh & Hansel, 2000). Once the punishment level has been established, the court is supposed to consider the needs of the offender and how these may best be addressed. However, these needs frequently are only vaguely specified and rarely assessed. One result is that priority implicitly and in practice may be given to punishment. This priority can be reinforced through various mechanisms that place greater discretion in the hands of prosecutors rather than judges. For example, laws that stipulate automatic sanctions for certain offenses do not eliminate discretion; instead, they shift it to prosecutors, who can determine whether and how to charge an offense (Feld, 1999; Mears, 2000; Sanborn, 1994; Singer, 1996). Consequently, in practice, many guideline systems make punishment a priority not just for youth who may be transferred but for all youth referred to juvenile court.

Sentencing guidelines have not gone unopposed. For example, research on the Texas Progressive Sanction Guidelines indicates that many judges resisted enactment of the Guidelines and then, once they became law, resisted using them (Mears, 2000). One reason is their belief that offense-based criteria provide too limited a basis for structuring decision-making. Thus, even though compliance with the Guidelines is voluntary, some judges feel that the Guidelines symbolize too narrow a focus, one that draws attention from factors they believe are more important, such as the age and maturity of the youth and their family and community contexts. Such concerns have been expressed about adult sentencing guidelines (e.g., see Forer, 1994). One difference with juvenile sentencing guidelines is that, despite the views of opponents, they generally state explicitly that there are multiple goals associated with sanctioning and that practitioners should consider a range of mitigating factors (Howell, 1995).

Balancing Discretion Versus Disparity and Consistency, and Procedural Versus Substantive Justice

In stark contrast to the early foundation of the juvenile court, many states today are intent on eliminating disparity and inconsistency in sentencing (Feld, 1999; Torbet et al., 1996). The widespread belief, evident in many sentencing guidelines, is that (a) judicial discretion causes disparity and inconsistency and (b) that offense-based systems can eliminate or reduce these problems. Both beliefs prevail despite the fact that little empirical evidence exists to support them (Mears & Field, 2000; Sanborn, 1994; Yellen, 1999). But the fact that such strategies may not work does not belie the underlying trend toward discovering ways to promote fairness and consistency in sentencing. Nor does it belie the fact that, as with adult sanctioning, there likely will continue to be an ongoing tension between the use of discretion and the need to have sanctions that are relatively similar for different populations and within and across jurisdictions.

This tension is captured in part by the distinction in the sociology of law between procedural and substantive justice. From the perspective of procedural justice, fairness emerges from decisions that are guided by established rules and procedures for sanctioning cases that exhibit specific characteristics. By contrast, from the perspective of substantive justice, fairness emerges from decisions that are guided by consideration of the unique situational context and characteristics of the defendant (Gould,1993; Ulmer & Kramer, 1996).

In recent years, and as exemplified by the creation of offense-based sentencing guidelines, juvenile justice systems increasingly are focusing on procedural justice. In the case of transfer particularly, the Supreme Court and state legislatures have attempted to ensure that there is procedural parity with adult proceedings. Yet despite the increased proceduralization, for most cases facing the juvenile courts, substantive justice also remains a priority, especially when sanctioning first-time and less serious offenders. In these instances, states have devised strategies, outlined in their guidelines, that promote diversion, rehabilitation, and treatment.

Maintaining the View That Most Youth Are 'Youth,' Not Adults

Public opinion polls show that whereas most people consistently support rehabilitative sanctioning of youth, they also support punitive, get-tough measures for serious and violent offenders (Roberts & Stalans, 1998). Moreover, even when the public supports transferring youth to the adult system, they generally prefer youth to be housed in separate facilities and to receive individualized, rehabilitative treatment (Schwartz, Guo, & Kerbs, 1993). The apparent contradiction likely constitutes the primary reason that wholesale elimination of the juvenile justice system has not prevailed. In the debate about abolishing the juvenile court, this fact frequently is omitted, perhaps because so much attention has centered on changes in transfer laws. Indeed, were one to focus solely on recent trends in transfer, one might conclude that an eventual merging of juvenile and adult systems is inevitable (Feld, 1999).

Yet the focus and structure of juvenile sentencing guidelines, which explicitly call for rehabilitation and early intervention, suggest otherwise. In contrast to get-tough developments in the criminal justice system (Clark et al., 1997), most states—even those without guideline systems—have struggled to maintain a focus not only on the most violent offenders but also on efficient and effective intervention with less serious offenders. This trend is reflected in the proliferation of alternative, or specialized, courts, including community, teen, drug, and mental health courts (Butts & Harrell, 1998; Office of Justice Programs, 1998; Santa Clara County Superior Court, 2001). These courts focus on timely and rehabilitative sanctioning that draws on the strengths of families and communities and the cooperation and assistance of local and state agencies.

Some authors suggest that these courts threaten the foundation of the juvenile court (Butts & Harrell, 1998). But specialized courts can be viewed as symbolic of the reemergence of the juvenile justice system as historically conceived—namely, as a system designed to intervene on an individualized, case-by-case basis, addressing the particular risks and needs of offenders (Butts & Mears, 2001). Indeed, to this end, many guidelines promote diversion of first- and second-time, less serious offenders from formal processing to informal alternatives available through specialized courts.

Limited Conceptualization and Assessment of the Implementation and Effects of Changes in the Juvenile Justice System

One last and prominent trend in juvenile justice bears emphasizing—the lack of systematic attention to conceptualizing and assessing the implementation and effects of recently enacted laws. A focus on sentencing guidelines illustrates the point: Few states have systematically articulated precisely what the goals of the guidelines are, how specifically the guidelines are expected to achieve these goals, or what in fact the effects of the guidelines have been (Coolbaugh & Hansel, 2000; Fagan & Zimring, 2000; Mears, 2000).

One example common to many guidelines is the focus on consistency. Several questions illustrate the point. What exactly does *consistency* mean? Is it identical sentencing of like offenders within jurisdictions? Across jurisdictions? Does it involve similar weighting of the same factors by all judges or judges within each jurisdiction in a state? Across states? Apart from definitional issues, does consistency lead to reduced crime or increased perceptions of fairness? If so, how? What precisely are the mechanisms by which increased consistency would lead to changes in crime or perceptions of fairness? The failure to address these questions means that it is impossible to assess whether there has been more or less consistency resulting from guideline systems.

Similar questions about many other aspects of recent juvenile justice reforms remain largely unaddressed, with two unfortunate consequences. First, as noted above, it is impossible to assess the effects of the reforms without greater clarity concerning their goals and the means by which these goals are to be reached. As a result, it is difficult if not impossible to make informed policy decisions, including those focusing on maintaining or eliminating the juvenile justice system (Schneider, 1984; Singer, 1996). Second, without conceptualization and assessment of the effects of recent reforms, there is an increased likelihood that research on delimited aspects of juvenile justice systems will be generalized into statements about entire systems, even though there may be little to no correspondence between the two.

Conclusion

Recent changes to juvenile justice systems throughout the United States indicate a trend toward developing more efficient and effective strategies for balancing different and frequently competing goals. This trend is evident in recent juvenile sentencing guidelines. As the above discussion demonstrates, guidelines focus on more than transferring the most serious offenders to the criminal justice system. They also focus on balancing competing goals, reducing discretion and promoting fair and consistent sanctioning, and tempering procedural with substantive justice. More generally, guidelines aim to preserve the notion that youth are not adults.

One result of such trends is increasing interest in alternative administrative mechanisms for processing youthful offenders. Specialized "community," "teen," "drug," "mental health," and other such courts have been developed to do what the original juvenile court was supposed to do—provide individualized and rehabilitative sanctioning. But the "modern" approach involves doing so in a more timely and sophisticated fashion, and in a way that draws on the cooperation and assistance of local and state agencies as well as families and communities.

In the new millennium, juvenile justice thus involves more than an emphasis on due process and punishment. It also involves substantive concerns, including a range of competing goals, a belief in the special status of childhood, and the desire to develop more effective strategies for preventing and reducing juvenile crime.

By focusing on sentencing guidelines, these types of issues become more apparent, highlighting the need for researchers to look beyond transfer laws in assessing recent juvenile justice reforms. Indeed, there is a need for research on many new and different laws, polices, and programs in juvenile justice, most of which remain unassessed. As we enter the new millennium, it will be critical to redress this situation, especially if we are to move juvenile justice beyond "juvenile" versus "adult" debates and to develop more efficient and effective interventions.

References

Bazemore, G., & Umbreit, M. (1995). Rethinking the sanctioning function in juvenile court: Retributive or restorative responses to youth crime. *Crime & Delinquency*, 41, 296–316.

Bishop, D. M., & Frazier, C. E. (2000). Consequences of transfer. In J. Fagan & F. E. Zimring (Eds.), *The changing boundaries of juvenile justice: Transfer of adolescents to the criminal court* (pp. 227–276). Chicago: University of Chicago Press.

Bishop, D. M., Lanza-Kaduce, L., & Frazier, C. E. (1998). Juvenile justice under attack: An analysis of the causes and impact of recent reforms. *Journal of Law and Public Policy*, 10, 129–155.

Butts, J. A., & Harrell, A. V. (1998). *Delinquents or criminals? Policy options for juvenile offenders*. Washington, DC: The Urban Institute.

Butts, J. A., & Mears, D. P. (2001). Reviving juvenile justice in a get-tough era. *Youth & Society*, 33, 169–198.

Butts, J. A., & Mitchell, O. (2000). Brick by brick: Dismantling the border between juvenile and adult justice. In C. M. Friel (Ed.), *Criminal justice 2000: Boundary changes in criminal justice organizations* (Vol. 2, pp. 167–213). Washington, DC: National Institute of Justice.

Clark, J., Austin, J., & Henry, D. A. (1997). *"Three strikes and you're out": A review of state legislation.* Washington, DC: National Institute of Justice.

Coolbaugh, K., & Hansel, C. J. (2000). *The comprehensive strategy: Lessons learned from the pilot sites.* Washington, DC: Office of Juvenile Justice and Delinquency Prevention.

Corriero, M. A. (1999). Juvenile sentencing: The New York youth part as a model. *Federal Sentencing Reporter*, 11, 278–281.

Dawson, R. O. (1996). *Texas juvenile law* (4th ed.). Austin: Texas Juvenile Probation Commission.

Cullen, F. T., & Gendreau, P. (2000). Assessing correctional rehabilitation: Policy, practice, and prospects. In J. Horney (Ed.), *Criminal justice 2000: Policies, processes, and decisions of the criminal justice system* (Vol. 3, pp. 109–175). Washington, DC: National Institute of Justice.

Demleitner, N. V. (1999). Reforming juvenile sentencing. *Federal Sentencing Reporter*, 11, 243–247.

Fagan, J., & Zimring, F. E. (Eds.). (2000). *The changing borders of juvenile justice.* Chicago: University of Chicago Press.

Feld, B. C. (1999). *Bad kids: Race and the transformation of the juvenile court.* New York: Oxford University Press.

Forer, L. (1994). *A rage to punish: The unintended consequences of mandatory sentencing.* New York: Norton.

Gould, M. (1993). Legitimation and justification: The logic of moral and contractual solidarity in Weber and Durkheim. *Social Theory*, 13, 205–225.

Guarino-Ghezzi, S., & Loughran, E. J. (1996). *Balancing juvenile justice.* New Brunswick, NJ: Transaction.

Howell, J. C. (1995). *Guide for implementing the comprehensive strategy for serious, violent, and chronic juvenile offenders.* Washington, DC: Office of Juvenile Justice and Delinquency Prevention.

Lieb, R., & Brown, M. E. (1999). Washington state's solo path: Juvenile sentencing guidelines. *Federal Sentencing Reporter*, 11, 273–277.

Lipsey, M. W. (1999). Can rehabilitative programs reduce the recidivism of juvenile offenders? An inquiry into the effectiveness of practical programs. *Virginia Journal of Social Policy and Law*, 6, 611–641.

Mears, D. P. (2000). Assessing the effectiveness of juvenile justice reforms: A closer look at the criteria and impacts on diverse stakeholders. *Law and Policy*, 22, 175–202.

Mears, D. P., & Field, S. H. (2000). Theorizing sanctioning in a criminalized juvenile court. *Criminology*, 38, 101–137.

National Criminal Justice Association. (1997). *Juvenile justice reform initiatives in the states: 1994–1996.* Washington, DC: Office of Juvenile Justice and Delinquency Prevention.

Office of Justice Programs. (1998). *Juvenile and family drug courts: An overview.* Washington, DC: Author.

Roberts, J. V., & Stalans, L. J. (1998). Crime, criminal justice, and public opinion. In M. Tonry (Ed.), *The handbook of crime and punishment* (pp. 31–57). New York: Oxford University Press.

Sanborn, J. A. (1994). Certification to criminal court: The important policy questions of how, when, and why. *Crime & Delinquency*, 40, 262–281.

Santa Clara County Superior Court. (2001). *Santa Clara County Superior Court commences juvenile mental health court.* San Jose, CA: Author.

Schneider, A. L. (1984). Sentencing guidelines and recidivism rates of juvenile offenders. *Justice Quarterly*, 1, 107–124.

Schwartz, I. M., Guo, S., & Kerbs, J. J. (1993). The impact of demographic variables on public opinion regarding juvenile justice: Implications for public policy. *Crime & Delinquency*, 39, 5–28.

Singer, S. I. (1996). Merging and emerging systems of juvenile and criminal justice. *Law and Policy*, 18, 1–15.

Snyder, H. N., & Sickmund, M. (1999). *Juvenile offenders and victims: 1999 national report*. Washington, DC: Office of Juvenile Justice and Delinquency Prevention.

Texas Criminal Justice Policy Council. (2001). *The impact of progressive sanction guidelines: Trends since 1995*. Austin, TX: Author.

Torbet, P., Gable, R., Hurst, H. IV, Montgomery, I., Szymanski, L., & Thomas, D. (1996). *State responses to serious and violent juvenile crime*. Washington, DC: Office of Juvenile Justice and Delinquency Prevention.

Ulmer, J. T., & Kramer, J. H. (1996). Court communities under sentencing guidelines: Dilemmas of formal rationality and sentencing disparity. *Criminology, 34,* 383–407.

Utah Sentencing Commission. (1997). *Juvenile sentencing guidelines manual*. Salt Lake City, UT: Author.

Wilson, J. J., & Howell, J. C. (1993). *Comprehensive strategy for serious, violent, and chronic juvenile offenders: Program summary*. Washington, DC: Office of Juvenile Justice and Delinquency Prevention.

Yellen, D. (1999). Sentence discounts and sentencing guidelines. *Federal Sentencing Reporter, 11,* 285–288. ✦

Chapter 10

Teen Courts

A Focus on Research

Jeffrey A. Butts and Janeen Buck

Editor's Introduction

Chapter 9 argued that today the juvenile court has become more *offense-oriented*. This is an important change, since originally the juvenile court was very *offender-oriented*—it focused on juveniles and their needs and problems rather than on the offenses they committed. The chapter concluded that increasing numbers of juveniles are being transferred out of the juvenile court in two directions. In one direction are "community," "teen," "drug," and "mental health" courts that are doing what the original juvenile court did—providing individualized and rehabilitative sanctioning. In the other direction are the (adult) criminal courts, where increasing numbers of juveniles are simply punished for their offenses.

Juveniles transferred to the criminal courts will be examined in the chapters in Part VI. Here, Chapter 10 looks at the most important and rapidly spreading of the new specialized courts: teen courts.[1] This report is based on a survey of 300 teen courts nationwide, conducted in 1998.

It is interesting that the rapid spread of these new courts may reflect the same problem that led to the establishment of the original juvenile court, as described in Chapter 2. The original juvenile court was founded in 1899 because the criminal court provided only harsh punishments for responding to juvenile offenders. As a result, officials often had to choose between punishing a juvenile harshly and doing nothing at all. Eventually, these officials concluded that both of these options increased delinquency, and they established the juvenile court as a "middle ground" to provide lenient punishments for a wider number of juveniles.

Adapted from Jeffrey A. Butts and Janeen Buck, "Teen Courts: A Focus on Research," *Juvenile Justice Bulletin*. Washington, DC: Office of Juvenile Justice and Delinquency Prevention, 2000. Copyright is not claimed in this article, a publication of the United States government.

One of the points emphasized in Chapter 9 is that today, teen courts provide some sanction for every offense, even though these sanctions are often very lenient. It points out that many of these juveniles would have received no punishment at all if they had been handled in juvenile court. Thus, it appears that the juvenile court today is in the same situation that the criminal court was in 1899. And it appears that "teen courts" today are spreading rapidly for the same reason that the juvenile courts spread rapidly in the early years of the twentieth century: they provide lenient options for responding to a wider range of juvenile offending.

Regardless of whether that is the case, teen courts seem to be a promising method for reducing offending in juveniles. Chapter 10 concludes by reviewing research on their effectiveness, and even more recent research has continued to find reductions in recidivism in first-, second-, and even third-time juvenile offenders, compared to those handled in regular juvenile courts.

Notes

1. From only a handful in the 1960s, the number of teen courts had grown to about 675 by the year 2000 and about 880 by 2004. See Deborah Kirby Forgays and Lisa DeMilio, "Is Teen Court Effective for Repeat Offenders?: A Test of the Restorative Justice Approach," *International Journal of Offender Therapy and Comparative Criminology* 49 (1):107–118, February 2005. Another rapidly spreading specialized court is the juvenile drug court. See Jeffrey Butts and John Roman, eds., *Juvenile Drug Courts and Teen Substance Abuse*, Urban Institute Press, Washington DC, 2004.

2. For example, for first-time offenders see Andrew Rasmussen, "Teen Court Referral, Sentencing, and Subsequent Recidivism: Two Proportional Hazards Models and a Little Speculation," *Crime & Delinquency* 50(4):615–35, October 2004. For second-time offenders, see Forgays and DeMilio, op. cit. Even third-time offenders may experience reduced recidivism—Andrew J. Dick, Reed Geertsen, and Randall M. Jones ("Self-Reported Delinquency Among Teen Court Participants," *Journal for Juvenile Justice and Detention Services* 18(1):33–49, Spring 2003) found reduced recidivism for "early" offenders but not for those who had broken the law four times or more.

❖ ❖ ❖

The Teen Court Concept

Teen courts are generally used for younger juveniles (ages 10 to 15), those with no prior arrest records, and those charged with less serious law violations (e.g., shoplifting, vandalism, and disorderly conduct). Typically, young offenders are offered teen court as a voluntary alternative in lieu of more formal handling by the traditional juvenile justice system. . . .

Teen courts differ from other juvenile justice programs because young people rather than adults determine the disposition, given a broad array of sentencing options made available by adults overseeing the program. Teen court defendants may go through an intake process, a preliminary review of charges, a court hearing, and sentencing, as in a regular juvenile court. In a teen court, however, other young people are responsible for much of the process. Charges may be presented to the court by a 15-year-old "prosecutor." Defendants may be represented by a 16-year-old "defense attorney." Other youth may serve as jurors, court clerks, and bailiffs. In some teen courts, a youth "judge" (or panel of youth judges) may choose the best disposition or sanction for each case. In a few teen courts, youth even determine whether the facts in a case have been proven by the prosecutor (similar to a finding of guilt). . . .

Adults are also involved in teen courts. They often administer the programs, and they are usually responsible for essential functions such as budgeting, planning, and personnel. In many programs, adults supervise the courtroom activities, and they often coordinate the community service placements where youth work to fulfill the terms of their dispositions. In some programs, adults act as the judges while teens serve as attorneys and jurors. The key to all teen court programs, however, is the significant role youth play in the deliberation of charges and the imposition of sanctions on young offenders.

Proponents of teen court argue that the process takes advantage of one of the most powerful forces in the life of an adolescent—the desire for peer approval and the reaction to peer pressure. According to this argument, youth respond better to prosocial peers than to adult authority figures. Thus, teen courts are seen as a potentially effective alternative to traditional juvenile courts staffed with paid professionals such as lawyers, judges, and probation officers. Teen court advocates also point out that the benefits extend beyond defendants. Teen courts may benefit the volunteer youth attorneys and judges, who probably learn more about the legal system than they ever could in a classroom. The presence of a teen court may also encourage the entire community to take a more active role in responding to juvenile crime. Teen courts offer at least four potential benefits:

- **Accountability.** Teen courts may help to ensure that young offenders are held accountable for their illegal behavior, even when their offenses are relatively minor and would not likely result in sanctions from the traditional juvenile justice system.

- **Timeliness.** An effective teen court can move young offenders from arrest to sanctions within a matter of days rather than the months that may pass with traditional juvenile courts. This rapid response may increase the positive impact of court sanctions, regardless of their severity.

- **Cost savings.** Teen courts usually depend heavily on youth and adult volunteers. If managed properly, they may handle a substantial number of offenders at relatively little cost to the community. The average annual cost for operating a teen court is $32,822 (National Youth Court Center, unpublished data).

- **Community cohesion.** A well-structured and expansive teen court program may affect the entire community by increasing public appreciation of the legal system, enhancing community-court relationships, encouraging greater respect for the law among youth, and promoting volunteerism among both adults and youth. . . .

Program Characteristics

Recent growth in the number of teen court programs nationwide was reflected in the brief tenure of the programs responding to the national survey. Of all the programs that responded, 13 percent had been in operation less than 1 year and 42 percent had been in operation for only 1 to 3 years. More than two-thirds (67 percent) of all teen courts had been in existence for less than 5 years. . . .

Many teen courts that responded to the survey were closely affiliated with the traditional justice system. . . . Courts, law enforcement agencies, juvenile probation offices, or prosecutors' offices operated slightly more than half (52 percent) of the programs responding to the survey. More than one-third (37 percent) of the programs were affiliated with the courts and 12 percent with law enforcement. Private agencies operated one-quarter (25 percent) of the teen court programs. . . .

Most teen court and youth court programs were relatively small. . . . More than half (59 percent) of the programs responding to the survey handled 100 or fewer cases annually. Just 13 percent of the programs handled more than 300 cases per year. . . .

Very few programs relied on private funding to meet their operational costs. . . . More than half (59 percent) of the teen courts received no private funding; 16 percent of the programs received up to one-fifth of their funding from private sources, and 11 percent received between one-fifth and one-half from private sources. . . .

Client Characteristics

Teen courts usually handle relatively young offenders with no prior arrests. Survey respondents reported that, on average, 24 percent of their cases involved youth under age 14 and 66 percent involved youth under age 16. More than one-third (39 percent) of the teen courts accepted only first-time offenders and another 48 percent reported that they "rarely" accepted youth with prior arrest records. Nearly all programs (98 percent) reported that they "never" or "rarely" accepted youth with prior felony arrests. Most programs (91 percent) also indicated that they "never" or "rarely" accepted youth who previously had been referred to a juvenile court.

To assess the nature of those cases typically handled in teen court, the survey asked each program to review a list of offenses and to indicate whether the program received such cases "very often," "often," "rarely," or "never." The offenses most likely to be received "often" or "very often" were theft (93 percent), minor assault (66 percent), disorderly conduct (62 percent), possession or use of alcohol (60 percent), and vandalism (59 percent). . . .

Sanctions

The principal goal of teen court is to hold young offenders accountable for their behavior. In a system of graduated sanctions, there is a consequence for every offense. Every youth who has admitted guilt or who is found guilty in teen court receives some form of sanction. In many communities, teen court sanctions do more than punish the offender. Sanctions encourage young offenders to repair at least part of the damage they have caused to the community or to specific victims. Offenders are often ordered to pay restitution or perform community service. Some teen courts require offenders to write formal apologies to their victims; others require offenders to serve on a subsequent teen court jury. Many courts use other innovative dispositions, such as requiring offenders to attend classes designed to improve their decisionmaking skills, enhance their awareness of victims, and deter them from future theft.

Survey respondents were asked to assess a list of typical sanctions and indicate how frequently the program used each one (i.e., "very often," "often," "rarely," or "never"). Community service was the most commonly used sanction. . . . Nearly all (99 percent) of responding teen courts reported using community service "often" or "very often." Other frequently used sanctions included victim apology letters (86 percent), written essays (79 percent), teen court jury duty (74 percent), drug/alcohol classes (60 percent), and restitution (34 percent). . . .

Courtroom Models

NYCC [The National Youth Court Center] divides the courtroom approaches used by teen courts into four types . . . : adult judge, youth judge, peer jury, and youth tribunal (National Youth Court Center, 2000). Findings from the national survey suggested that the adult judge model was the most popular. Nearly half (47 percent) of the responding courts used only the adult judge model. When the number of cases handled by adult judges in programs using a mix of courtroom models was added, the adult judge model accounted for more than half (60 percent) of all teen court cases.

The next most prevalent courtroom model was the peer jury, which accounted for 22 percent of all teen court cases. More than one in four (26 percent) teen court programs used this model for at least part of their caseloads. The youth judge and tribunal models were the least used, with each accounting for just 7 percent of all cases.

The use of courtroom models varied somewhat according to the agency sponsoring the program. . . . The adult judge model was the most popular among teen courts operated by local courts and probation agencies (58 percent) and those hosted by schools, private agencies, and other not-for-profit organizations (48 percent). There was no dominant model, however, among programs operated by law enforcement agencies or prosecutors. In fact, more than one-third (34 percent) of those programs used mixed models (i.e., a combination of two or more courtroom models). . . .

Differences by Courtroom Model

The characteristics of teen courts were notably different when the analysis controlled for courtroom model. . . . For example, programs using the youth judge model were among the newest teen court programs. Fewer than one-fifth (19 percent) of these programs had been in operation for 5 years or more, compared with 31 percent of adult judge programs, 35 percent of programs using peer juries, and 34 percent of programs using the youth tribunal model. Most (58 percent) youth judge programs had been in operation for less than 2 years at the time of the survey. . . .

Youth judge programs were also the smallest programs in terms of their annual caseloads. Only 14 percent of programs using the youth judge model reported more than 100 cases per year, compared with 40 percent of programs using the adult judge model and 38 percent of programs using peer juries.

Programs using the peer jury model were the least likely to depend on private funding. Nearly four-fifths (78 percent) of peer jury programs received no private funding and only 13 percent received more than one-third of their funding from private sources. For most other courtroom models, nearly half of the programs responding to the survey reported receiving some private funding (i.e., 45 percent of adult judge programs, 47 percent of youth judge programs, and 48 percent of youth tribunal programs).

Programs using the youth judge and youth tribunal models were more likely to allow juveniles to plead innocence or guilt and to hold trials. About one-third (35 percent) of programs using the youth judge model and 44 percent of those using the youth tribunal model held trials.

About 80 percent of teen court programs responding to the survey had a paid, full-time or part-time program director. Programs using the peer jury model were least likely to have paid program directors (58 percent). Likewise, these programs were least likely to operate during the summer months (53 percent). . . .

Of the four major program models, youth tribunal programs were the most likely to accept referrals for youth with prior arrest records. Only 28 percent of programs using the youth tribunal model reported that they would "never" accept youth with prior arrests, compared with at least 40 percent for all other program models. Just 39 percent of tribunal programs indicated that they would "never" accept youth with prior juvenile court referrals, compared with 50 percent or more among the other types of teen court models. . . .

Recidivism

Recidivism would seem to be an obvious focus for evaluation studies of teen courts, but only a handful of evaluations have measured postprogram recidivism. . . . Most evaluations of teen court recidivism have employed relatively simple research designs. Even some of the best studies (Minor et al., 1999; LoGalbo, 1998; Swink, 1998; Wells, Minor, and Fox, 1998) have relied on data from a single group of teen court cases at a single point in time. Often, researchers have failed to use comparison groups or pre- and postmeasures. Thus, it is impossible to test the assumption that recidivism outcomes are due to teen court rather than to other factors (e.g., the type of youth selected for teen court may be unlikely to recidivate).

Only three published studies (Hissong, 1991; North Carolina Administrative Office of the Courts, 1995; Seyfrit, Reichel, and Stutts, 1987) have used reasonably appropriate comparison groups to measure the possible effects of teen courts on recidivism. . . . Hissong's evaluation of an Arlington, TX, teen court compared recidivism among teen court defendants with a group of non-teen-court participants matched on sex, race, age, and offense. The analysis suggested that teen court participants were significantly less likely to reoffend than the comparison group (24 percent versus 36 percent). Several important elements of the study, however, were poorly documented.

The definition of recidivism used in the analysis (presumably rear-rest) is unclear. The duration of the followup period is not described (subjects may have had different periods of risk), and there is a range of unexplored potential differences between the treatment group and the comparison group.

The North Carolina study used a comparison group that consisted of 97 cases diverted by police during a 6-month period prior to imple-mentation of the teen court in Cumberland, NC. Researchers hypoth-esized that these youth would have been referred to teen court had the program been in existence. Teen court and comparison group cases were matched using several factors, including demographic characteristics and offense type, and researchers tracked the recidi-vism of both groups. The study failed to find statistically significant differences in the recidivism of the two groups. In fact, the analysis seemed to favor the comparison group. After 7 months, 20 percent of teen court participants had reoffended, compared with just 9 percent of the comparison group. The study also found little difference be-tween the two groups in average time before a new offense (4.1 months for teen court offenders versus 4.6 months for the compari-son group). Youth who successfully completed the teen court pro-gram were less likely to reoffend than were youth who began but failed to complete the program (11 percent compared with 42 per-cent), but this finding may reflect the greater tendency of low-risk youth to complete the program.

Seyfrit and her colleagues (1987) tracked recidivism outcomes for 52 youth referred to a Columbia County, GA, teen court during an 18-month period in the early 1980's. They also collected data for a comparison group of 50 youth matched on demographics and of-fenses. The study found little difference between the two groups. Al-though 12 percent of the comparison group recidivated during the followup period, the same was true for 10 percent of the teen court defendants. Like the North Carolina study, the Seyfrit study was un-able to control statistically for different periods of opportunity to reoffend. The followup periods ranged from 6 to 18 months, which reduced the researchers' ability to infer any real differences in the re-cidivism of the two groups.

Other Outcomes

Several studies have suggested that teen courts may have effects on youth other than reduced recidivism. These potential benefits include client satisfaction with the teen court experience (Colydas and McLeod, 1997; McLeod, 1999; Reichel and Seyfrit, 1984; Swink, 1998; Wells, Minor, and Fox, 1998), enhanced perceptions of procedural justice

(Butler-Mejia, 1998), improved attitudes toward authority (LoGalbo, 1998; Wells, Minor, and Fox, 1998), and greater knowledge of the legal system (LoGalbo, 1998; Wells, Minor, and Fox, 1998). . . .

For example, McLeod's (1999) survey of former teen court participants found that at least 90 percent of youth referred to the Colonie (NY) Youth Court during 1997 and 1998 believed that the experience increased their understanding of the legal system, helped them improve their behavior, and helped them become more responsible. Nearly all survey respondents (95 percent) reported that going through teen court caused them to "make more thoughtful decisions." Nearly three in five (58 percent) reported better communication with their parents, and half (50 percent) reported improved grades in school. However, the study's very low response rate (24 percent of youth surveyed) raised the possibility that the youth responding to the followup survey may have been the most compliant and prosocial youth in the sample.

LoGalbo's (1998) evaluation of the Sarasota County, FL, teen court program also found that teen court positively affected defendant attitudes toward authority and understanding of the legal process. LoGalbo surveyed 111 youth immediately after their initial interview with teen court staff and again upon completion of the program. The survey asked participants about their knowledge of Florida laws and the justice system, their attitudes toward nine authority figures (e.g., police officer, judge, parent, teacher), their attitudes toward teen court and toward themselves, and their perception of the fairness of teen court procedures. The study found teen court participation was associated with increased self-esteem and positive attitudes toward select authority figures (e.g., judges). The analysis also suggested that recidivism was less likely among defendants with improved attitudes toward authority figures.

Strong client satisfaction was also reported by researchers in Kentucky. Exit interviews conducted by Wells and colleagues (1998) revealed high levels of satisfaction among 123 teen court participants, with 84 percent indicating that their sentences were fair. Several positive features of the teen court experience were cited by the Kentucky subjects, including "educational advantages" (37 percent) and the actual sentences youth received (21 percent). Teens also consistently indicated that the opportunity to serve as a teen court juror was an important, positive aspect of the teen court process. . . .

Conclusion

State and local jurisdictions across the country are embracing teen court as an alternative to the traditional juvenile justice system for their youngest and least serious offenders. Many jurisdictions report that teen court increases young offenders' respect for the justice system and reduces recidivism by holding delinquent youth accountable for what is often their first offense. Moreover, a teen court may be able to act more quickly and more efficiently than a traditional juvenile court. Researchers are beginning to accumulate a body of findings on the effectiveness of teen courts, but more detailed information is needed for future practice and policy development. . . .

References

Butler-Mejia, K. 1998. Seen but not heard: The role of voice in juvenile justice. Unpublished master's thesis. Fairfax, VA: George Mason University.

Colydas, V., and McLeod, M. 1997. Colonie (NY) youth court evaluation. Unpublished manuscript. Troy, NY: Russell Sage College.

Hissong, R. 1991. Teen court—Is it an effective alternative to traditional sanctions? *Journal for Juvenile Justice and Detention Services* 6:14–23.

LoGalbo, A.P. 1998. Is teen court a fair and effective juvenile crime diversion program? Unpublished manuscript. Tampa, FL: University of South Florida, New College.

McLeod, M. 1999. Satisfaction with youth court proceedings: A follow-up analysis of the Colonie (NY) youth court. Paper presented at the annual meeting of the American Society of Criminology, Toronto, Canada.

Minor, K.I., Wells, J.B., Soderstrom, I.R., Bingham, R., and Williamson, D. 1999. Sentence completion and recidivism among juveniles referred to teen courts. *Crime and Delinquency* 45:467–480.

National Youth Court Center. 2000. How teen/youth courts operate. National Youth Court Center Web Site. Lexington, KY: American Probation and Parole Association. On the World Wide Web: www.youthcourt.net/.

North Carolina Administrative Office of the Courts. 1995. *Report on the Teen Court Programs in North Carolina*. Raleigh, NC: North Carolina Administrative Office of the Courts.

Reichel, P., and Seyfrit, C. 1984. A peer jury in juvenile court. *Crime and Delinquency* 30:423–438.

Seyfrit, C.L., Reichel, P., and Stutts, B. 1987. Peer juries as a juvenile justice diversion technique. *Youth and Society* 18:302–316.

Swink, M.I. 1998. Onondaga County youth court recidivism rates. Unpublished manuscript. Syracuse, NY: Syracuse University, Maxwell School of Citizenship and Public Affairs.

Wells, J. B., Minor, K.I., and Fox, J.W. 1998. *An Evaluation of Kentucky's 1997–98 Teen Court Program*. Richmond, KY: Eastern Kentucky University, Center for Criminal Justice Education and Research. ✦

Youthful Offenders in Criminal Court

C hapter 9 concluded that juveniles today are being transferred out of the juvenile court in two directions. Chapter 10 looked at transfers in one direction—to the new "teen" courts. Now the chapters in Part VI looks at transfers in the other direction—to the (adult) criminal courts.

The first of these chapters is a case study of a criminal court in New York City that exclusively holds trials for 13- to 15-year-olds who are being prosecuted as adults. The second chapter argues that juveniles should not be subject to the death penalty. The argument is based on biological and psychological research on the brain functioning of adolescents. ✦

Chapter 11

Prosecuting Adolescents in Criminal Courts

Criminal or Juvenile Justice?

Aaron Kupchik

Editor's Introduction

Transfers to criminal court are part of the "get tough" movement with juvenile offenders. The goal is to increase the *certainty* and *severity* of punishments, and thereby to reduce the subsequent *recidivism* of the youthful offenders who are transferred.

In general, however, studies find that youths transferred to criminal court tend to reoffend more quickly and more often than comparable youth who are retained in juvenile court.[1] The problem may be that transfer to criminal court does not increase the certainty or severity of punishments, compared to retaining the youth in juvenile court.

A recent study of 393 youth transferred to criminal courts during the 1990s in Cook County (Chicago) illustrates the problem with certainty and severity.[2] Sixty-six percent of the youths were transferred for drug offenses, but 37 percent of these drug cases were not prosecuted at all in criminal courts, and 74 percent of those that were prosecuted were sentenced to probation rather than incarceration. Thus, only 16 percent of the transferred drug cases (which were two-thirds of all transferred cases) actually resulted in a prison sentence. This certainly is different from what the law would seem to intend.

An explanation for the high rate of acquittals may be the increased adversarial atmosphere in criminal courts, including the right to a jury trial. In the juvenile courts, in contrast, there are no juries and there is a tendency for all parties to focus on the broader needs of the juveniles rather than the fine points of the evidence. Cases that might have been transferred to criminal court

Adapted from Aaron Kupchik. 2003. "Prosecuting Adolescents in Criminal Courts: Criminal or Juvenile Justice?" *Social Problems* 50 (3):439–60. Copyright © 2003 by the University of California Press. Reprinted by permission.

tend to have a very high adjudication (conviction) rate if they are retained in juvenile court.

A separate problem is the low rate of incarceration for those who are convicted. Here, the problem may be that in most states, the criminal court judge must sentence these young offenders to the adult prison system.[3] Because of many well-known problems with this practice (including prison rape), criminal court judges may be reluctant to incarcerate these offenders. In contrast, in cases that might have been transferred to criminal court, juvenile court judges are quite happy to send offenders to juvenile institutions.

If these explanations are correct, then the problem faced by officials today is quite similar to the one faced by officials one hundred years ago when the original juvenile court was founded. As described in Chapter 2, at that time few lenient options were available so officials were forced to choose between harshly punishing a youth and doing nothing at all. Both of these options seemed likely to increase future offending, and as a practical matter officials often chose to do nothing rather than to harshly punish. The juvenile court was founded to provide a "middle ground" between these two bad options.

Perhaps transfers to criminal court are a "symbol" of toughness against juveniles that do little to achieve that goal.[4] Whether or not that is true, increasing numbers of youths nationwide are being transferred to criminal courts and tried as adults. Chapter 11 presents an observational study of a criminal court in New York City exclusively devoted to prosecuting 13- to 15-year-olds as adults. The author found that trials in this court were conducted according to a criminal court model—a formal adversarial proceeding focused on the offense. However, at sentencing, the court shifted to something that was more like a juvenile court—an informal nonadversarial proceeding focused on the offender and oriented toward rehabilitation. The author concludes that, at least to some extent, this court "reproduced" the juvenile court in the sentencing phase.

Notes

1. Jeffrey A. Butts and Daniel P. Mears, "Reviving Juvenile Justice in a Get-Tough Era," *Youth & Society* 33(2):175–80, December 2001. A possible problem with these studies is "selection bias"—i.e., even controlling for present offense and prior record, it is possible that "worse" kids are transferred to criminal courts and that this causes the increased rate of recidivism. See David L. Myers, "The Recidivism of Violent Youths in Juvenile and Adult Court: A Consideration of Selection Bias," *Youth Violence and Juvenile Justice* 1(1):79–101 (2003). The solution to that problem would be to do a randomized controlled study. One could, for example, take all cases selected for transfer in a high-transfer jurisdiction (e.g., Miami), and then randomly retain half those cases in juvenile court. A follow-up study could compare the recidivism of the two groups, which would determine whether transfer increases recidivism or whether "worse" cases are selected for transfer. But this type of study has not been allowed in any jurisdiction.

2. Juvenile Transfer Advocacy Unit, "Transfers to Adult Court in Cook County: The Status of Automatic Transfers to Adult Court in Cook County, Illinois; Oct. 1990 to Sept. 2000," http://www.jjustice.org/template.cfm?page_id=46. It is interesting

to note that, as in the New York City court described below, virtually all the transferred youth in Chicago were minorities, with less than 1 percent white.

3. This is not true of all states—see the discussion of "blended sentences" in Chapter 1. In four states, a criminal court judge can sentence youthful offenders to a juvenile institution for an initial period of time, with later transfer to an adult institution (criminal-inclusive blend), and in eight additional states a criminal court judge may sentence a youthful offender to either the juvenile or the adult correctional system (criminal-exclusive blend).

4. Butts and Mears, op. cit.

✦ ✦ ✦

Prosecuting adolescents in criminal (adult) court has become more common over the past twenty years; virtually every state has revised its laws to facilitate the transfer of adolescents from juvenile to criminal courts (Snyder and Sickmund 1999; Zimring 1998). Some jurisdictions establish categories of offenders and offenses that are transferred automatically to criminal court, while others allow a prosecutor or judge discretion over selecting youth for transfer (Feld 1998). Despite the increasing use of transfer to criminal court, we know little about how criminal court actors evaluate and attribute responsibility to adolescents prosecuted in criminal court. Some prior research suggests that this jurisdictional transfer may not eliminate an offender-oriented, rehabilitation-focused, informal style of justice associated with "juvenile justice" throughout the 20th century (Singer 1996; Singer, Fagan, and Liberman 2000). The focus on individualized rehabilitation associated with juvenile justice (see Platt 1977; Rothman 1980; Ryerson 1978) is at odds with the formal, offense-based and punitive model of justice normally associated with "criminal justice" in criminal courts (Feld 1999; Hagan, Hewitt, and Alwin 1979; Zimring 2000). As a result, the transfer of adolescents to criminal court creates a potential conflict for court actors who process juveniles in criminal courts previously reserved primarily for adults.

These two models of justice vary from one another along three major dimensions: (1) evaluative criteria, (2) sentencing goals, and (3) formality of court proceedings. The criminal justice model commonly associated with criminal courts involves offense-based evaluative criteria and punitive sentencing within a formal court environment. In contrast, relative to a criminal justice model, a juvenile justice model relies on offender-based evaluative criteria and pursues a sentencing goal of rehabilitation, within a less formal court environment. Given this disparity between juvenile justice and criminal justice models, it is not clear which, if either, guides case processing when adolescents are prosecuted and sentenced in criminal court.[1]

The incongruity between an adolescent's apparent immaturity and a formal criminal court environment may cause tensions and practical difficulties that must be resolved by criminal court personnel processing youthful defendants. It is entirely possible that criminal court decision-makers are unable to ignore adolescents' immaturity, or to hold adolescent defendants to the same standards of responsibility as adult defendants. However, we know little about the strategies used by local legal communities to deal with this potential incongruity, or about how jurisdictional transfer policies (mandating that adolescents be transferred to adult court) are filtered through local legal cultures of criminal courts (see Ulmer and Kramer 1998). It is unclear whether criminal courts prosecuting adolescents (1) apply an offense-based and punishment-focused model, treating young offenders as criminals deserving of punishment; (2) reintroduce individualized evaluative criteria and rehabilitative sentencing goals, treating young offenders as children in need of guidance (Platt 1977); or (3) rely on a new model of justice.

In this article I use a case study of a criminal court specializing in the prosecution of adolescents to answer this question. The data come from observations of courtroom proceedings and interviews with court personnel. After analyzing the data, I identify contradictions between criminal and juvenile models of justice in this setting, and show how court actors resolve these contradictions throughout the various phases of case processing. . . .

New York State Juvenile Offender Law

To answer my research questions I use a case study of a New York City criminal court specializing in adolescent offenders. I use this research site because statutes governing the jurisdictional boundary between juvenile and criminal courts in New York reflect nationwide trends in the transfer of adolescents to criminal court.[2]

In New York, all offenders 16 years or older are considered adults, and many offenders younger than 16 are prosecuted in criminal court as well. In 1978, New York passed the "Juvenile Offender Law," which mandates that 14- and 15-year-olds (at the time of their offenses) who are charged with any of 17 designated felony offenses, and 13-year-olds charged with murder, are excluded from juvenile court. While these individuals (hereafter Juvenile Offenders, or JOs) can be transferred back to juvenile court, their cases originate in criminal court. The rules and procedures for prosecuting JOs match those of criminal court in general, but the sentences legislatively prescribed for JOs are less severe (regarding time sentenced to incarceration) than those for adult defendants (Singer 1996).

Enacted in 1978, the JO Law was the predecessor to many other states' transfer laws. Increasing numbers of states are now moving toward this model of transfer and away from a traditional model in which a judge decides which adolescents are to be transferred (Feld 1998). New York criminal courts therefore offer a well-established model for understanding recent trends in prosecuting adolescents in criminal courts.

In 1993, following the lobbying efforts of an influential judge and a grant from a private funding agency, each county in New York City other than Staten Island began to prosecute JOs in a specialized criminal court "part"[3] (Liberman, Raleigh, and Solomon 2000). As a result, most JO cases that continue past the initial stage of arraignment (which takes place in a lower court before being transferred up to the [Supreme Court]) are now prosecuted in a specialized criminal court part in each county before a criminal court judge who specializes in JO cases. . . .

Data and Methods

This research was conducted in one of the specialized criminal "youth part" courts in New York City. The data come from observations of court proceedings and interviews with the criminal court community (judge, prosecutors, and defense attorneys). I collected observational data during approximately 30 visits to court over the course of six months, during which I observed 290 hearings: 124 sentencing hearings, 145 regularly scheduled hearings to review the status of cases, and 21 plea allocutions (hearings in which defendants plead guilty). Rather than following individual cases (which can take years for completion), I attended all court "calendar" days; calendar days are days in which all active cases not on trial are scheduled for whatever action or hearing type is required. This procedure ensured that I observed the full array of the court's caseload, because all cases appear on calendar days at some time. I also observed two trials. . . .

The characteristics of the defendants and crimes committed for the cases I observed are consistent with the results of a city-wide report that documents case flow in this particular court part, among others (Criminal Justice Agency 2001). The majority of defendants are younger than 16-years-old and face serious felony charges; to be classified as a Juvenile Offender (JO) one must be 13-, 14- or 15-years-old and be charged with one of 17 serious felony charges.[4] A small number of older offenders, usually slightly older adolescents, are prosecuted in the court if they are co-defendants of JOs. The modal charge category faced by the defendants in the court (of the 17 JO eligible charges) is robbery, but all 17 JO-eligible charges are represented. Overall, approximately half of the defendants whose cases I observed have prior arrest records.[5] The vast majority of cases result in conviction, usually through plea bargain. According to the city-wide report referred to above, slightly more than half of the defendants sentenced in this court are incarcerated, with most of the rest receiving probation (Criminal Justice Agency 2001). As evidenced by the high proportion of defense attorneys paid for by the court, most defendants who appear before the court are poor. And, very few white adolescents are prosecuted in this court. According to a recent city-wide report on minority overrepresentation among JO defendants, only 4 percent of JO cases filed in criminal court—and 2 percent of cases convicted there—involved white defendants. With regard to other racial categories, 66 percent of JO cases filed were against African American defendants, and 30 percent involved Hispanic defendants[6] (Liberman, Winterfield, and McElroy 1996). The vast majority of defendants spoke English fluently, as measured by the rarity of language interpreters (an attorney or judge requested an interpreter for a defendant in only 8 of the 290 hearings). . . .

Case Processing Prior to Sentencing: Criminal Justice

Prior to sentencing,[7] the behaviors of the court actors in this court are consistent with the criminal justice model previously outlined; the court operates like a formal, offense-oriented criminal court rather than an informal, offender-oriented juvenile court. This stage involves a formal, adversarial process with a goal of determining guilt or innocence. Hearings follow a typical pattern whereby the prosecutor presents evidence to strengthen the State's case against the defendant, the defense attorney refutes the prosecutor's case by pointing out weaknesses in the quality of the evidence, and the judge ensures that statutes are properly followed and defendants' rights are respected. Juvenile justice-oriented concerns such as the defendant's social, educational, and family background, or future consequences for the offender, are rarely, if ever, discussed during this stage of case processing. Drawing on previous organizational studies of juvenile and criminal courts, I illustrate the formal, offense-focused style of proceedings in this stage by highlighting four dimensions of court organization and interaction: (1) the style of interaction, (2) the courtroom workgroup, (3) language, and (4) the defendant's role in case processing (see Eisenstein et al. 1988; Emerson 1969; Ulmer 1997; Ulmer and Kramer 1996, 1998).

Style of Interaction

The courtroom workgroup members maintain a formal legal atmosphere regarding the style of interaction used in court. Court actors' beliefs in reduced culpability for adolescents are suppressed during the early stages of case processing. Instead, they behave in a formal manner that resembles the official criminal court environment in which they work, and only discuss offense-oriented factors such as evidence, prior offending records, and offense severity.

Prior to sentencing, the members of this workgroup—the prosecutor, defense attorney, and judge—assume adversarial roles in discussing characteristics and severity of alleged offenses. . . . Much of this jockeying back and forth occurs during off-the-record discussions at the judge's bench (bench conferences) during which the prosecutor and defense attorney posture for an advantage and the judge mediates between them. During these bench conferences the prosecutor and defense attorney each estimate the strength of the other side's case and decide how to proceed. For the defense this information dictates whether the defendant pleads guilty, and if so, for how severe a sentence she can negotiate. For the prosecution this information determines whether to offer a more enticing plea bargain or, occasionally, whether or not the case should be dismissed. The judge mediates the negotiations by prodding each for information, making rulings when either side (usually the defense) submits a legal motion, and suggesting resolutions to disagreements. . . .

Courtroom Workgroup

Prior to the sentencing phase, the courtroom workgroup is limited to three legal actors: the judge, defense attorney, and prosecutor. No other court professionals or sponsoring agencies, such as social workers or counseling professionals, are involved in this early phase. The only exceptions are when police officers or other witnesses are required to testify under oath about the actual offense, or when the department of probation becomes involved in establishing a defendant's guilt for a violation of probation. Instead of expanding the workgroup to include treatment professionals, the probation department, defendants, or other individuals and agencies as in juvenile court (see Emerson 1969), the legal sufficiency of conviction is limited to discussions by the defense attorney, prosecutor, and judge.

Language

The language used in this court prior to sentencing is of a formal, ceremonial nature characteristic of a criminal court (Carlen 1976). Such formality is illustrated by the judge's referrals to himself as "the court"; for example, the judge always says "the court understands" rather than "I understand." The language used by the defense attorneys and prosecutor mirrors this level of decorum. The defense attorney and prosecutor may use less formal language when they approach the judge's bench for off-the-record conversations, but never on-the-record in open court. On the rare occasion that an attorney breaches this norm, the judge rebukes her immediately, reminding her she is in a formal court of law and should behave accordingly.

Defendant's Role

The interaction between the court actors and defendants during early stages of case processing exhibits the formal style of criminal court as well. Defendants in court have no active role in court hearings prior to formal conviction. They stand silently for every hearing with their hands behind their backs, even when they are not handcuffed. The judge almost never addresses a defendant or directly involves her in any way. If a defendant attempts to speak to the judge for any reason, the judge will stop her immediately and instruct her to speak to her attorney, who can then address the court. This practice stands in contrast to juvenile courts, where judges often directly address defendants in all phases of processing (Emerson 1969).

Case Processing During the Sentencing Phase: Juvenile Justice

Contrary to the tenor of court hearings prior to sentencing, case processing during the sentencing phase reflects the juvenile justice model. Offender-oriented factors arise as prominent evaluative criteria, as court actors begin to discuss offenders' social, educational, and family backgrounds (see Bortner 1982; Emerson 1969). Rehabilitation emerges as the primary goal of sentencing. And, courtroom workgroup members' routine interaction and language patterns adhere less strictly to formal procedural rules. . . . Again, I demonstrate the model of justice used in this stage of case processing by examining the style of interaction among court actors, the make-up of the courtroom workgroup, the language used in court, and the defendant's role in case processing.

Style of Interaction

The noticeably adversarial and competitive nature of the courtroom workgroup changes abruptly once court actors begin to discuss sentencing. At this point, court actors cooperate with one another to a greater extent than before and collectively fashion appropriate sentences for individual defendants. The prosecutor typically lobbies for a harsher sanction than requested by the defense attorney. However, the distance between their views is smaller and their differences more nuanced than was the case during their debate of guilt vs. innocence during the earlier phase. . . .

Courtroom Workgroup

Recall that prior to the sentencing phase the judge focuses narrowly on respecting defendants' due process rights and ensuring that the State's case is sufficient for conviction and legally assembled (with evidence collected and argued in accordance with the law). He does so by moderating the adversarial dialogue between defense and prosecution and deciding on motions and debates between these two sides. Yet during the sentencing phase he leads case processing rather than moderating it. Moreover, he widens the courtroom work group by requesting the involvement of representatives from treatment program agencies, who allow him to discuss a broader array of offender-oriented information and focus on rehabilitation as a sentencing goal.

Following conviction, the judge's demeanor changes markedly and he acts according to the juvenile justice ideals he espouses. Aside from leading hearings and fashioning his own sentences, the judge also gathers information on the defendant's home life and educational background, and fashions a treatment program that fits each defendant's individual needs. Sending defendants to counseling programs prior to final sentencing ensures that they will be supervised and able to access treatment services. These programs then send representatives to court who can report on each defendant, including matters such as the offender's educational background, occupational skills, mental, learning, or behavioral disabilities, and family support and supervision.

Thus, as a result of an expanded courtroom workgroup that grows to include treatment program representatives, court actors begin to consider characteristics of offenders during the sentencing stage. Armed with a greater array of information about individual offenders than in earlier hearings, the judge often uses this information in deciding on a defendant's status. . . .

The role of the prosecutor is diminished during the sentencing phase. Having already requested a particular sentence, the prosecutor has little to add other than repeating the previous request. Moreover, the judge focuses court proceedings on the defendant's character and continuing behavior during the sentencing phase, and the prosecutor has no information on these subjects.

Language

The language used in sentencing hearings is far less formal than the ceremonial language of earlier hearings. The judge comments frequently on the defendant's character and openly makes character judgments (see Emerson 1969)—this occurs most often in cases in which the judge thinks the defendant has not complied with his previous court orders. . . . This type of judgmental discourse poses a sharp contrast to the formal nature of hearings prior to sentencing, where guilt or innocence was discussed strictly in legal terms.

Defendant's Role

Perhaps the most striking difference between the two phases is the involvement of the defendant. The defendant plays a central role in sentencing hearings, often through direct exchange with the judge. Here the judge may ask specific questions of the juvenile, or ask for a general report from her. Recall that prior to sentencing the judge does not tolerate any discussion from the defendant without mediation by her attorney. . . .

Conclusion

By drawing on varying forms of court organization and interaction processes in the two phases of court processing, this court is able to create a new form of justice that borrows principles and practices from both juvenile and criminal models of justice. The result is a hybrid form of justice, a sequential justice model that incorporates elements of a criminal justice model (offense-based evaluative criteria and procedural formality) during early stages of case processing, and juvenile justice (offender-based evaluative criteria, procedural informality, and a goal of rehabilitation) during later stages. I demonstrate this distinction among phases of case processing by reference to four contextual dimensions: the style of interaction, courtroom workgroups, language, and the defendant's role in court hearings. Previously, only one study has discussed the possible reproduction of juvenile justice in criminal courts, and it did so without access to qualitative data concerning how these courts process defendants (Singer et al. 2000). My results diverge from this previous research by finding that the model of justice is contingent on the stage of case processing, rather than a sustained reproduction of juvenile justice. . . .

The extent to which this sequential model may be generalized, or true in other jurisdictions that prosecute adolescents in criminal courts, remains to be tested by further research. Given the resilience of the belief in reduced culpability of adolescents that I find in this court, one might expect this culturally rooted idea to cause a strain for other criminal court communities prosecuting adolescents. Moreover, the method of transfer to adult court examined here is perhaps the most rapidly proliferating method, as a greater numbers of states have both recently lowered their jurisdictional boundaries between juvenile and criminal courts and barred greater numbers of offenders from juvenile court by statutory exclusion (Feld 1998, 2000). In addition, the sentencing scheme in this court—fixed sentencing with room for judicial discretion (by giving Youthful Offender status)—is similar to that of criminal courts in many other states (see Savelsberg 1992) and increasingly common with regard to the criminal court prosecution of adolescents (Feld 1998). Because New York's method of prosecuting adolescents in criminal court demonstrates increasingly common characteristics of states' efforts to criminalize delinquency, there is ample cause to think that the process I find here may be generalizable to other courts as well. . . .

Notes

1. This is not to say that these orientations are mutually exclusive, or that either type of Court fully resembles either "juvenile justice" or "criminal justice." Rather, these concepts are ideal types that have traditionally been used to compare the two types of courts. Hence, they are useful for illustrating the difficulties of merging the two domains by prosecuting children as if they were adults.

2. Between 1978 and 1994, 44 states amended their juvenile justice Statutes to increase their ability to transfer adolescents younger than 18 to criminal court (Torbet et al, 1996). In 1995, 17 states further expanded their juvenile justice laws to this end. Today, all fifty states have the ability to transfer juveniles to adult court (Snyder and Sickmund 1999; U.S. General Accounting Office 1995). Moreover, many states recently revised their laws to remove the judge's power of discretion regarding which adolescents are transferred, and either allow prosecutors this discretion or establish categories of offenses and offenders that are automatically transferred so criminal court (Feld 1998).

3. In New York, courtrooms with assigned judges are called court "parts."

4. The charges include various degrees of murder, kidnapping, arson, robbery, assault, manslaughter, burglary, rape, and possession of a weapon.

5. This is demonstrated by data from cases in 1992–1993 from the same courts, and involving defendants charged with the same offenses. In that prior research, approximately 50 percent of the sampled 15- and 16-year-olds in the data set have prior arrest records (Kupchik, Fagan, and Liberman 2003). Additionally, in about half the cases I observed for this study a prior arrest record was mentioned by the prosecuting attorney.

6. The available data are taken from police reports, and only include these three categories. Therefore, the data do not distinguish between African American defendants and defendants of Caribbean descent, nor

between white Hispanic and black Hispanic defendants. Juveniles classified as "other ethnicity" comprised 3 percent of the sample and were removed from the analysis of Liberman and associates (1996).

7. I refer to the sentencing phase not as a formally declared hearing following official conviction, but as discussions that involve a consideration of sentence assuming conviction. These discussions often precede formal conviction, but do not occur until all workgroup members have implicitly agreed that the case will soon lead to conviction, at which point they begin to negotiate a sentence in exchange for a guilty plea.

References

Bortner, M. A. 1982. *Inside a Juvenile Court: The Tarnished Ideal of Individualized Justice*. New York: New York University Press.

Carlen, Pat. 1976. *Magistrate's Justice*. London: Martin Robertson.

Criminal Justice Agency. 2001. Annual Report on the Adult Court Case Processing of Juvenile Offenders in New York City, January through December 2000. New York: Criminal Justice Agency.

Eisenstein, James, Roy Flemming, and Peter Nardulli. 1988. *The Contours of Justice: Communities and Their Courts*. Boston: Little, Brown.

Emerson, Robert M. 1969. *Judging Delinquents: Context and Process in Juvenile Court*. Chicago: Aldine.

Feld, Barry C. 1998. "Juvenile and Criminal Justice Systems' Responses to Youth Violence." Pp. 189–261 in *Youth Violence*, edited by Michael Tonry and Mark H. Moore. Chicago: University of Chicago Press.

———. 1999. *Bad Kids: Race and the Transformation of Juvenile Court*. New York: Oxford University Press.

———. 2000. "Legislative Exclusion of Offenses from Juvenile Court Jurisdiction: A History and Critique." Pp. 83–144 in *The Changing Borders of Juvenile Justice*, edited by Jeffrey Fagan and Franklin E. Zimring. Chicago: University of Chicago Press.

Hagan, John, John D. Hewitt, and Duane F. Alwin. 1979. "Ceremonial Justice: Crime and Punishment in a Loosely Coupled System." *Social Forces* 58:506–27.

Kupchik, Aaron, Jeffrey Fagan, and Akiva Liberman. 2003. "Punishment, Proportionality and Jurisdictional Transfer of Adolescent Offenders: A Test of the Leniency Gap Hypothesis." *Stanford Law and Policy Review* 14:57–83.

Liberman, Akiva, William Raleigh, and Freda Solomon. 2000. Specialized Court Parts for Juvenile Offenders in New York City's Adult Felony Courts: Case Processing in 1994–1995 and 1995–1996. New York: New York City Criminal Justice Agency.

Liberman, Akiva, Laura Winterfield, and Jerome McElroy. 1996. Minority Over-Representation Among Juveniles in New York City's Adult and Juvenile Court Systems During Fiscal Year 1992. New York: New York City Criminal Justice Agency.

Platt, Anthony. 1977. *The Child Savers: The Invention of Delinquency*. 2nd ed. Chicago: University of Chicago Press.

Rothman, David J. 1980. *Conscience and Convenience: The Asylum and its Alternative in Progressive America*. Boston: Little, Brown.

Ryerson, Ellen. 1978. *The Best Laid Plans: America's Juvenile Court Experiment*. New York: Hill and Wang.

Savelsberg, Joachim. 1992. "Law that Does Not Fit Society: Sentencing Guidelines as a Neoclassical Reaction to the Dilemmas of Substantivized Law." *American Journal of Sociology* 97:1346–81.

Singer, Simon I. 1996. *Recriminalizing Delinquency: Violent Juvenile Crime and Juvenile Justice Reform*. New York: Cambridge University Press.

Singer, Simon I., Jeffrey Fagan, and Akiva Liberman. 2000. "The Reproduction of Juvenile Justice in Criminal Court: A Case Study of New York's Juvenile Offender Law." Pp. 353–77 in *The Changing Borders of Juvenile Justice*, edited by Jeffrey Fagan and Franklin E. Zimring. Chicago: University of Chicago Press.

Snyder, Howard and Melissa Sickmund. 1999. *Juvenile Offenders and Victims: A National Report.* National Center for Juvenile Justice. Washington, DC: U.S. Department of Justice, Office of Juvenile Justice and Delinquency Prevention.

Torbet, Patricia, Richard Gable, Hunter Hurst IV, Imogene Montgomery, Linda Szymanski, and Douglas Thomas. 1996. State Responses to Serious and Violent Juvenile Crime. Washington, DC: Office of Juvenile Justice and Delinquency Prevention.

Ulmer, Jeffery T. 1997. *Social Worlds of Sentencing: Court Communities Under Sentencing Guidelines.* New York: SUNY Press.

Ulmer, Jeffery T. and John H. Kramer. 1996. "Court Communities Under Sentencing Guidelines: Dilemmas of Formal Rationality and Sentencing Disparity." *Criminology* 34:383–407.

———. 1998. "The Use and Transformation of Formal Decision-Making Criteria: Sentencing Guidelines, Organizational Contexts, and Case Processing Strategies." *Social Problems* 45:248–67.

U.S. General Accounting Office. 1995. *Juveniles Processed in Criminal Court and Case Dispositions.* Washington, DC: General Accounting Office.

Zimring, Franklin E. 1998. *American Youth Violence.* New York: Oxford University Press.

———. 2000 "The Punitive Necessity of Waiver." Pp. 207–25 in *The Changing Borders of Juvenile Justice,* edited by Jeffrey Fagan and Franklin E. Zimring. Chicago: University of Chicago Press. ✦

Chapter 12

Less Guilty by Reason of Adolescence

Developmental Immaturity, Diminished Responsibility, and the Juvenile Death Penalty

Laurence Steinberg and Elizabeth S. Scott

Editor's Introduction

Until recently, the death penalty was available in many states for offenders who committed capital offenses on or after their 16th birthdays. But on March 1, 2005, the United States Supreme Court held that "The Eighth and Fourteenth Amendments forbid imposition of the death penalty on offenders who were under the age of 18 when their crimes were committed."[1] The majority opinion of the Supreme Court repeatedly cited the article presented below as Chapter 12.

This chapter focuses on the death penalty for juveniles, but it really addresses a much broader issue: mitigation of punishments for juvenile offenders. In Chapter 2, ("The Cycle of Juvenile Justice"), mitigation was said to exist at almost all times and in almost all places. And in Chapter 11, on the criminal court in New York City, the author spoke of "the resilience of the belief in reduced culpability of adolescents that I find in this court" and suggested that this idea might "cause a strain" for court personnel who prosecute adolescents: "It is entirely possible that criminal court decision-makers are unable to ignore adolescents' immaturity, or to hold adolescent defendants to the same standards of responsibility as adult defendants."

Laurence Steinberg and Elizabeth S. Scott. 2003. "Less Guilty by Reason of Adolescence: Developmental Immaturity, Diminished Responsibility, and the Juvenile Death Penalty." *American Psychologist* 58(12):1009–1018. Copyright © 2003 by the American Psychological Association. Adapted with permission.

Chapter 12 reviews a variety of recent research relevant to mitigation, including physiological studies of brain development and functioning that shows the physical differences between adolescent and adult brains. In the end, the chapter concludes that it is appropriate to mitigate the punishments for juveniles, and that it is particularly appropriate to do so with respect to the death penalty.

In some ways, this article reinvents the wheel. It uses modern scientific methods to examine an issue that people have been examining with their own eyes since the dawn of time, and uses sophisticated scientific analysis to reach the same conclusion that virtually everyone else has reached using common sense.

The problem, of course, is that although mitigation is found at *almost* all times and places, many of the recent "get tough" reforms in juvenile justice in the United States have abandoned it. These reforms often take the view that juveniles have the same responsibility for their actions as adults—they are simply "small adults." Therefore, juveniles are given the same punishments as adults: "If you're old enough to do the crime, you're old enough to do the time."

Chapter 12 takes a very different view. Given the characteristics of juvenile brain functioning, the article concludes that most juvenile offenders do not belong in criminal courts at all. Rather, in their view, the best policy is one in which "most youths are dealt with in a separate justice system, in which rehabilitation is a central aim, and none are eligible for the ultimate punishment of death." Clearly, society must respond to the offending behavior of juveniles, but not by treating juveniles as if they simply are "small adults."

Note

1.   *Roper, Superintendent, Potosi Correctional Center v. Simmons*, (03-633) 112 S.W.3d 397. Argued October 13, 2004 and decided March 1, 2005.

✦ ✦ ✦

We argue that emerging knowledge about cognitive, psychosocial, and neurobiological development in adolescence supports the conclusion that juveniles should not be held to the same standards of criminal responsibility as adults. Under standard, well-accepted principles of criminal law, the developmental immaturity of juveniles mitigates their criminal culpability and, accordingly, should moderate the severity of their punishment. . . .

In general, factors that reduce criminal culpability can be grouped roughly into three categories. The first category includes endogenous impairments or deficiencies in the actor's decision-making capacity that affect his or her choice to engage in criminal activity. The incapacity—or diminished capacity—may be due to mental illness or mental retardation, extreme emotional distress, or susceptibility to influence or domination (Kadish, 1987).

Under the second category, culpability is reduced when the external circumstances faced by the actor are so compelling that an ordinary (or "reasonable") person might have succumbed to the pressure in the same way as did the defendant (Morse, 1994). The extraordinary circumstances could involve duress, provocation, threatened injury, or extreme need. A person who commits a crime in response to these circumstances typically receives less punishment than one who commits a comparable crime under less compelling conditions.

The third category of mitigation includes evidence that the criminal act was out of character for the actor and that, unlike the typical criminal act, his or her crime was not the product of bad character. For example, a reduced sentence might result if the crime was a first offense; if the actor expressed genuine remorse or tried to mitigate the harm; if the actor had a history of steady employment, fulfillment of family obligations, and good citizenship; or, more generally, if the criminal act was aberrant in light of the defendant's established character traits and respect for the law's values (United States Sentencing Commission, 1998).

Developmental Immaturity and Mitigation

Each of the categories of mitigation described in the previous section is important to an assessment of the culpability of adolescents who become involved in crime, and each sheds light on differences between normative adolescents and adults. First, and most obviously, adolescents' levels of cognitive and psychosocial development are likely to shape their choices, including their criminal choices, in ways that distinguish them from adults and that may undermine competent decision making. Second, because adolescents' decision-making capacities are immature and their autonomy constrained, they are more vulnerable than are adults to the influence of coercive circumstances that mitigate culpability for all persons, such as provocation, duress, or threat. Finally, because adolescents are still in the process of forming their personal identity, their criminal behavior is less likely than that of an adult to reflect bad character. Thus, for each of the sources of mitigation in criminal law, typical adolescents are less culpable than are adults because adolescent criminal conduct is driven by transitory influences that are constitutive of this developmental stage.

Deficiencies in Decision-Making Capacity

It is well established that reasoning capabilities increase through childhood into adolescence and that preadolescents and younger teens differ substantially from adults in their cognitive abilities (Keating, 1990). These basic improvements in reasoning are complemented by increases in specific and general knowledge gained through education and experience and by improvements in basic information-processing skills, including attention, short- and long-term memory, and organization (Siegler, 1997). Although few psychologists would challenge the assertion that most adults have better reasoning skills than preadolescent children, it is often asserted that, by mid-adolescence, teens' capacities for understanding and reasoning in making decisions roughly approximate those of adults (Fischhoff, 1992; Furby & Beyth-Marom, 1992). Indeed, advocates for adolescent self-determination made this argument in support of adolescent abortion rights (American Psychological Association, 1990; Melton, 1983). However, as we and our colleagues have argued in several recent articles, there is good reason to question whether age differences in decision making disappear by mid-adolescence, particularly as capacities may be manifested in the real-world settings in which choices about criminal activity are made (Scott, Reppucci, & Woolard, 1995; Steinberg & Cauffman, 1996). Laboratory studies that are the basis of the assertion that adolescents' reasoning ability is equivalent to that of adults are only modestly useful in understanding how youths compare with adults in making choices that have salience to their lives or that are presented in stressful, unstructured settings in which decision makers must rely on personal experience, knowledge, and intuition (Cauffman & Steinberg, 2000; Scott et al., 1995; Steinberg, 2003; Steinberg & Cauffman, 1996). In typical laboratory studies of decision making, individual adolescents are presented with hypothetical dilemmas under conditions of low emotional arousal and then asked to make and explain their decisions. In the real world, and especially in situations in which crimes are committed, however, adolescents' decisions are not hypothetical, they are generally made under conditions of emotional arousal (whether negative or positive), and they usually are made in groups. In our view, it is an open and unstudied question whether, under real-world conditions, the decision making of mid-adolescents is truly comparable with that of adults.

More important, even when teenagers' cognitive capacities come close to those of adults, adolescent judgment and their actual decisions may differ from that of adults as a result of psychosocial immaturity. Among the psychosocial factors that are most relevant to understanding differences in judgment and decision making are (a) susceptibility to peer influence, (b) attitudes toward and perception of risk, (c) future orientation, and (d) the capacity for self-management. Whereas cognitive capacities shape the process of decision making, psychosocial immaturity can affect decision-making outcomes, because these psychosocial factors influence adolescent values and preferences in ways that drive the cost-benefit calculus in the making of choices. In other words, to the extent that adolescents are less psychosocially mature than adults, they are likely to be deficient in their decision-making capacity, even if their cognitive processes are mature (Cauffman & Steinberg, 2000; Scott et al., 1995; Steinberg & Cauffman, 1996).

There is considerable evidence that the four dimensions of psychosocial maturity described in the previous paragraph continue to develop during the adolescent years. First, substantial research supports the conventional wisdom that, even in middle adolescence, teenagers are more responsive to peer influence than are adults. Studies in which adolescents are presented with hypothetical dilemmas in which they are asked to choose between an antisocial course of action suggested by their peers and a prosocial one of their own choosing indicate that susceptibility to peer influence increases between childhood and early adolescence as adolescents begin to individuate from parental control, peaks around age 14, and declines slowly during the high school years (Berndt, 1979; Steinberg & Silverberg, 1986). Peer influence affects adolescent judgment both directly and indirectly. In some contexts, adolescents make choices in response to direct peer pressure to act in certain ways. More indirectly, adolescents' desire for peer approval—and fear of rejection—affect their choices, even without direct coercion. Peers also provide models for behavior that adolescents believe will assist them in accomplishing their own ends (Moffitt, 1993).

Second, it is well established that over an extended period between childhood and young adulthood, individuals become more future-oriented. Studies in which individuals are asked to envision themselves or their circumstances in the future find that adults project out their visions over a significantly longer time frame than do adolescents (Greene, 1986; Nurmi, 1991). In addition, in studies in which individuals are queried about their perceptions of the short-term and longer term pros and cons of various sorts of risk taking (e.g., the risk of having unprotected sex, Gardner & Herman, 1990) or asked to give advice to others about risky decisions (e.g., whether to have cosmetic surgery; Halpern-Felsher & Cauffman, 2001), adolescents tend to discount the future more than adults do and to weigh more heavily short-term consequences of decisions—both risks and benefits—in making choices. There are at least two plausible explanations for this age difference in future orientation. First, owing to cognitive limitations in their ability to think in hypothetical terms, adolescents simply may be less able than adults to think about events that have not yet occurred (i.e., events that may occur sometime in the future). Second, the weaker future orientation of adolescents may reflect their more limited life experience. For adolescents, a consequence 5 years in the future may seem very remote in relation to how long they have been alive; teens may simply attach more weight to short-term consequences because they seem more salient to their lives (Gardner, 1993).

Third, adolescents differ from adults in their assessment of and attitude toward risk. In general, adolescents use a risk-reward calculus that places relatively less weight on risk, in relation to reward, than that used by adults. When asked to advise peers on making a potentially risky decision, for example (e.g., whether to participate in a study of an experimental drug), adults spontaneously mentioned more potential risks than did adolescents (Halpern-Felsher & Cauffman, 2001). In addition, experimental studies that use gambling tasks show that, compared with those of adults, adolescents' decisions are more driven by rewards and less by risks (see Furby & Beyth-Marom, 1992).

A number of explanations for this age difference have been offered. First, youths' relatively weaker risk aversion may be related to their more limited time perspective, because taking risks is less costly for those with a smaller stake in the future (Gardner & Herman, 1990). Second, adolescents may have different values and goals than do adults, leading them to calculate risks and rewards differently (Furby & Beyth-Marom, 1992). For example, the danger of some types of risk taking (e.g., driving well over the speed limit) could constitute reward for an adolescent but a cost to an adult. In addition, considerable evidence indicates that people generally make riskier decisions in groups than they do alone (Vinokur, 1971); there is evidence both that adolescents spend more time in groups than do adults and, as noted earlier, that adolescents are relatively more susceptible to the influence of others.

Fourth, although more research is needed, the widely held stereotype that adolescents are more impulsive than adults finds some support in research on developmental changes in impulsivity and self-reliance over the course of adolescence. As assessed on standardized self-report personality measures, impulsivity increases between middle adolescence and early adulthood and declines thereafter, and gains in self-management skills take place during early, middle, and late adolescence (Greenberger, 1982; Steinberg & Cauffman, 1996). Studies using the Experience Sampling Method, in which individuals are paged several times each day and asked to report on their emotions and activities, indicate that adolescents have more rapid and more extreme mood swings (both positive and negative) than adults, which may lead them to act more impulsively (Larson, Csikszentmihalyi, & Graef, 1980). Taken together, these findings indicate that adolescents may have more difficulty regulating their moods, impulses, and behaviors than do adults.

Most of the developmental research on cognitive and psychosocial functioning in adolescence measures behaviors, self-perceptions, or attitudes, but mounting evidence suggests that at least some of the differences between adults and adolescents have neuropsychological and neurobiological underpinnings. What is most interesting is that studies of brain development during adolescence, and of differences in patterns of brain activation between adolescents and adults, indicate that the most important developments during adolescence occur in regions that are implicated in processes of long-term planning, the regulation of emotion, impulse control, and the evaluation of risk and reward (Spear, 2000). For example, changes in the limbic system around puberty may stimulate adolescents to seek higher levels of novelty and to take more risks and may contribute to increased emotionality and vulnerability to stress (Dahl, 2001). At the same time, patterns of development in the prefrontal cortex, which is active during the performance of complicated tasks involving long-term planning and judgment and decision making, suggest that these higher order cognitive capacities may be immature well into late adolescence (Giedd et al., 1999; Sowell, Thompson, Holmes, Jernigan, & Toga, 1999). At this point, the connection between neurobiological and psychological evidence of age differences in decision-making capacity is indirect and suggestive.

However, the results of studies using paper-and-pencil measures of future orientation, impulsivity, and susceptibility to peer pressure point in the same direction as the neurobiological evidence, namely, that brain systems implicated in planning, judgment, impulse control, and decision making continue to mature into late adolescence. Thus, there is good reason to believe that adolescents, as compared with adults, are more susceptible to influence, less future oriented, less risk averse, and less able to manage their impulses and behavior, and that these differences likely have a neurobiological basis. The important conclusion for our purposes is that juveniles may have diminished decision-making capacity compared with adults because of differences in psychosocial capacities that are likely biological in origin. . . .

Heightened Vulnerability
to Coercive Circumstances

The psychosocial immaturity of adolescents contributes to their diminished capacity (the first category of mitigation), but it is important to another source of mitigation as well. As we noted earlier,
criminal culpability can be reduced on the basis of circumstances
that impose extraordinary pressures on the actor. The criminal law
does not require exceptional fortitude or bravery of citizens and, in
general, recognizes mitigation where an ordinary (or in legal par-
lance, "reasonable") person might have responded in the same way as
the defendant under similar circumstances. In evaluating the behavior of an adolescent in responding to extenuating circumstances,
however, the correct basis for evaluation is not comparison of the actor's behavior with that of an "ordinary" adult but rather with that of
an "ordinary" adolescent (*In re William G.*, 1987; Scott & Steinberg,
2003).

Because of their developmental immaturity, normative (i.e., "ordinary") adolescents may respond adversely to external pressures that
adults are able to resist. If adolescents are more susceptible to hypothetical peer pressure than are adults (as noted earlier), it stands to
reason that age differences in susceptibility to real peer pressure will
be even more considerable. Thus, it seems reasonable to hypothesize
that a youth would succumb more readily to peer influence than
would an adult in the same situation. Similarly, if adolescents are
more impulsive than adults, it may take less of a threat to provoke an
aggressive response from a juvenile. And, because adolescents are
less likely than adults to think through the future consequences of
their actions, the same level of duress may have a more disruptive impact on juveniles' decision making than on that of adults. In general,
legal judgments about mitigation should consider the extent to which
developmentally normal adolescents are more susceptible to external
pressures than are adults. Adolescents' claim to mitigation on this
ground is particularly compelling in that, as legal minors, they lack
the freedom that adults have to extricate themselves from a
criminogenic setting (Fagan, 2000).

Although plausible inferences can be drawn about how developmental influences may affect adolescents' responses to external pressures, we do not have sufficient research comparing the behavior of
adolescents and adults at varying levels of duress, provocation, or coercion. Some social psychological research has examined contextual
influences on decision making—for example, the literature on the
risky shift, which shows that individuals take more risks in groups
than when alone (Vinokur, 1971)—but this research has not exam-

ined whether the impact of different contextual factors varies as a function of the decision maker's age. Further, as we noted earlier, studies comparing the decision making of adolescents with that of adults have intentionally minimized the influence of contextual factors that could affect the decision-making process differently for individuals of different ages. Recent evidence on age differences in the processing of emotionally arousing information supports the hypothesis that adolescents may tend to respond to threats more viscerally and emotionally than adults (Baird, Gruber, & Fein, 1999), but far more research on this topic is needed.

Unformed Character as Mitigation

In addition to the mitigating effects of adolescents' diminished decision-making capacity and greater vulnerability to external pressures, youthful culpability is also mitigated by the relatively unformed nature of their characters. As we have noted, the criminal law implicitly assumes that harmful conduct reflects the actor's bad character and treats evidence that this assumption is inaccurate as mitigating of culpability (Duff, 1993; Vuoso, 1986). For most adolescents, the assumption is inaccurate, and thus their crimes are less culpable than those of typical criminals.

The emergence of personal identity is an important developmental task of adolescence and one in which the aspects of psychosocial development discussed earlier play a key role. As documented in many empirical tests of Erikson's (1968) theory of the adolescent identity crisis, the process of identity formation includes considerable exploration and experimentation over the course of adolescence (Steinberg, 2002a). Although the identity crisis may occur in middle adolescence, the resolution of this crisis, with the coherent integration of the various retained elements of identity into a developed self, does not occur until late adolescence or early adulthood (Waterman, 1982). Often this experimentation involves risky, illegal, or dangerous activities like alcohol use, drug use, unsafe sex, and antisocial behavior. For most teens, these behaviors are fleeting; they cease with maturity as individual identity becomes settled. Only a relatively small proportion of adolescents who experiment in risky or illegal activities develop entrenched patterns of problem behavior that persist into adulthood (Farrington, 1986; Moffitt, 1993). Thus, making predictions about the development of relatively more permanent and enduring traits on the basis of patterns of risky behavior observed in adolescence is an uncertain business. At least until late adolescence, individuals' values, attitudes, beliefs, and plans are likely to be tentative and exploratory expressions rather than enduring representations of personhood. Thus, research on identity development in adolescence supports the view that much youth crime stems from normative experimentation with risky behavior and not from deep-seated moral deficiency reflective of "bad" character. One reason the typical delinquent youth does not grow up to be an adult criminal is that the developmentally linked values and preferences that drive his or her criminal choices as a teenager change in predictable ways as the youth matures.

The distinction between youthful criminal behavior that is attributable to characteristics that adolescents outgrow and conduct that is attributable to relatively more permanent elements of personality is captured in Moffitt's (1993) work on the developmental trajectories of antisocial behavior. In her view, adolescent offenders fall into one of two broad categories: adolescence-limited offenders, whose anti-social behavior begins and ends during adolescence, and a much smaller group of life-course-persistent offenders, whose antisocial behavior begins in childhood and continues through adolescence and into adulthood. According to Moffitt, the criminal activity of both groups during adolescence is similar, but the underlying causes of their behavior are very different. Life-course-persistent offenders show longstanding patterns of antisocial behavior that appear to be rooted, at least in part, in relatively stable psychological attributes that are present early in development and that are attributable to deficient socialization or neurobiological anomalies. Adolescence-limited offending, in contrast, is the product of forces that are inherent features of adolescence as a developmental period, including peer pressure, experimentation with risk, and demonstrations of bravado aimed at enhancing one's status in the social hierarchy of the peer group. By definition, the causes of adolescence-limited offending weaken as individuals mature into adulthood.

In view of what we know about identity development, it seems likely that the criminal conduct of most young wrongdoers is quite different from that of typical adult criminals. Most adults who engage in criminal conduct act on subjectively defined preferences and values, and their choices can fairly be charged to deficient moral character. This cannot be said of typical juvenile actors, whose behaviors are more likely to be shaped by developmental forces that are constitutive of adolescence. To be sure, some adolescents may be in the early stages of developing a criminal identity and reprehensible moral character traits, but most are not. Indeed, studies of criminal careers indicate that the vast majority of adolescents who engage in criminal or delinquent behavior desist from crime as they mature into adulthood (Farrington, 1986). Thus the criminal choices of typical young offenders differ from those of adults not only because the choice, qua choice, is deficient as the product of immature judgment, but also because the adolescent's criminal act does not express the actor's bad character.

The notion that individuals are less blameworthy when their crimes are out of character is significant in assessing the culpability of typical young offenders. In one sense, young wrongdoers are not like adults whose acts are less culpable on this ground. A claim that an adult's criminal act was out of character requires a demonstration that his or her established character is good. The criminal choice of the typical adolescent cannot be evaluated in this manner because the adolescent's personal identity is in flux and his or her character has not yet stabilized. However, like the adult offender whose crime is mitigated because it is out of character, adolescent offenders lack an important component of culpability—the connection between a bad act and a bad character.

The fact that antisocial activity in adolescence is not usually indicative of bad character also raises important questions about the construct validity of juvenile psychopathy, a "diagnosis" that has recently received considerable attention (Edens, Skeem, Cruise, & Cauffman, 2001; Forth & Burke, 1998; Seagrave & Grisso, 2002; Steinberg, 2002b). Labeling an individual as a psychopath—perhaps the quintessential case of "bad character"—implies that the individual's antisocial behavior is due to fixed aspects of his or her personality. But, as we have suggested, this assumption is difficult to defend as applied to individuals whose identity development is still under way. (Indeed, it is for this very reason that the diagnosis of antisocial personality disorder is not made prior to the age of 18; American Psychiatric Association, 1994). Although the notion that some juvenile offenders are actual or "fledgling" psychopaths has become increasingly popular in legal and psychological circles, no data exist on the stability or continuity of psychopathy between adolescence and adulthood. In the absence of evidence that juveniles who, on the surface, resemble adult psychopaths (e.g., juveniles who are callous, manipulative, and antisocial) actually become adult psychopaths, it would seem unwise to use this label when describing an adolescent.

Our analysis also clarifies why the crime of the adult actor with "adolescent" traits warrants a different response than does that of the typical young offender. Although most impulsive young risk takers who focus on immediate consequences will mature into adults with different values, some adult criminals have traits that are similar to their younger counterparts. In the case of the adult, however, the predispositions, values, and preferences that motivate him or her most likely are characterological and are unlikely to change predictably with the passage of time. Adolescent traits that contribute to criminal conduct are normative in adolescence, but they are not typical of adulthood. In an adult, these traits are often part of the personal identity of an individual who is not respectful of the values of the criminal law and who deserves full punishment when he or she violates its prohibitions. . . .

Developmental Immaturity, Diminished Culpability, and the Juvenile Crime Policy

. . . If, in fact, adolescent offenders are generally less culpable than their adult counterparts, how should the legal system recognize their diminished responsibility? An important policy choice is whether immaturity should be considered on an individualized basis, as is typical of most mitigating conditions, or as the basis for treating young law violators as a separate category of offenders (Scott & Steinberg, 2003).

We believe that the uniqueness of immaturity as a mitigating condition argues for the adoption of, or renewed commitment to, a categorical approach, under which most youths are dealt with in a separate justice system, in which rehabilitation is a central aim, and none are eligible for the ultimate punishment of death. Other mitigators—emotional disturbance and coercive external circumstances, for example—affect criminal choices with endless variety and have idiosyncratic effects on behavior; thus, individualized consideration of mitigation is appropriate where these phenomena are involved. In contrast, the capacities and processes associated with adolescence are characteristic of individuals in a relatively defined group, whose development follows a roughly systematic course to maturity, and whose criminal choices are affected in predictable ways. . . .

In our view, however, there is sufficient indirect and suggestive evidence of age differences in capacities that are relevant to criminal blameworthiness to support the position that youths who commit crimes should be punished more leniently than their adult counterparts. . . . The Supreme Court has repeatedly emphasized that the death penalty is acceptable punishment only for the most blameworthy killers (*Gregg v. Georgia*, 1976; *Lockett v. Ohio*, 1978). All other developed countries have adopted a policy that assumes that adolescents, because of developmental immaturity, simply do not satisfy this criterion. The United States should join the majority of countries around the world in prohibiting the execution of individuals for crimes committed under the age of 18.

References

American Psychiatric Association (1994). Diagnostic and statistical manual of mental disorders (4th ed.). Washington, DC: Author.

American Psychological Association (1990). Brief for Amicus Curiae in support of appellees, Hodgson v. Minnesota 497 U.S. 417, No. 88-805. Washington, DC: Author.

Baird, A., Gruber, S., & Fein, D. (1999). Functional magnetic resonance imaging of facial affect recognition in children and adolescents. Journal of the American Academy of Child and Adolescent Psychiatry, 38, 195–199.

Berndt, T. (1979). Developmental changes in conformity to peers and parents. Developmental Psychology, 15, 608–616.

Cauffman, E., & Steinberg, L. (2000). (Im)maturity of judgment in adolescence: Why adolescents may be less culpable than adults. Behavioral Sciences and the Law, 18, 1–21.

Dahl, R. (2001). Affect regulation, brain development, and behavioral/emotional health in adolescence. CNS Spectrums, 6, 1–12.

Duff, R. (1993). Choice, character, and criminal liability. Law and Philosophy, 12, 345–383.

Edens, J., Skeem, J., Cruise, K., & Cauffman, E. (2001). The assessment of juvenile psychopathy and its association with violence: A critical review. Behavioral Sciences and the Law, 19, 53–80.

Erikson, E. (1968). Identity: Youth and crisis. New York: Norton.

Fagan, J. (2000). Contexts of choice by adolescents in criminal events. In T. Grisso & R. Schwartz (Eds.), Youth on trial: A developmental perspective on juvenile justice (pp. 371–401). Chicago: University of Chicago Press.

Farrington, D. (1986). Age and crime. In M. Tonry & N. Morris (Eds.), Crime and justice: An annual review of research (pp. 189–217). Chicago: University of Chicago Press.

Fischhoff, B. (1992). Risk taking: A developmental perspective. In J. Yates (Ed.), Risk-taking behavior (pp. 133–162). New York: Wiley.

Forth, A., & Burke, H. (1998). Psychopathy in adolescence: Assessment, violence and developmental precursors. In D. Cooke, A. E. Forth, & R. D. Hare (Eds.), Psychopathy: Theory, research and implications for society (pp. 205–229). Boston: Kluwer Academic.

Furby, L., & Beyth-Marom, R. (1992). Risk taking in adolescence: A decision-making perspective. Developmental Review, 12, 1–44.

Gardner, W. (1993). A life-span rational choice theory of risk taking. In N. Bell & R. Bell (Eds.), Adolescent risk taking (pp. 66–83). Newbury Park, CA: Sage.

Gardner, W., & Herman, J. (1990). Adolescents' AIDS risk taking: A rational choice perspective. In W. Gardner, S. Millstein, & B. Wilcox (Eds.), Adolescents in the AIDS epidemic (pp. 17–34). San Francisco: Jossey-Bass.

Giedd, J., Blumenthal, J., Jeffries, N., Castllanos, F., Liu, H., & Zijdenbos, A. et al. (1999). Brain development during childhood and adolescence: A longitudinal MRI study. Nature Neuroscience, 2, 861–863.

Greenberger, E. (1982). Education and the acquisition of psychosocial maturity. In D. McClelland (Ed.), The development of social maturity (pp. 155–189). New York: Irvington.

Greene, A. (1986). Future-time perspective in adolescence: The present of things future revisited. Journal of Youth and Adolescence, 15, 99–113.

Gregg v. Georgia 428 U.S. 153 (1976).

Halpern-Felsher, B., & Cauffman, E. (2001). Costs and benefits of a decision: Decision-making competence in adolescents and adults. Journal of Applied Developmental Psychology, 22, 257–273.

In re William G. (1987) 963 Pacific Reporter 2d 187 (Ariz. App. Div.).

Kadish, S. (1987). Excusing crime. California Law Review, 75, 257–296.

Keating, D. (1990). Adolescent thinking. In S. S. Feldman & G. R. Elliot (Eds.), At the threshold: The developing adolescent (pp. 54–89). Cambridge, MA: Harvard University Press.

Larson, R., Csikszentmihalyi, M., & Graef, R. (1980). Mood variability and the psychosocial adjustment of adolescents. Journal of Youth and Adolescence, 9, 469–490.

Lockett v. Ohio 438 U.S. 586 (1978).

Melton, G. B. (1983). Toward "personhood" for adolescents: Autonomy and privacy as values in public policy. American Psychologist, 39, 99–103.

Moffitt, T. (1993). Adolescence-limited and life-course-persistent antisocial behavior: A developmental taxonomy. Psychological Review, 100, 674–701.

Morse, S. (1994). Culpability and control. Pennsylvania Law Review, 142, 1587–1660.

Nurmi, J. (1991). How do adolescents see their future? A review of the development of future orientation and planning. Developmental Review, 11, 1–59.

Scott, E., Reppucci, N., & Woolard, J. (1995). Evaluating adolescent decision making in legal contexts. Law and Human Behavior, 19, 221–244.

Scott, E., & Steinberg, L. (2003). Blaming youth. Texas Law Review, 81, 799–840.

Seagrave, D., & Grisso, T. (2002). Adolescent development and the measurement of juvenile psychopathy. Law and Human Behavior, 26, 219–239.

Siegler, R. (1997). Children's thinking (3rd ed.). Englewood Cliffs, NJ: Prentice Hall.

Sowell, E., Thompson, P., Holmes, C., Jernigan, T., & Toga, A. (1999). In vivo evidence for post-adolescent brain maturation in frontal and striatal regions. Nature Neuroscience, 2, 859–861.

Spear, P. (2000). The adolescent brain and age-related behavioral manifestations. Neuroscience and Biobehavioral Reviews, 24, 417–463.

Steinberg, L. (2002a). Adolescence (6th ed.). New York: McGraw-Hill.

Steinberg, L. (2002b). The juvenile psychopath: Fads, fictions, and facts. National Institute of Justice Perspectives on Crime and Justice: 2001 Lecture Series, 5, 35–64.

Steinberg, L. (2003). Is decision-making the right framework for the study of adolescent risk-taking? In D. Romer (Ed.), Reducing adolescent risk: Toward an integrated approach (pp. 18–24). Thousand Oaks, CA: Sage.

Steinberg, L., & Cauffman, E. (1996). Maturity of judgment in adolescence: Psychosocial factors in adolescent decision-making. Law and Human Behavior, 20, 249–272.

Steinberg, L., & Silverberg, S. (1986). The vicissitudes of autonomy in early adolescence. Child Development, 57, 841–851.

United States Sentencing Commission (1998). United States sentencing guidelines manual: Section 5K2.20. Washington, DC.

Vinokur, A. (1971). Review and theoretical analysis of the effects of group processes upon individual and group decisions involving risk. Psychological Bulletin, 76, 231–250.

Vuoso, G. (1986). Background, responsibility, and excuse. Yale Law Review, 96, 1661–1686.

Waterman, A. (1982). Identity development from adolescence to adulthood: An extension of theory and a review of research. Developmental Psychology, 18, 341–358. ✦

Juvenile Corrections

The two chapters in Part VII provide overviews of two very different juvenile corrections systems in two very different states. Looking at these two states gives a sense of the range and diversity of youth corrections systems nationwide.

The first chapter looks at the state of California, which has the largest juvenile corrections system in the country and perhaps in the world. This system emphasizes largeness—for example, California recently held nearly 20,000 youths in secure facilities statewide and the largest such facility housed about 1,600 youths.

The second chapter looks at the state of Missouri. This smaller state has a juvenile corrections system that emphasizes smallness—for example, Missouri recently held only 180 youths in secure facilities statewide and the largest such facility housed around 35 youths. ✦

Chapter 13

Youth Corrections in California

David Steinhart and Jeffrey A. Butts

Editor's Introduction

California's juvenile corrections system strongly emphasizes confinement of juvenile offenders, as opposed to programs (other than standard probation and parole) that handle juveniles in the community. The counties run two types of confinement facilities: detention centers ("juvenile halls") and "probation camps." A third type is run by the state: the institutions of the California Youth Authority (CYA).

Detention centers provide temporary confinement for juveniles who have been arrested but whose cases have not been completely processed by the juvenile courts. After processing, these juveniles are supposed to leave the detention center and go either to a "placement" (i.e., either an institutional placement or a community placement) or back to their own homes. However, nearly half of the juveniles in these facilities are "post-disposition" cases—i.e., their court processing is completed. There are many reasons for these youth remaining in detention centers, including the lack of space in the state-run and private facilities to which these youths should be sent.

Many of the counties in California also run *probation camps* that provide relatively short-term placements for a variety of offenders. Some of these camps are highly secure (i.e., with locks and fences) while others are *non-secure*. Some of the non-secure (or "open") facilities are in out-of-the-way places, which make it inconvenient to run away. Other facilities are *staff-secure,* which means that staff make sure the kids stay put. But on the whole, youth placed in non-secure facilities are trusted to remain there on their own.

The *institutions* of the California Youth Authority are the largest and the most "prison-like" juvenile confinement facilities in the state—the largest of these facilities has 1,600 beds. This system is quite expensive—the most recent estimate is that each youth in a CYA institution costs the state $71,700 per year.[1] It also has been plagued with high recidivism rates—a 2004 study con-

Adapted from David Steinhart and Jeffrey A. Butts. 2002. "Youth Corrections in California." Washington, DC: The Urban Institute. Copyright © 2002 by the Urban Institute.

ducted by the CYA itself found that three-fourths of youths released from the system were rearrested within a three-year period.[2]

Finally, there have been widespread abuses within its facilities, both recently and throughout its history.[3] On November 16, 2004, Governor Arnold Schwarzennegger announced a major reorganization of the CYA.[4] This action was taken in response to a series of scandals that had rocked the system. It also was in response to a class-action suit filed against the CYA for widespread abuses. The state settled this suit on January 31, 2005, by agreeing to undertake a wide range of reforms which re-emphasized rehabilitation and treatment instead of punishment.[5] However, no additional money was to be provided from the state budget to implement these reforms.[6]

Notes

1. Sele Nadel-Hayes and Daniel Macallair, "Restructuring Juvenile Corrections in California: A Report to the State Legislature." San Francisco: Center on Juvenile and Criminal Justice, September, 2005, p. 32.

2. B. Baily and G. Palmer, "High Rearrest Rate: Three-Fourths of Wards Released Over 13 Years Held on New Charges," *San Jose Mercury News*, October 17, 2004.

3. See, for example, "Special Report: Juvenile Injustice," *U.S. News and World Report*, August 3, 2004. For reports on abuses during the 1980s, see Lerner (1982, 1986) and DeMuro et al. (1988) in the reference list at the end of this chapter.

4. J. Warren, "State Youth Prisons on Road to Rehab," *Los Angeles Times*, November 17, 2004.

5. J. Warren, "For Young Offenders, A Softer Approach," *Los Angeles Times*, February 1, 2005.

6. Sele Nadel-Hayes and Daniel Macallair, op. cit.

✦ ✦ ✦

California places more juveniles in secure confinement than any other state in the country. On an average day, according to data from the Office of Juvenile Justice and Delinquency Prevention, nearly 20,000 youths are held in the state's secure facilities. In recent years, California accounted for one in five confined juveniles nationwide, even though it contained 13 percent of the juvenile population (Sickmund and Wan 1999). . . .[1]

Youth Facilities

California divides control over juvenile confinement facilities between state and county governments. The state agency primarily responsible for incarcerating young offenders—the California Youth Authority—operates large institutions where (generally the most serious) offenders are committed by county juvenile courts for long-term placement. The state has little direct role in the operation of detention facilities (known as juvenile halls) or local commitment facilities (i.e., probation camps and ranches). These facilities are operated and funded by county governments, although the state does exercise some regulatory control over them through the California Board of Corrections. . . .

Detention

At the beginning of 2001, there were 58 detention facilities (or juvenile halls) located in 51 California counties. These facilities had a combined capacity of nearly 7,000 beds (California Board of Corrections 2001a). The highest, single-day population reported during 2000 for juvenile halls statewide was 7,805, or more than 10 percent over capacity. The size of detention facilities in California ranges from small, special purpose facilities in rural and alpine counties to very large centers (300 beds or more) in major metropolitan counties such as Los Angeles, Orange, and San Diego. The size of California's juvenile detention system—whether measured as rated capacity or average daily population—increased steadily during the 1990s. . . .

Factors Affecting the Use of Detention. The average citizen probably believes that increases or decreases in the size of juvenile detention systems are related to rising or falling juvenile crime rates. Changes in serious juvenile crime, however, cannot account for recent trends in California's use of detention. Between 1990 and 2000, the average daily population of youth in the state's juvenile detention facilities increased approximately 20 percent. The number of juvenile felony arrests during this period, however, dropped 30 percent, from 91,373 to 63,889 (California Department of Justice 2001). Juvenile arrests for property felonies dropped 42 percent, while arrests for violent felonies fell 19 percent and felony drug arrests declined 24 percent among juveniles. . . . The recent growth in detention, therefore, must be due to factors other than the pressures of arrest trends. . . .

The Role of Policy and Practice. . . . Under California law, probation officers have authority in most cases to release minors without detention prior to a court hearing. If released before a court hearing, arrested youth tend to stay out of custody all through the judicial process, thus avoiding further growth in the detention population. To help probation officers make these intake decisions, all large metropolitan probation departments (e.g., Los Angeles, San Francisco, Orange, San Diego, Santa Clara, Sacramento) use objective risk assessment instruments to screen youth based upon their apparent need for secure detention. Even where risk assessment instruments are used, however, they may be an ineffective means of controlling the juvenile hall population, either because the assessment criteria themselves are designed to detain youth for a wide variety of behaviors or because probation officers can easily override the screening instrument in favor of secure custody. Moreover, Proposition 21 imposed new limits on the discretion of probation officers to release minors at intake, by requiring that youth arrested for more serious crimes be detained until a court hearing.

Other local juvenile justice practices can influence the size of the detention population. One critical factor is the average length of time it takes to move a case through court. Some county court systems are more efficient than others and are able to move minors more quickly through the process, minimizing the total time minors spend in predisposition custody. According to the state Board of Corrections, the average length of stay for all California juvenile detention facilities in 2000 was 27 days. This was longer than the average of 22½ days reported in 1999. Even small increases in average length of stay can have a multiplier effect on the total number of bed-days needed in a detention facility or its average daily population (ADP). . . .

Post-Disposition Cases. The traditional function of juvenile detention is to establish physical custody over youth accused of serious crimes before and during the court process, much like an adult jail. Detention ensures a youth's attendance at court hearings and serves the public safety by preventing new offenses while the court process is under way. Geared toward short-term stays, detention facilities and detention staff are not generally equipped to provide treatment or specialized programming for young offenders. Nevertheless, California's juvenile detention facilities often contain large numbers of minors that have already completed the court process—that is, post-disposition cases. Some of these youth stay in custody for many months following court processing.

Post-disposition detention cases generally fall into three categories: youth serving time in a "commitment program" within the detention center, those waiting in the detention facility for a court-ordered placement, and those who have been returned to detention for a probation violation or a placement failure. During the first three months of 2001, nearly half (47 percent) of all youth in California's juvenile halls were post-disposition cases, compared with 36 percent during the same period in 1999 (California Board of Corrections 2001b). . . .

Alternatives to Secure Detention. Some jurisdictions across the United States rely on an array of supervision alternatives to limit the use of their juvenile detention facilities (Schwartz and Barton 1994). Supervision options can include home detention programs, day-reporting centers, work-service programs for probation violators, and even electronic monitoring for certain offenders. California policy-makers have not often made strong funding commitments to the development of local supervision alternatives.

Counties may have been reluctant to develop supervision alternatives for economic reasons. With few exceptions, California counties are responsible for the full cost of placing youth in the type of programs that often serve as alternatives to detention. Even though many such programs have lower operating costs than secure detention, new programs also have start-up costs that must be fully supported by county budgets. Thus, economic disincentives to the development of supervision alternatives may have encouraged county officials to "stay the course" and continue to rely on detention for a wide range of juvenile offenders.

Local policymakers' emphasis on secure custody is not due simply to a lack of alternatives. State and local officials in California have long preferred to make broad use of detention. In 1994, California approved some of the nation's most stringent prison terms for chronic adult offenders ("three strikes and you're out") and during the same year changed its juvenile justice laws making it easier to try minors as adults and increasing penalties across the board. Even as juvenile crime rates began to drop in the mid-1990s, many California counties continued to rely heavily on secure detention despite chronic crowding, high operating costs, and undiminished demands for ever-larger facilities. In such an environment, there was often little enthusiasm for community-based detention alternatives. . . .

Probation Camps and Ranches

California also maintains a large, separate network of local placement facilities for juvenile offenders. Falling somewhere between the traditional arrangements of local detention and state sponsored corrections, these programs, known as probation "camps" or "ranches," are local commitment programs for youth that have been adjudicated under the delinquency jurisdiction of county juvenile courts. As of 2001, according to the state Board of Corrections, California counties were operating 5,100 probation camp beds. . . .

Not every county has a probation camp or ranch for juvenile offenders. Los Angeles County, with 20 probation camps, represents nearly half the state's camps and ranches. Another 26 counties have at least one camp, while 31 counties have no camp facility at all. . . .

The character and quality of camp programs may be quite different from county to county. The juvenile probation camp system in Los Angeles County is unique, both in California and in the United States. With more than 2,000 beds across 20 separate facilities, Los Angeles County operates a diverse local care system for adjudicated

juveniles. Los Angeles camps run the gamut from higher security facilities housing juveniles adjudicated for violent crimes to boot camp
programs and mental health facilities.[2] Los Angeles's local residential
facilities provide the juvenile justice system with a broader menu of
dispositional options for adjudicated delinquents as well as reduce
the county's utilization of Youth Authority beds, even for juveniles adjudicated for serious and violent crimes. . . . Unlike California's detention facilities, which are persistently crowded in some of the largest
counties, probation camps and ranches are rarely filled beyond their
rated capacities. During 2000, California's probation camps and
ranches had an 89 percent average occupancy rate.

The Dispositional Continuum. Probation camps and ranches are
an important resource for the California juvenile justice system. In
recent years, the state's camps and ranches have held an average of
4,500 juveniles per day, according to the California Board of Corrections. About 20,000 juveniles per year are admitted to camps and
ranches, where the average length of stay is two to three months.
Were these offenders to be committed to the California Youth Authority instead, they would serve much longer sentences, use far more bed
space, and consume even more resources.

The commitment of a juvenile offender to a county probation
camp is a less severe disposition than commitment to the Youth Authority. Most camps and ranches in California counties are semi-
secure or non-secure facilities, without locked cells or (in many
cases) fenced perimeters. By contrast, the institutions of the Youth
Authority are more prison-like, with more expensive security features, and contain larger populations, averaging 600 beds per institution. The average stay in CYA institutions is also much longer, more
than 10 times the average stay in local probation camps. . . .[3]

California Youth Authority

California runs the world's largest network of youth incarceration
facilities—a set of institutions and camps holding more than 7,000
youth per day known collectively as the "California Youth Authority,"
or CYA. . . . CYA facilities are spread throughout the state, with populations that vary by age, gender, security level, and county of origin.

The institutions range from prison-like facilities including the
large (1,200 beds) Stark Training School in Chino to the campus-like
environments of the Fred C. Nelles and O. H. Close facilities for younger male offenders. . . . The CYA also runs several rural conservation
camps for youth committed to its custody.

Each youth committed to the Youth Authority by a juvenile court is
first referred to one of three reception centers for diagnostic testing,
classification, and assignment to an institution. The CYA maintains

two institutions that serve as reception centers for male offenders, one for the northern region of the state and one for the southern region. The correctional facility for females (Ventura) includes its own reception and diagnostic unit for committed females.

Commitments and Institutional Populations. The young offenders held in CYA institutions are a more diverse population than would be found in many state juvenile justice systems. The Youth Authority is responsible for young offenders committed to its custody by either juvenile or criminal courts. Approximately 15 percent of offenders held by the CYA are actually young adults sentenced to the California Department of Corrections (CDC) by an adult court who are sent to the Youth Authority to serve their sentence (California Youth Authority 2001). A handful of these youth may complete their sentences in CYA facilities, but most are transferred to state prison at some point during their sentence. The Youth Authority's jurisdiction for young offenders, both juvenile and young adult, ends on the offender's 25th birthday.

Juveniles in California may be sentenced directly to the Department of Corrections, whether by juvenile or criminal court. According to California law, young offenders must be at least 16 to be housed in a state (adult) prison. Many serious offenses, however, are barred from CYA jurisdiction. When an adult court in California convicts a minor under age 16 of a crime for which Youth Authority commitment is barred, state law provides that the minor may be temporarily housed at CYA, but transfer to a state prison facility is mandatory by age 18. In recent years, state lawmakers and voters have made it harder for minors convicted in adult courts to be sentenced to the CYA. The passage of Proposition 21 in March 2000 further narrowed CYA eligibility criteria by increasing the number of offenses for which CYA commitment is expressly prohibited.

Length of Stay Policies. Policies regarding offender length of stay are a critical determinant of the demand for confinement space in California. The length of offender commitments to CYA is not controlled either by the committing court or by CYA. Instead, the length of time each youth spends with the Youth Authority is established by a separate state entity known as the Youthful Offender Parole Board (YOPB). In other words, sentences at CYA are indeterminate. Upon admission, each youth is given a parole consideration date by the YOPB. Whether an individual youth is actually released at that time depends on the Board's review of the youth's behavior during the period of commitment. Young offenders with particularly poor behavior may experience longer periods of confinement in CYA institutions than they would have as adults sentenced to state prison for similar offenses. The only limit on sentence length in CYA facilities is that youthful offenders cannot be institutionalized longer than the maximum adult determinate term, or the maximum age of CYA jurisdiction, whichever comes first.

The bifurcation of control over the use of CYA confinement—with custodial and program responsibility held by the Youth Authority and release power maintained by the Youthful Offender Parole Board—was blamed in the past for contributing to crowding in CYA institutions. An analysis by DeMuro and his colleagues in 1988 found that the population of offenders held in CYA institutions had doubled between 1978 and 1988, not because crime rates or commitments from county courts had increased, but because actions by the YOPB effectively doubled the average length of stay for CYA commitments in these years (DeMuro, DeMuro, and Lerner 1988). In 1988, CYA institutional populations had ballooned to nearly 9,000 offenders, approximately 150 percent of their design capacity. The California legislature, facing large increases in the cost of running CYA institutions given their rising population levels, began to place limits on YOPB confinement policies. The population in CYA institutions soon began to recede. By 1996, however, average length of stay had started to increase again, putting renewed pressure on institutional space. The new increases in length of stay, however, were due at least in part to rising rates of juvenile violent crime, causing more juveniles with longer sentences to be committed to CYA. In 1996, the average length of stay in CYA institutions (including parole violators) was 22½ months. By 2000, the average stay had increased to more than 27 months. . . .

Conditions of Confinement. . . . In 1999, the state inspector general's office confirmed reports that youth had been abused at several CYA institutions. The incidents included sealing rooms and spraying youth with mace, slamming them into walls, forcing youth into cells with human waste on the floors, or staging "Friday night fights" between institutionalized youth. The allegations were reminiscent of earlier studies that described abuses in CYA facilities. Between 1984 and 1990, for example, Commonweal produced three books on the CYA, citing a pattern of fear and gang violence in the institutions and blaming the problems on crowding in the institutions and on the state's policy of allowing counties to commit too many property and drug offenders to CYA (Lerner 1982, 1986). Near the end of 1999, in the wake of renewed negative publicity about the Youth Authority, California's governor fired his recently appointed CYA director and instructed the Youth and Adult Corrections Agency to take steps to renew the quality and safety of CYA's institutions and programs. Several steps were taken by state corrections officials to improve conditions in CYA facilities, including upgrades of education and mental health services for confined youth.

Private Placememnts. The availability of private facilities may be another critical factor in determining the future demand for confinement space in California's youth corrections facilities. On any given day in California, there are approximately 6,000 youth in private foster care placements under the supervision of county probation departments. Most of these youth (about 80 percent) can be found in a network of group homes that are designed to house six or more youth at a time. In addition, most of them are likely to have been made wards of the local juvenile court in response to criminal violations (under Welfare and Institutions Code Section 602), but some may have been adjudicated and placed in residential care for non-criminal (status) offenses (under Welfare and Institutions Code Section 601). Private facilities that house probation youth in California vary greatly in location, size, and treatment focus, from large campus providers like Boys Republic (which operates a 200-bed campus in Chino as well as smaller group homes) to small "mom and pop" homes housing 6 to 12 youths in residential neighborhoods. . . . The fact that nearly half of the state's juvenile detention population consists of post-disposition minors may be due in part to the extended delays in arranging placements that have been ordered by juvenile courts. . . .

Notes

1. Juveniles are youths between the ages of 10 and 17 who are legally under the jurisdiction of the juvenile court. Not all youths under age 18 are legal juveniles. Some states consider 17-year-olds and even 16-year-olds as adults for the purposes of criminal prosecution. California law sets the upper age of juvenile court jurisdiction at age 17.

2. A description of the Los Angeles Probation Camp system can be found at http://probation.co.la.ca.us.

3. Average length of stay for first-time CYA commitments was 33 months in 2000, compared to 2½ months in local probation camps.

References

California Board of Corrections. 2001a. "Juvenile Detention Profile Survey—2000 Annual Report." Sacramento, Calif.: California Board of Corrections.
———. 2001b. "Juvenile Detention Profile Survey, 1st Quarter 1999 through 1st Quarter 2001." Sacramento, Calif.: California Board of Corrections.
California Department of Justice. 2001. "Criminal Justice Profiles (Statewide and County) through Calendar Year 2000." Sacramento, Calif.: Criminal Justice Statistics Center, California Department of Justice.
California Youth Authority. 2001. "Department Description." Sacramento, Calif.: California Youth Authority.
DeMuro, Paul, Anne DeMuro, and Steve Lerner. 1988. Reforming the CYA: How to End Crowding, Diversify Treatment and Protect the Public without Spending More Money. Bolinas, Calif.: Commonweal Research Institute.

Lerner, Steve. 1982. The CYA Report, Part I: Conditions of Life at the California Youth Authority. Bolinas, Calif.: Commonweal Research Institute.

———. 1986. The CYA Report, Part II: Bodily Harm: The Pattern of Fear and Violence at the California Youth Authority. Bolinas, Calif.: Commonweal Research Institute.

Schwartz, Ira M., and William H. Barton, eds. 1994. Reforming Juvenile Detention: No More Hidden Closets. Columbus: Ohio State University Press.

Sickmund, Melissa, and Wan, Yi-chun. 1999. "Census of Juveniles in Residential Placement Databook." http://www.ojjdp.ncjrs.org/ojstatbb/cjrp/. ✦

Chapter 14

Small Is Beautiful
The Missouri Division of Youth Services

Dick Mendel

Editor's Introduction

California's troubled youth corrections system emphasizes institutions but has been very expensive with high recidivism rates and many problems of abuse. A very different system is found in Missouri. This state closed its only large juvenile institution in 1983 and recently was holding only 180 youths in secure confinement statewide.[1] Most of its facilities are small, holding fewer than 35 youths, with a strong emphasis on treatment and rehabilitation.

The results are promising. The state claims a lower recidivism rate and lower costs than several other comparable states. In addition, the Missouri system has been free of the types of scandals and abuses that have plagued the California system.

While these results are promising, it is difficult to directly compare the two systems because the states themselves are so different. In addition, different states often have slightly different measures of recidivism, which makes their results difficult to compare. Nevertheless, these two states represent the range and diversity of juvenile corrections throughout the United States. At this point, it seems more likely that Missouri's system, rather than California's, represents the future of juvenile corrections.

Note

1. Richard A. Mendel, *Less Cost, More Safety: Guiding Lights for Reform in Juvenile Justice.* Washington, DC: American Youth Policy Forum, 2001, p. 9.

✦ ✦ ✦

Adapted from Dick Mendel, "Small is Beautiful: The Missouri Division of Youth Services," *AdvoCasey* 5(1), Spring, 2003 (published by the Annie E. Casey Foundation, Baltimore, MD, www.aecf.org).

J ust a hundred yards south of the Missouri River, a few blocks off the main drag in Boonville, Missouri, population 8,000, lies an arresting site: a 158-acre campus of grim two-story brick residence halls, surrounded by a chain-link fence adorned with razor wire at eye-level and topped with a menacing barbed-wire overhang.

Think of it as a portrait of America's approach to juvenile corrections.

In state after state, the greatest budget expenditures for juvenile corrections and the greatest number of incarcerated youth are concentrated in large, congregate-care "training schools," most of them located in country towns like Boonville. Nationwide, 52 percent of juveniles confined in 1997 were held in facilities with more than 110 offenders.

In these training schools, young offenders—most of them minorities, often from the cities—spend months or years, typically housed in small cells, disconnected from their families and neighborhoods. They are disconnected as well from the social forces that drove them to criminality—and to which they will sooner or later return.

The facilities employ teachers and typically some certified counselors as well, but youth spend much of their time under the watchful gaze of "correctional officers," often high school graduates, some with little training in or affinity for counseling or youth development. Or, if youth misbehave, they languish alone—locked down in isolation cells.

Training school confinement is often justified as a necessary step to protect the public. Yet only 27 percent of incarcerated youth nationwide have been found guilty of a violent felony. Most have committed only property or drug crimes, or disorderly conduct, sometimes only misdemeanors or "status offenses" (like truancy or alcohol possession) that would not be crimes if committed by an adult. Nonetheless, recidivism studies routinely find that half or more of training school youth are convicted of a new offense within three years of release.

The Rear-View Mirror

Here in Missouri, though, this troubling portrait of juvenile corrections can be seen only in the rear-view mirror.

From 1887 until 1983, the Boonville Training School was Missouri's primary correctional facility for boys, holding up to 650 teens at a time. Though its stated mission was rehabilitative, the reality at Boonville was often brutal.

Soon after losing his job in 1949, for instance, former Boonville Superintendent John Tindall, a would-be reformer, described the facility in the St. Louis Post-Dispatch: "I saw black eyes, battered faces, broken noses among the boys," Tindall wrote. "The usual corrective procedure among the guards was to knock a boy down with their fists, then kick him in the groin. . . . Many of the men were sadists."

Three boys died inside the facility in 1948 alone.

Conditions remained problematic throughout the 1950s, '60s, and '70s, reports University of Missouri law professor Douglas Abrams, who recently completed a history of the state's juvenile courts. A 1969 federal report condemned Boonville's "quasi-penal-military" atmosphere, particularly the practice of banishing unruly youth to "the Hole"—a dark, solitary confinement room atop the facility's administration building.

Then in 1983, Missouri shut down the Boonville training school.

Missouri's Division of Youth Services (DYS) began in the 1970s to experiment with smaller correctional programs. Liking the results, and tired of the endless scandals at Boonville, the state donated the facility to the state's Department of Corrections, which turned it into an adult penitentiary.

In place of Boonville, as well as a training school for girls in Chillicothe that closed in 1981, DYS secured smaller sites across the state—abandoned school buildings, large residential homes, a convent—and outfitted them to house delinquent teens. The largest of the new units housed only three dozen teens.

DYS divided the state into five regions, so confined youth could remain within driving distance of their homes and families. And it began staffing its facilities primarily with college-educated "youth specialists," rather than traditional corrections officers.

Over the next decade, DYS developed a distinctive new approach to juvenile corrections—one that relies on group process and personal development, rather than punishment and isolation, as the best medicines for delinquent teens.

Today, the available data suggest that Missouri achieves far more success than most other states in reducing the future criminality of youthful offenders. Missouri also rises above the pack in protecting the safety of confined youth, preventing abuses, and fostering learning.

"I think it's a great system," says Barry Krisberg, president of the National Council on Crime and Delinquency. "More than any other state in the country, Missouri provides a positive, treatment-oriented approach that's not punitive or prison-like."

Small Is Beautiful

According to both Missouri insiders and national justice experts, Missouri's switch to smaller facilities was crucial to improving its juvenile corrections system. "The most important thing in dealing with youthful offenders is the relationships," says veteran juvenile justice consultant Paul DeMuro, "the one-on-one relationships formed between young people and staff. And not just the line staff. It's critical that the director of the facility know every kid by name." Ned Loughran, executive director of the Council of Juvenile Correctional Administrators, agrees that "small is extremely important."

"The kids coming into juvenile facilities need a lot of specialized attention," Loughran says. "A small facility allows the staff to get to know the kids on a very individual basis."

Large facilities routinely suffer with high rates of staff turnover and absenteeism, Loughran adds, "so the kids spend a lot of time sitting in their rooms. . . . With large [facilities] it's like going to a large urban high school. Kids get lost, and these kids can't afford to get lost."

Small Isn't Everything

Smaller facilities, however, are not a magic bullet for juvenile corrections reform. Kentucky has long housed delinquent teens in small facilities, but a federal investigation in 1995 found that Kentucky was ignoring abuse complaints, using isolation cells excessively, and providing substandard education and mental health programming. (Since then, Kentucky has beefed up staff training and closed its worst facilities.)

In Missouri, small facilities likewise produced no immediate miracles. Initially, chaos reigned inside many of the new sites, recalls Gail Mumford, who began working with DYS in 1983 and now serves as the division's regional administrator for the northwest corner of the state.

"It was really crazy," says Mumford. "We didn't know what we were doing. The boys ran us ragged [at first]. They were acting up every day, sometimes every hour."

But conditions in Missouri's small facilities steadily improved as DYS tinkered with staffing patterns, invested in staff training, built case management and family counseling capabilities, and invested in community-based services to monitor and support teens after they leave custody.

Led by its charismatic director, Mark Steward, who has overseen the agency since 1988, DYS also built an enviable base of political support across the Missouri political spectrum. Before his untimely death in 2000, Democratic Governor Mel Carnahan frequently invited Steward to bring DYS youth for visits to his office in the state capitol. Likewise, conservative state Supreme Court Judge Stephen Limbaugh, a cousin of commentator Rush Limbaugh, is also a longtime DYS supporter.

Remodeling the Schoolhouse

In what was once an elementary school on the northern fringes of Kansas City, 15 miles from downtown, the Northwest Regional Youth Center is home to 30 serious youth offenders.

Inside, the facility has been redesigned from its schoolhouse days. But there are no cells inside, no iron bars. In fact, once you pass through a metal detector at the front door, there are few locked doors and little security hardware of any type—just video cameras whose monitors line a wall of the central office.

"Why I think they're such a good system is that they have preserved the community aspect even in the secure programs," says Loughran. "When you visit, you can see that they're not institutional. They've been able to preserve . . . a family atmosphere."

The main lobby of the Northwest Center is furnished with couches and rugs. Handmade posters produced by facility residents hang on one wall, and an upright piano hugs another. Along the third wall stands an elaborate fountain, constructed by residents in the late '90s, that empties into an oval pond that brims with oversized goldfish.

Three of the old school's classrooms remain just that, classrooms, and three others have been turned into dormitories—each an open room furnished with two-level bunk beds and dressers.

These dorms, in turn, are each part of a larger "pod" where residents spend the majority of their time. Each pod also includes a living room furnished with couches and coffee tables, plus a "treatment room" where the team meets for an hour each afternoon and youth talk about their personal histories, their future goals, and the roots of their delinquent behavior.

A Focus on Treatment

It is this emphasis on treatment, and the underlying philosophy behind it, that sets Missouri apart. Like a growing number of states, Missouri employs mental health counselors to work with youth and their families, and it partners with outside psychiatrists to ensure that confined youth receive appropriate psychotropic medications.

But while some states concentrate therapy in these occasional services, Missouri infuses treatment into every aspect of its correctional programs. From the day they enter a DYS facility, Missouri youth spend virtually every moment with a team of 9–11 other teens. The teams eat together, sleep together, study together, shower together—

always under the supervision of two trained youth specialists (or during the school day, one youth specialist and one teacher).

At least five times per day the teams "check in" with one another—telling their peers and the staff how they feel physically and emotionally. And at any time, youth are free to call a "circle"—in which all team members must stand facing one another—to raise concerns or voice complaints. Thus, at any moment the focus can shift from the activity at hand—education, exercise, clean-up, a bathroom break—to a lengthy discussion of behaviors and attitudes. Staff members also call circles frequently to enforce expectations regarding safety, courtesy, and respect.

At the Northwest Center, efforts to establish a positive environment are clearly paying off. "I remember my first day," recalled Dawson, a Northwest resident, before leaving the facility last year. "People were helping each other, people were interacting with each other in ways you weren't used to. You ain't used to a total stranger helping you out to a degree that any average person wouldn't."

Line of Body

The final pillar of Missouri's rehabilitative process takes place in the treatment rooms, where teams meet each afternoon. Some days the teens participate in "group-builders"—shared activities designed to build comradery and help teens explore issues like trust, perceptions, and communication. But in many meetings one particular teen will make a presentation to the group about his or her life.

In the "life history" session, teens are asked to—and often do—talk about wrenching experiences in their lives: domestic abuse, violence, sexual victimization, and family negligence. They are also encouraged to speak about their crimes and other misdeeds.

In the "genogram," teens produce and then explain a coded family tree detailing domestic violence, alcoholism, drug addiction, criminality, and illiteracy in their families, as a first step toward exploring the roots of their own behavior problems. In the "line of body," confined adolescents trace their bodies onto a large sheet of paper and then write in the physical and mental traumas they have suffered during their young lives. . . .

When Martin, a 15-year-old chronic offender in the Northwest Regional Youth Center's "A Team," completed the exercise last year, his illustration was covered with scars. Martin's feet had been broken at ages 11 and 12, and "both feet carried me in and out of evil," he wrote. Both hands were scarred from fighting, Martin said, and stained through contact with drugs, stolen property, and "negative sexual relations." One arm had burns suffered while smoking marijuana, the other arm a knife wound.

But it was around his head that Martin had suffered the deepest trauma: sleep problems (ages 11–15); emotional scars from physical and sexual abuse (ages 2–15), including sexual assaults by his own father at age 7; brain injuries from a nearly successful suicide attempt (age 11); and "brain fried" from his abuse of "pills, weed, meth, alcohol, shrooms, and opium"(ages 8–15).

Sadly, this long list of wounds is not atypical of the boys and girls committed to DYS. Of the 12 teens in the Northwest Center's A Team in the first half of 2002, nine suffered from parental abuse or neglect; 12 had alcoholic or drug-addicted parents; and six had parents who had served time behind bars, including two boys whose fathers were in prison for murder.

A Safe Space

According to Vicky Weimholt, the DYS deputy director in charge of treatment, convincing delinquent teens to open up about their troubled pasts is critical in reversing behavior problems. And the keys to getting teens talking are physical and emotional safety. "Without safety," she says, "you're really very limited in what you can do.

"Our staff are always there, and they will not let you get hurt," Weimholt explains. "And on the emotional side, you can't underestimate the power of group work. There are nine or ten other kids in the same circumstances, facing the same problems. . . . There's safety in knowing that I'm not the only one going through this."

In promoting safety, DYS staff shun most of the tactics commonly used in training schools. Even when they act out, youth are almost never held in isolation. The Northwest Regional Youth Center has no isolation cells. DYS staff do not employ "hog ties," "four-point restraints," or handcuffs to stifle youth who become violent.

Instead, Missouri staff train the teams themselves to restrain any youth who threatens the group's safety. Only staff members may authorize a restraint, but once they do team members grab arms and legs and wrestle their peer to the ground. Once down, the team holds on until the young person regains his or her composure.

Ned Loughran, the correctional administrators' director, sharply criticizes this practice, which has been abandoned by nearly every other state. "You shouldn't have juvenile offenders putting their hands on other juvenile offenders," he says. "These kids come in with all kinds of aggression."

But DYS Director Mark Steward defends youth restraints on both practical and therapeutic grounds. "We don't have 200-kid facilities with 100 staff we can call in to break things up," he says. And even if they did have the staffing, "if we had to wait for the staff to arrive [whenever a fight broke out], someone's gonna get their head beat in."

Steward says that in the 15 years he's been leading DYS, there has never been a serious injury during a restraint, never a lawsuit or a formal complaint filed by parents. Steward also cites the infrequent use of restraints in DYS facilities and the near-absence of serious fights among youth.

On the Northwest Center's A Team, for instance, not a single fight broke out from February to November 2002, and only six restraints were called—all for the same young man, Isaiah, an emotionally disturbed 17-year-old on heavy medications.

"The kids are the only ones who can stop the fights and keep it safe," Steward says. "So it works much better to give them the responsibility."

Community Connection

The small scale and therapeutic, family-oriented atmosphere distinguish Missouri's juvenile facilities from the training schools common throughout most of America. The differences do not end when Missouri teens walk out the doors of a DYS facility. More than most states, Missouri supports youth through the tricky transition when they leave facilities and return home.

"Large, locked, secure training schools frequently fall prey to an institutional culture in which the measures of success relate only to compliance with rules and norms," writes Johns Hopkins University criminologist David Altschuler, the nation's foremost expert on so-called "aftercare" for juvenile offenders.

"Progress within such settings is generally shortlived, unless it is followed up, reinforced, and monitored in the community," Altschuler complains, and in most jurisdictions, "the complexity and fragmentation of the justice system works against the reintegration of offenders back into the community."

Missouri, by contrast, makes aftercare a core component of its correctional approach. It assigns one "service coordinator" to oversee each young person from the time they enter DYS custody until he or she is discharged—usually after three to six months on aftercare. These coordinators—unlike the parole officers employed by most states—decide when the young person will leave residential care, and they already have longstanding relationships with teens when they do head home.

While on aftercare, youth meet and speak frequently with their service coordinators, and many youth are also assigned a "tracker"—typically a college student, or a resident of the youth's home community—who meets with them several times per week, monitors their progress, and helps them find jobs.

Missouri also operates 11 nonresidential "day treatment" centers from 8 A.M. to 3 P.M. each school day, which serve as a step-down for many teens after leaving a DYS facility. (DYS also assigns some youth—typically younger teens with lesser offending histories—directly to day treatment.)

Well-Spoken Teens

Word of Missouri's unique juvenile corrections system has begun to spread. National Public Radio aired a feature about DYS in 2001, and the nonpartisan American Youth Policy Forum dubbed Missouri a "guiding light" for juvenile justice reform. As a result, the state hosts frequent tours for policymakers and juvenile justice practitioners from other states.

Visitors often respond with surprise, even amazement, at the feeling of safety and optimism inside the facilities, and at the ability of Missouri youth to articulate a positive message and dispel the negative stereotypes that typically surround delinquent teens.

After touring St. Louis-area DYS facilities in December 2002, David Addison, chief juvenile public defender for Baltimore County, Maryland, said, "I was very impressed with the professionalism of the staff, and I was impressed that the kids really understood what the program was all about. They were able to express it a lot better than a lot of the staff could explain it here in Maryland."

Diane Winston, a Louisiana state legislator who toured DYS facilities in late 2002, says that "the kids we met had definitely gone through a process of change. They had a lot of new tools for coping when they get out. . . .

"In Louisiana, we have what Missouri had 20 years ago, which is warehousing kids in facilities that isolate and punish our juvenile offenders," Winston added. "In Missouri, they've broken it down into smaller therapeutically focused centers where they really are changing behaviors. . . ."

DYS Director Mark Steward takes DYS youth every year to visit with and testify before state legislators in Jefferson City, Missouri's capital, and Steward sponsors countless facility tours for influential leaders all over the state.

Linda Luebbering, who once analyzed the DYS budget for the Missouri Division of Budget and Planning and is now the budget division's director, vividly recalls her first visit to a DYS facility.

"I was surprised that I was walking into a facility like that—these were hard-core kids—and I was completely comfortable to go up and talk to them about their treatment," Luebbering says. "I ended up in a long conversation with a very well-spoken young man. Only afterward did Mark [Steward] tell me that this kid had committed murder. It made a big impression on me."

Measuring Outcomes

Historically, DYS has not measured the long-term re-offending rates of program graduates. For years it reported only the number of youth returned to its own custody for crimes and rule violations committed before their 17th birthdays—but not how many were convicted or sentenced as adults.

In April 2000, Missouri's state auditor criticized this oversight, and since then DYS has tracked the number of youth who end up in Missouri's adult corrections system. (DYS still lacks the ability to calculate the number of youth convicted of new offenses following release, the most common measure of recidivism.)

The most recent DYS recidivism report, compiled in February 2003, shows that 70 percent of youth released in 1999 avoided recommitment to a correctional program within three years.

Of 1,386 teens released from DYS custody in 1999, just 111 (8 percent) were sentenced to state prison or a state-run 120-day adult incarceration program within 36 months of release, and 266 (19 percent) were sentenced to adult probation. The new report also shows that 94 youth were recommitted to DYS for new offenses following release. (Another 134 youth returned to DYS residential facilities temporarily for breaking rules while on aftercare. DYS does not consider these cases failures or include them in its recidivism data.)

Compared to states that measure recidivism in similar ways, these success rates are exceptional. For instance, a 2000 recidivism study in Maryland found that 30 percent of youth released from juvenile corrections facilities in 1997 were incarcerated as adults within three years. In Louisiana, 45 percent of youth released from residential programs in 1999 returned to juvenile custody or were sentenced to adult prison or probation by mid-2002.

In Florida, 29 percent of youth released from a juvenile commitment program in 2000–2001 were returned to juvenile custody or sentenced to adult prison or probation within 12 months; the comparable figure in Missouri is just 9 percent.

Missouri's lower recidivism rates do not come with a high price tag. The total DYS budget for 2002 was $58.4 million—equal to $103 for each young person statewide between the ages of 10 and 16. By contrast, Louisiana spends $270 per young person 10–16, Maryland spends roughly $192 for each youth ages 10–17, and Florida spends approximately $271. (Juvenile courts in Maryland and Florida have jurisdiction over youth up to age 17, while Missouri and Louisiana juvenile laws cover youth only up to age 16.)

In addition, not a single Missouri teen has committed suicide under DYS custody in the 20 years since Boonville closed. Lindsay Hayes, a researcher with the National Center on Institutions and Alternatives, reports that 110 youth suicides occurred nationwide in juvenile facilities from 1995 to 1999 alone.

Missouri's educational outcomes are also promising. Though DYS youth enter custody at the 26th percentile of Missouri students in reading and the 21st percentile in math, and many have not attended school regularly for years, three-fourths made more academic progress than a typical public school student in 2002, and 222 DYS youth earned their GEDs.

Unfinished Business

Even with these encouraging signs, some limitations remain apparent in Missouri's youth corrections efforts.

While the DYS philosophy places strong emphasis on families, and the regional approach keeps most teens close to home, only 40 percent of DYS youth participated in family therapy last year. And in many cases, this therapy involved only handful of sessions just prior to release. Moreover, DYS therapists need not be licensed. Most are former direct care staff who have undertaken 150 hours of additional in-house training.

DYS has also suffered in recent years from a lingering state budget crisis. Salaries have been frozen since 2000, which has sapped morale and led some valued staffers to leave. The budget squeeze has also reduced DYS's ability to help youth from deeply troubled families. Funding for "independent living" programs is increasingly scarce, forcing DYS to return some youth to chaotic and unhealthy homes. Budget shortages have also limited DYS's ability to help youth prepare for work and careers.

Providing Opportunity

Despite these limitations, 70 percent of Missouri youth stay out of serious trouble for three years after leaving DYS facilities. Even at the

Northwest Regional Youth Center, which receives the most serious offenders in the Kansas City region—including many youth who've
failed in other programs—half of the graduates succeed for three
years.

Among youth released from the Northwest Center's A Team in
2002, none had returned to state custody as of March 2003. Martin,
whose "line of body" revealed head-to-toe scars, is back in high
school earning good grades. Isaiah, the heavily medicated youth, has
lived at home for five months without incident. Jerome, an athletic
Kansas City teen with a long history of car thefts, is mentoring younger children in an afterschool project. Roger, a one-time gang member and drug dealer, joined the military. Craig, a former heroin user
and dealer, found work in a hospital.

Only one teen, Dawson, appears to be in serious jeopardy. A mus-
cular African-American teen from one of Kansas City's toughest east-
side neighborhoods, Dawson was born to an addicted mother and a
father he never knew. He was taken in by a neighborhood family at
age 4 but never bonded with his stepfather, and his behavior grew increasingly reckless in adolescence. By 16, when he entered the Northwest Center, Dawson had been arrested for burglary, assault, drug
possession, and driving in a stolen car. . . .

At Northwest, Dawson earned a GED, made plans to attend college
and play football, and acquired a new demeanor of thoughtfulness
and self-respect. In April 2002, a month after leaving the facility,
Dawson explained that "I'm glad [for my time at Northwest]. I
learned a lot there. I got to chance to think about my priorities, become more of a man."

But Dawson had not lifted a finger yet to pursue college or find
work. He partied with friends, stayed out till all hours and then slept
till noon in his stepparents' large but crumbling prairie box home.
Still, he insisted that he would never return to the corner drug
trade—the vocation of choice for most of his neighborhood peers.

"It's just not tempting to me," he said. "I know I've got skills. I've
got a future, and I'm not going to do anything that could put me in
prison and take that away from me."

Asked if he also worried about the morality of selling drugs,
Dawson paused a moment, then responded: "Honestly, most of the
reason I won't do it is for me, but yeah, I know what drugs do. When
a little kid don't have no mommy or daddy because they're off doing
drugs, that ain't right. I don't want to be part of that."

Despite his strong words, Dawson never applied to college. He
even declined to interview for subsidized jobs lined up by DYS staff.
And sadly, as his aftercare period ended in the summer of 2002, both
Dawson's service coordinator and a DYS tracker spotted him on a no-
torious drug corner.

Tales like Dawson's leave Mark Steward philosophical—but no less certain of Missouri's unconventional, smaller-is-better approach to juvenile corrections.

"All we can do is to give these kids a chance," Steward says. "We teach them to look at themselves. We put them in a safe and stable and supportive environment—some of them for the first time in their lives. We help them see opportunities and make choices about their futures, but in the end it's still up to them.

"With us, they have an opportunity. Send them to a typical training school, where staff intimidates them and they have to fight to survive, and they've got no shot." ✦

Part VIII

What Works? Prevention and Rehabilitation

A t the beginning of the twentieth century, there was a broad social movement in American that was concerned with youth in general and with boys in particular. That movement was associated with an image of youth as *malleable*. Young people were imagined as being similar to wet clay, which you can shape and mold and form into anything you want. You can make it into something beautiful or useful—a bowl, a vase, a statue. Or you could make it into an ugly and useless lump. Once the clay sets, once it hardens, its shape cannot be changed without breaking.

Youth were conceptualized in exactly this way: adults could shape and mold and form them into productive citizens or into predatory criminals. However they were shaped, these youth would soon "harden" and then they no longer could be changed. This image resulted in the founding of many organizations designed to shape, mold, and form youth into productive citizens, including not only the original juvenile court in 1899, but also the Boy Scouts and the YMCA.[1]

Today, "get tough" reforms in juvenile justice are premised on the opposite image: youthful offenders are "hardened" criminals. Because young offenders are not "malleable," the appropriate policy response is to "lock 'em up and throw away the key." Other programs, however, retain the traditional assumption that juveniles are malleable: prevention programs and rehabilitation programs. Both these programs contain the idea of malleability, but there is a difference between them.

Rehabilitation programs take youths who, in one way or another, already have been "shaped" and "molded" and "formed" into youthful offenders. Rehabilitation programs try to "re-form" them into productive citizens. Like clay that already has been molded into one thing, this can be a difficult task—it seems it would be easier to work with clay that has not already been shaped into something that you don't want. This is the idea of prevention: it would be better if we prevented youths from being shaped and formed and molded into offenders in the first place.

The research reported in these two chapters finds that both rehabilitation and prevention work, in terms of reducing recidivism
among serious juvenile offenders. But consistent with the image of
wet clay, research finds that we get bigger payoffs from prevention
programs than we get from rehabilitation programs.

Note

1.   E.g., see David I. Macleod, *Building Character in the American Boy—The
     Boy Scouts, YMCA, and Their Forerunners, 1870–1920,* University of
     Wisconsin Press, Madison, 2004; Kenneth B. Kidd, *Making American
     Boys,* University of Minnesota Press, Minneapolis, 2005. ✦

Chapter 15

Blueprints for Violence Prevention

Sharon Mihalic, Abigail Fagan, Katherine Irwin, Diane Ballard,
and Delbert Elliott

Editor's Introduction

Chapter 15 looks at 11 prevention programs that have been selected as "model programs" by the "Blueprints" project, a large program funded by the Office of Juvenile Justice and Delinquency Prevention. These programs were selected on the basis of three criteria.

First, the program must be effective in preventing and/or reducing violence, delinquency, or drug use. This effectiveness must be demonstrated with research that uses a control group, where that group is formed either by random assignment or by matching.

Second, this crime prevention/reduction effect must be shown to persist over time—it is not sufficient to show that participants are better at the end of the program than they were at the beginning.

Third, the results must be replicated. In other words, it is not sufficient for these results to be achieved only once. The program must be able achieve similar results at some other place and some other time.

These are very stringent criteria, and only 11 programs have been found to meet all three of them.

Another 21 programs have been found to be effective in preventing or reducing these problem behaviors and many have shown that the effect persists over time. The problem is that, for the most part, these programs have not been replicated. The "Blueprints" project calls these "promising programs," as op-

Adapted from Sharon Mihalic, Abigail Fagan, Katherine Irwin, Diane Ballard, and Delbert Elliott, *Blueprints for Violence Prevention*, OJJDP Report, Office of Juvenile Justice and Delinquency Prevention, Washington, DC, July 2004. Copyright is not claimed in this article, a publication of the United States government.

posed to the "model programs" that meet all three criteria. These are not discussed in this chapter due primarily to space limitations. However, at least some of these "promising" programs probably will be designated as "model programs" in the future once their results have been replicated.

✦ ✦ ✦

Research has demonstrated that some violence prevention practices are more effective than others and some practices do not work at all (Sherman et al., 1998; Lipsey, 1992; Mihalic and Aultman-Bettridge, 2004). Moreover, as Elliott and Tolan (1998) note, "doing something is not always better than doing nothing," because some interventions (such as Scared Straight or other prison visitation programs) have been shown to be harmful to adolescents (Petrosino, Turpin-Petrosino, and Finckenauer, 2000). . . .

. . . This research demonstrates that behavioral, skills-oriented, and multimodal practices, in both criminal justice and other settings, can reduce crime (Lipsey, 1992). For example, family therapy and improving parenting practices have been shown to be key strategies in reducing crime and delinquency, by improving the youth's home environment, which can be the source of many problems (Sherman et al., 1998). Schools have also become a primary locus of prevention efforts as they contain both a ready delivery mechanism and a population base of students able to participate. Research in the area of school-based prevention demonstrates that school and discipline management interventions, interventions to establish norms and expectations for behavior, and instructional programs that teach social competency skills using cognitive-behavioral methods are all effective practices. In contrast, other types of programs (such as instructional programs that do not use cognitive-behavioral methods, therapeutic interventions such as counseling and social work, and recreation and leisure programs) are consistently ineffective in reducing outcomes related to violence and other antisocial behaviors (Gottfredson, 1998; Mihalic and Aultman-Bettridge, 2004). . . .

The following sections describe many of these strategies and provide information regarding the Blueprints programs that adopt each approach. . . . The programs are divided into two broad domains—those with an environmental focus (i.e., changing the family, school, and community environment) and those that focus on the individual, including cognitive-behavioral, mentoring, and community supervision and aftercare programs. . . .

Environmentally Focused Programs . . .

Nurse-Family Partnership

Nurse-Family Partnership (formerly Prenatal and Infancy Home Visitation by Nurses) sends nurses to the homes of low-income, first-time mothers, beginning during pregnancy and continuing for 2 years after the birth of the child. The program is designed to help women improve their prenatal health and the outcomes of pregnancy through the following methods:

- Encouraging good health habits.

- Teaching mothers the skills necessary to care for their infants and toddlers, in order to improve children's health and development.

- Improving women's own personal development, giving particular attention to the planning of future pregnancies, women's educational achievement, and parents' participation in the workforce.

The program has been tested with both white and African American families in rural and urban settings.

Nurse-Family Partnership has had positive outcomes on mothers' obstetrical health, psychosocial functioning, and other health-related behaviors (Olds et al., 1998). During the first 15 years after delivery of their first child, low-income, unmarried women who received nurse home visits had 31 percent fewer subsequent births, longer intervals between births (an average of 2 years), fewer months on welfare (60 months versus 90 months), 44 percent fewer behavioral problems due to alcohol and drug abuse, 69 percent fewer arrests, and 81 percent fewer criminal convictions than those in the control group. The program has also reduced rates of child abuse and neglect by helping young parents learn effective parenting skills and effective means of coping with a range of issues, including depression, anger, impulsiveness, and substance abuse. One study found that participation in the program was associated with a 79-percent reduction in state-verified cases of child abuse and neglect among mothers who were poor and unmarried. In their second year of life, nurse-visited children had 56 percent fewer visits to emergency rooms for injuries and ingestions than children who were not visited.

Long-term positive outcomes for adolescents have also been reported. Adolescents whose mothers received nurse home visits more than a decade earlier were 60 percent less likely to have run away, 56 percent less likely to have been arrested, and 80 percent less likely to have been convicted of a crime than adolescents whose mothers did not receive visits. They also smoked fewer cigarettes per day, consumed less alcohol in the past 6 months, and exhibited fewer behavioral problems related to alcohol and drug use.

Home visitation has also been found to be cost effective. An evaluation by Rand Corporation indicates that providing home visitation to low-income and unmarried mothers results in a savings to government and society. The savings exceed program costs by a factor of 4 by the time an intervention child reaches age 15; the return on the investment is realized by the child's fourth birthday (Karoly et al., 1998). Cost savings are primarily in reduced welfare and criminal justice expenditures, but also in increases in tax revenues (Olds et al., 1999).

Incredible Years: Parent, Teacher, and Child Training Series

The Incredible Years: Parent, Teacher, and Child Training Series is a comprehensive set of curriculums designed to promote social competence and prevent, reduce, and treat conduct problems in young children. The program targets children ages 2 to 8 who exhibit or are at risk for conduct problems. In all three programs, trained facilitators use videotaped scenes to encourage group discussion, problem solving, and sharing of ideas. The parent training component includes three series: BASIC, ADVANCE, and SCHOOL. BASIC is the core element of program delivery. The other two series, and the teacher and child training programs, are recommended elements of program delivery. BASIC teaches parents interactive play and reinforcement skills, nonviolent discipline techniques, logical and natural consequences, and problem-solving strategies. ADVANCE addresses family risk factors such as depression, marital discord, poor coping skills, poor anger management, and lack of emotional support. SCHOOL focuses on teaching ways to enhance youth's academic and social competencies.

The teacher training component helps strengthen classroom management skills. It seeks to help instructors encourage and motivate students, promote students' prosocial behavior and their cooperation with peers and teachers, teach anger management and problem-solving skills, and reduce classroom aggression.

The child training component, also known as the Dina Dinosaur curriculum, emphasizes skills related to developing emotional competency, having empathy with others and learning perspective, making and keeping friends, managing anger, solving interpersonal problems, following school rules, and succeeding at school. It is designed for use as a "pull out" treatment program for small groups of children who exhibit conduct problems, although it is also being tested as a preventive, classroomwide curriculum.

In six randomized trials, the parent training program has been shown to reduce children's conduct problems, increase positive affect and compliance to parental commands, and increase school bonding and involvement. These improvements have been sustained up to 3 years after the intervention (Webster-Stratton, 1990). In two randomized trials, the teacher program has been shown to reduce peer aggression in the classroom, increase positive interactions with teachers and peers, and improve school readiness (Webster-Stratton, Reid, and Hammond, 2000). In two randomized trials of the child program, conduct problems at home were reduced and cognitive problem-solving strategies with peers improved (Webster-Stratton and Hammond, 1997). (See Webster-Stratton et al., 2001, for a summary of all evaluations.)

Functional Family Therapy

Functional Family Therapy (FFT) is a short-term, family-based prevention and intervention program that has been successfully applied in a variety of contexts to treat high-risk youth and their families from different backgrounds. This multisystemic clinical program was specifically designed to help diverse populations of underserved and at-risk youth, ages 11 to 18, who often enter the system angry, without hope, and/or resistant to treatment. On average, participating youth and families attend 12 1-hour sessions spread over 3 months; more difficult cases require 26 to 30 hours of direct service. Therapists' caseloads average 12–16 families.

Three distinct treatment phases are offered in FFT:

- Phase 1, Engagement and Motivation, is designed to engage and motivate youth and families and help them face and overcome intense negative affects (such as hopelessness and anger) that prevent change.

- Phase 2, Behavior Change, focuses on the development and implementation of immediate and long-term behavior change plans that are culturally appropriate, context sensitive, and tailored to the unique characteristics of each family member.

- Phase 3, Generalization, helps families apply positive family change to other problem areas and/or situations, maintain changes, and prevent relapse. To ensure long-term support of changes, FFT links families with available community resources.

Program success with a wide range of interventionists, including paraprofessionals and trainees with various professional degrees, has been demonstrated and replicated for more than 25 years. Controlled comparison studies with followup periods of 1, 3, and 5 years have demonstrated significant and long-term reductions in youth re-offending, ranging from 25 percent to 60 percent, and also reductions in sibling entry into high-risk behaviors (Alexander et al., 2000). This program also has been demonstrated to be cost effective (Aos et al., 2001).

Multisystemic Therapy

Multisystemic Therapy (MST) provides cost-effective, community-based clinical treatment to violent and chronic juvenile offenders who are at high risk of out-of-home placement. The program is based on the philosophy that individuals live within a complex social network, encompassing individual, family, and extrafamilial (peer, school, and neighborhood) factors. Behavior problems can stem from and be maintained by problematic interactions within this social network, and MST specifically targets the multiple factors that can contribute to antisocial behavior. The overarching goal of the program is to help parents understand and help their children overcome behavior problems, including disengaging from deviant peers and overcoming poor school performance. To empower families, MST addresses identified barriers to effective parenting (e.g., parental drug abuse and mental health problems) and helps family members build an indigenous social support network involving friends, extended family, neighborhoods, and church members. In doing so, MST uses the strengths in each youth's social network to promote positive change in his or her behavior. Likewise, treatment is designed with input from the target family to increase family collaboration and participation.

Consistent with the program philosophy, and to enhance generalization to other settings, MST is typically provided in the home, school, and other community locations. Therapists with low case-loads (4–6 families)—and who are available 24 hours per day, 7 days per week—provide the treatment, placing developmentally appropriate demands for responsible behavior on youth and their families. Intervention plans include strategic family therapy, structural family therapy, behavioral parent training, and cognitive behavior therapies. The average duration of treatment is about 4 months, which includes approximately 60 hours of therapist-family contact.

Program evaluations have demonstrated 25 to 70 percent reductions in long-term rates of rearrest, and 47 to 64 percent reductions in out-of-home placements. Moreover, families receiving MST have shown extensive improvements in family functioning and decreases in youth's mental health problems. Positive results were maintained for nearly 4 years after treatment ended (Henggeler et al.,

2001). This program has been demonstrated to be cost-effective (Aos et al., 2001). . . .

Bullying Prevention Program

The Bullying Prevention Program focuses on restructuring the social environment of primary and middle schools in order to provide fewer opportunities for bullying behavior and to reduce the positive social rewards (such as peer approval and support) gained through bullying behavior. Overall, the program tries to create a school environment characterized by positive interest and involvement by adults and firm limits on unacceptable behavior; norm and rule violations consistently result in sanctions and adults act as authority figures and positive role models for youth. Although the Bullying Prevention Program actively involves students, adults in the school are seen as the driving force in changing the normative environment. To facilitate such a sweeping change, the program seeks to ensure that adults are aware of bullying problems and actively involved in their prevention, conveying the message that "bullying is not accepted in our class/school, and we will see to it that it comes to an end" (Olweus, Limber, and Mihalic, 1999).

The Bullying Prevention Program targets change in the school, classroom, and individual student. The program begins with the creation of a coordinating committee and a schoolwide survey assessing the extent and nature of the bullying problem. Following the survey, a school conference day is held to review questionnaire results. The coordinating committee then begins to plan strategies to change school-level conditions, such as creating a system of improved monitoring of students during recess and lunch times, and plans for parent and staff meetings to discuss the program and the progress of implementation. The classroom-level intervention involves the creation of class rules regarding bullying behavior and regular class meetings to discuss issues and/or rule infractions. In addition, parent-teacher meetings may occur to discuss elements of the program. The program is also implemented at the individual student level with individual intervention programs for bullies and their parents, and for victims and their parents, to ensure that any ongoing behavior is stopped and that victims receive needed support.

Research on the Bullying Prevention Program utilized a quasi-experimental design with time-lagged contrasts between age-equivalent groups (successive cohorts of children for particular grade levels), involving 2,400 students in grades 4 to 7 in 42 schools (28 elementary and 14 junior high) in Bergen, Norway. These students were followed for 2.5 years. The evaluation documented decreases of (typically) 50 percent or more in the frequency with which students reported being bullied by others. In addition, substantial reductions in student involvement in vandalism, fighting, thefts, and truancy were demonstrated. Several aspects of the social climate of the class showed marked improvement, including better order and discipline, improved social relationships, and increases in positive attitudes toward school (Olweus, Limber, and Mihalic, 1999). A program replication with 6,388 students in grades 4 through 6 in 39 schools in 3 matched pairs of rural South Carolina school districts revealed a decrease in the frequency with which intervention children bullied other children (by approximately 25 percent), while students in schools that were part of the control group reported a corresponding increase. Additionally, self-reported antisocial behavior increased in the control group, whereas no increase or a slower rate of increase with regard to general delinquency, vandalism, school misbehavior, and punishment for school-related misbehaviors was seen among the treated children (Olweus, Limber, and Mihalic, 1999).

Midwestern Prevention Project

The Midwestern Prevention Project (MPP) includes school normative environment change as one of many components of a comprehensive, 3- to 5-year community-based prevention program that targets "gateway" drug use of tobacco, alcohol, and marijuana—those substances that traditionally precede the use of other illicit substances. The program involves schools, parents, and community organizations, uses mass media to communicate messages regarding the dangers of gateway drug use, and seeks changes in health policies and community practices to reduce youth access to targeted substances. Each domain (school, parent, community organization, and health policy) is targeted in a specific timeline, beginning with the school intervention in the first year and ending with the health policy changes.

The school-based intervention is the central component of the program and is designed as a primary prevention program. The program begins in either sixth or seventh grade, depending on the school district and the grade that represents the transition to middle or junior high school. Ten to thirteen classroom sessions are delivered by teachers trained in the curriculum and may be facilitated by peer leaders who are nominated by the class and trained by teachers in the program components. The lessons focus on increasing drug resistance skills and also try to change the social climate of the school to encourage nondrug use norms. Five booster sessions are offered in the second year of the intervention to reinforce concepts learned previously, and followup peer counseling and support are made available through the high school years.

These school activities are followed by a parent component designed to develop norms within the family that discourage drug use through parent skills training sessions targeting parent-child communication and prevention support skills. This component continues throughout the middle/junior high school years. At the same time, a group composed of the school principal, teachers, parents, and peer leaders works to change the school climate by institutionalizing the school-based curriculum, helping to monitor drug use on the school grounds and in the community, and planning and implementing the parent training program.

The community component occurs during the last stages of the prevention effort and involves community leaders who create and implement drug abuse prevention services within the neighborhood, plan community activities that complement the school and family programs, and develop strategies to change health policies (such as local ordinances restricting cigarette smoking in public venues). This final goal is achieved through subcommittees of local government and community leaders and is largely directed at reducing supply of and demand for gateway substances. A mass media campaign using television, radio, and print outlets is delivered throughout the life of the project to convey to the larger community messages that are central to the student and parent skills training components of the program.

MPP was first evaluated in Kansas City using a quasi-experimental design in which schools (n=50) and communities were assigned to program conditions on the basis of scheduling flexibility and demographic matching where possible. Three sampling plans were used to collect data, including the random assignment of 8 schools to treatment or control groups that involved 1,607 students who were followed over a 3-year period. The program has demonstrated net reductions of up to 40 percent in adolescent daily smoking and marijuana use, along with smaller reductions in alcohol use, with the results maintained through high school graduation. Reductions in use of other illicit substances (amphetamines, LSD, and inhalants) have been shown for participating youth into early adulthood (age 23). The program has also demonstrated reductions in parents' use of alcohol and marijuana, and increased positive parent-child communication regarding drug use and abuse prevention. In addition, communities participating in MPP have reported that the program successfully facilitated the development of community services for drug abuse prevention (Pentz, Mihalic, and Grotpeter, 1997).

Individually Focused Programs . . .

Promoting Alternative Thinking Strategies

Promoting Alternative Thinking Strategies (PATHS) is a comprehensive program for promoting social and emotional competencies, including the understanding, expression, and regulation of emotions. The curriculum is designed for use by teachers and counselors throughout the year, with entire classrooms of children in kindergarten through fifth grade. PATHS has been researched with children in regular education classrooms and also with a variety of special needs students (e.g., deaf, hearing impaired, learning disabled, emotionally disturbed, mildly mentally delayed, and gifted). The curriculum provides teachers with systematic, developmentally based lessons, materials, and instructions for teaching their students emotional literacy, self-control, social competence, positive peer relations, and interpersonal problem-solving skills. More specifically, lessons include instruction in identifying and labeling feelings, expressing feelings, assessing the intensity of feelings, managing feelings, understanding the difference between feelings and behaviors, delaying gratification, controlling impulses, reducing stress, using self-talk, reading and interpreting social cues, understanding the perspectives of others, using steps for problem solving and decisionmaking, having a positive attitude toward life, increasing self-awareness, and enhancing verbal and nonverbal communication skills.

Focusing on these factors provides tools that enable youth to achieve academically and helps enhance classroom atmosphere and the learning process. In addition, promoting these developmental skills helps prevent or reduce behavioral and emotional problems. In fact, program evaluations based on various measures (such as teacher ratings and children's self reports) have demonstrated positive behavioral changes related to hyperactivity, peer aggression, and conduct problems (Greenberg, Kusche, and Mihalic, 1998). Using populations of normally adjusted students, behaviorally at-risk students, and deaf students, these effects also have been found for classrooms receiving the intervention compared with matched controls.

Life Skills Training

Life Skills Training (LST) is a 3-year intervention curriculum designed to prevent or reduce gateway drug use (tobacco, alcohol, and marijuana) by providing social resistance skills training to help students identify pressures to use drugs and resist drug offers (Dusenbury and Falco, 1995). LST is primarily meant to be implemented in school classrooms by teachers, but has also been successfully taught by health professionals and peer leaders. LST targets all middle/junior high school students, with an initial 15-lesson intervention offered in grade 6 or 7, depending on the school structure, and booster sessions taught in the following 2 years (10 sessions in year 2 and 5 sessions in year 3). Lessons average 45 minutes in length and can be delivered from once a day to once a week.

The three basic components of the program teach youth the following skills:

- Personal self-management skills (decisionmaking and problem solving, self-control skills for coping with anxiety, and self-improvement skills).

- Social skills (communication and general social skills).

- Information designed to effect youth's attitudes concerning drug use, to instill normative expectations concerning drugs, and to promote the development of skills for resisting negative influences from the media and peers regarding drug use.

Teachers use techniques such as direct instruction, demonstration, feedback, reinforcement, and practice.

Using outcomes averaged across more than a dozen studies, LST has been found to reduce alcohol, tobacco, and marijuana use by 50 to 75 percent for intervention students compared to control students. Reductions in smoking and the use of inhalants, narcotics, and hallucinogens have been demonstrated through the 12th grade (Botvin, Mihalic, and Grotpeter, 1998).

Project Towards No Drug Abuse

Project Towards No Drug Abuse (Project TND) is a targeted drug abuse prevention program with a focus on high school youth (ages 14 to 19) who are at risk for drug abuse.

The 12 classroom-based lessons, approximately 40 to 50 minutes each, are designed to be implemented over a 4-week period, although they could be spread out over as long as 5 weeks on the condition that all lessons are taught. The instruction to students provides cognitive motivation enhancement activities (to not use drugs), detailed information about the social and health consequences of drug use, correction of cognitive misperceptions and addresses topics including instruction in active listening, effective communication skills, stress management, coping skills, tobacco cessation techniques and self-control to counteract risk factors for drug abuse relevant to older teens.

Project TND has been tested in three true experimental field trials, involving one or two program conditions that were compared to a standard care control condition. A total of 3,000 youth from 42 schools were involved across the three trials. At 1-year followup relative to comparisons, participants who received the 12-session program experienced: a 27 percent prevalence reduction in 30-day cigarette use, a 22 percent prevalence reduction in 30-day marijuana use, a 26 percent prevalence reduction in 30-day hard drug use, a 9 percent prevalence reduction in 30-day alcohol use among baseline drinkers, and a 25 percent prevalence reduction in 1-year weapons carrying among males. . . .

Big Brothers Big Sisters of America

Big Brothers Big Sisters of America (BBBSA), with a network of more than 500 local agencies throughout the nation, maintaining more than 145,000 one-to-one relationships between youth and volunteer adults, operates as the largest and best-known mentoring program in the country. BBBSA began in the early 20th century by targeting youth in need of socialization, firm guidance, and connection with positive adult role models. Today, the program serves youth ages 6–18, a significant number of whom are from disadvantaged, single-parent households. Volunteer mentors are screened and trained, and matches are carefully made using established procedures and criteria. Mentors meet with youth partners at least three times a month for 3 to 5 hours to participate in activities determined by the interests of the child and the volunteer, such as taking a walk, attending a school activity or sporting event, playing a game, visiting the library, or just sharing thoughts and ideas about life. The program's hallmark is the supervision of the match relationship, which includes regular, scheduled visits and phone conversations among the mentor, the parent, and the child.

An 18-month evaluation of eight BBBSA affiliates found that, compared with a control group waiting for a match, youth in the mentoring program were 46 percent less likely to start using drugs, 27 percent less likely to start drinking, and 32 percent less likely to hit someone. Mentored youth also skipped half as many days of school as control youth, had better attitudes and performance in school, and had improved peer and family relationships (McGill, Mihalic, and Grotpeter, 1997). . . .

Multidimensional Treatment Foster Care

Multidimensional Treatment Foster Care (MTFC) is a cost-effective alternative to group or residential treatment, incarceration, and hospitalization for adolescents who have problems with chronic antisocial behavior, emotional disturbance, and delinquency. MTFC provides short-term (approximately 7 months), highly structured and therapeutic care in foster families to decrease delinquent behavior and increase participation in developmentally appropriate prosocial activities, including school, sports, and hobbies. The program recruits, trains, and supervises foster families in the community to provide participating youth with close supervision, fair and consistent limits, predictable consequences for rule-breaking, a supportive relationship with an adult, and an environment that reduces exposure to delinquent peers.

Youth participate in individual, skills-focused therapy provided weekly. The role of the therapist is to support the youngster's adjustment in the MTFC home where the main treatment effect is expected to occur. School attendance, behavior, and homework completion are closely monitored, and interventions are conducted as needed for youth in the schools.

Youth also participate in a structured daily behavior management program implemented in the MTFC home. A case manager, with the help of the MTFC parents, develops an individualized daily program for each youth that specifies the youth's schedule of activities and behavioral expectations and sets the number of points he or she can earn for satisfactory performance. The goal of the point program is to give MTFC parents a vehicle for providing the youngster with frequent positive reinforcement for normative and prosocial behaviors, and to give the youngster a clear message about how he or she is doing. Three levels of supervision are defined in MTFC:

• Level 1 requires adult supervision at all times.

• Level 2 grants youth limited free time in the community.

• Level 3 allows for some peer activities that require less structure.

The program relies on routine consultation with and ongoing supervision of MTFC parents and youth by case managers. Parents are called daily for a report on the youth's progress, and they also attend weekly group meetings. This ongoing consultation helps the MTFC parents to manage difficult adolescent problem behavior in a therapeutic way.

Family therapy is provided for the youth's biological (or adoptive) families in either a group or individual format. Family therapy typically includes a focus on problem solving and communication skills, methods for de-escalating family conflict, and instruction on how to advocate for school services for the youth. They are also taught to use the same type of structured supervision used in the MTFC home to increase the likelihood of success when the youth returns home.

Evaluations of MTFC demonstrate that participating youth had significantly fewer arrests (an average of 2.6 offenses versus 5.4 offenses) during a 12-month followup compared with a control group of youth who participated in residential group care programs. During the first 2 years after program completion, youth who participated in the MTFC program spent significantly fewer days in lockup than youth who were placed in other community-based programs. In addition, significantly fewer MTFC youth were ever incarcerated following treatment (Chamberlain, 1990). An additional evaluation of youth ages 9–18 leaving state mental hospital settings showed that MTFC youth were placed out of the hospital at a significantly higher rate than control youth (Chamberlain and Mihalic, 1998).

References

Alexander, J.F., Pugh, C., Parsons, B.V., Sexton, T., Barton, C., Bonomo, J., Gordon, D., Grotpeter, J.K., Hansson, K., Harrison, R., Mears, S., Mihalic, S.F., Ostrum, N., Schulman, S., and Waldron, H. 2000. Functional Family Therapy. In *Blueprints for Violence Prevention: Book 3*, edited by D.S. Elliot. Boulder, CO: Center for the Study and Prevention of Violence, Institute of Behavioral Science, University of Colorado.

Aos, S., Phipps, P., Barnoski, R., and Lieb, R. 2001. *The Comparative Costs and Benefits of Programs To Reduce Crime, Version 4.0*. Olympia, WA: Washington State Institute for Public Policy.

Botvin, G., Mihalic, S., and Grotpeter, J. 1998. Life Skills Training. In *Blueprints for Violence Prevention: Book 5*, edited by D.S. Elliot. Boulder, CO: University of Colorado, Institute of Behavioral Science, Center for the Study and Prevention of Violence.

Chamberlain, P. 1990. Comparative evaluation of specialized foster care for seriously delinquent youths: A first step. *Community Alternatives: International Journal of Family Care* 2:21–36.

Chamberlain, P., and Mihalic, S. 1998. Multidimensional Treatment Foster Care. In *Blueprints for Violence Prevention: Book 8*, edited by D.S. Elliot. Boulder, CO: University of Colorado, Institute of Behavioral Science, Center for the Study and Prevention of Violence.

Dusenbury, L., and Falco, M. 1995. Eleven components curricula. *Journal of School Health* 65:420–425.

Elliott, D.S., and Tolan, P.H. 1998. Youth violence, prevention, intervention, and social policy. In *Youth Violence: Prevention, Intervention, and Social Policy*, edited by D.J. Flannery and C.R. Huff. Washington, DC: American Psychiatric Press, pp. 3–46.

Gottfredson, D. 1998. School-based crime prevention. In *Preventing Crime: What Works, What Doesn't, What's Promising: A Report to the United States Congress*, edited by L.W. Sherman, D.C. Gottfredson, D. MacKenzie, J. Eck, P. Reuter, and S. Bushway. Washington, DC: U.S. Department of Justice, Office of Justice Programs, National Institute of Justice.

Greenberg, M., Kusche, C., and Mihalic, S. 1998. Promoting Alternative Thinking Strategies. In *Blueprints for Violence Prevention: Book 2*, edited by D.S. Elliott. Boulder, CO: University of Colorado, Institute of Behavioral Science, Center for the Study and Prevention of Violence.

Henggeler, S.W., Mihalic, S.F., Rone, L., Thomas, C., and Timmons-Mitchell, J. 2001. Multisystemic Therapy. In *Blueprints for Violence Prevention: Book 6*, edited by D.S. Elliott. Boulder, CO: University of Colorado, Institute for Behavioral Science, Center for the Study and Prevention of Violence.

Karoly, L.A., Greenwood, P.W., Everingham, S.S., Hoube, J., Kilburn, M.R., Rydell, C.P., Sanders, M., and Chiesa, J. 1998. *Investing in Our Children: What We Know and Don't Know About the Costs and Benefits of Early Childhood Interventions*. Washington, DC: RAND Corporation.

Lipsey, M.W. 1992. The effect of treatment on juvenile delinquents: Results from meta-analysis. In *Psychology and Law*, edited by F. Losel, D. Bender, and T. Bliesener. New York, NY: Walter de Gruyter.

McGill, D.E., Mihalic, S.F., and Grotpeter, J.K. 1997. Big Brothers Big Sisters of America. In *Blueprints for Violence Prevention: Book 2*, edited by D.S. Elliott. Boulder, CO:

University of Colorado, Institute of Behavioral Science, Center for the Study and Prevention of Violence.

Mihalic, S.F., and Aultman-Bettridge, T. 2004. A guide to effective school-based prevention programs. In *Policing and School Crime*, edited by W.L. Turk. Englewood Cliffs, NJ: Prentice Hall Publishers.

Olds, D.L., Henderson, C.R., Kitzman, H.J., Eckenrode, J.J., Cole, R.E., and Tatelbaum, R.C. 1999. Prenatal and infancy home visitation by nurses: Recent findings. *The Future of Children* 9:44–65.

Olds, D., Hill, P., Mihalic, S., and O'Brien, R. 1998. Prenatal and infancy home visitation by nurses. In *Blueprints for Violence Prevention: Book 7*, edited by D.S. Elliott. Boulder, CO: University of Colorado, Institute of Behavioral Science, Center for the Study and Prevention of Violence.

Olweus, D., Limber, S., and Mihalic, S.F. 1999. Bullying Prevention Program. In *Blueprints for Violence Prevention: Book 9*, edited by D.S. Elliott. Boulder, CO: University of Colorado, Institute of Behavioral Science, Center for the Study and Prevention of Violence.

Pentz, M.A., Mihalic, S., and Grotpeter, J. 1997. The Midwestern Prevention Project. In *Blueprints for Violence Prevention: Book 1*, edited by D.S. Elliott. Boulder, CO: University of Colorado, Institute of Behavioral Science, Center for the Study and Prevention of Violence.

Petrosino, A., Turpin-Petrosino, C., and Finckenauer, J. 2000. Well-meaning programs can have harmful effects! Lessons from experiments of programs such as Scared Straight. *Crime and Delinquency* 46:354–379.

Sherman, L.W., Gottfredson, D.C., MacKenzie, D., Eck, J., Reuter, P., and Bushway, S. 1998. *Preventing Crime: What Works, What Doesn't, What's Promising: A Report to the United States Congress*. Washington, DC: U.S. Department of Justice, Office of Justice Programs, National Institute of Justice.

Webster-Stratton, C. 1990. Long-term follow-up of families with young conduct-problem children: From preschool to grade school. *Journal of Clinical Child Psychology* 19:144–149.

Webster-Stratton, C., and Hammond, M. 1997. Treating children with early-onset conduct problems: A comparison of child and parent training interventions. *Journal of Consulting and Clinical Psychology* 65:93–109.

Webster-Stratton, C., Mihalic, S., Fagan, A., Arnold, D., Taylor, T., and Tingley, C. 2001. The Incredible Years: Parent, Teacher and Child Training Series. In *Blueprints for Violence Prevention: Book 11*, edited by D.S. Elliott. Boulder, CO: University of Colorado, Institute of Behavioral Science, Center for the Study and Prevention of Violence.

Webster-Stratton, C., Reid, J., and Hammond, M. 2000. Preventing conduct problems, promoting social competence: A parent and teacher training partnership for a multi-ethnic, Head Start population. Unpublished. Seattle, WA: University of Washington, School of Nursing, Department of Family and Child Nursing, Parenting Clinic. ✦

Chapter 16

Effective Intervention for Serious Juvenile Offenders

Mark W. Lipsey, David B. Wilson, and Lynn Cothern

Editor's Introduction

Chapter 16 examines a large number of specific rehabilitation programs, with a focus on their effectiveness in reducing the recidivism of serious, violent, and chronic juvenile offenders. The question is one that repeatedly arises in this book: are juvenile offenders "malleable" in the sense that they can be shaped and molded and formed into future productive citizens? Or are they "hardened" criminals, as argued by "get tough" advocates? This question, of course, is most important when it is asked about the most serious juvenile offenders.

After reviewing the research, it seems that the situation is not nearly as bleak as the "get tough" advocates assert, but it also seems that rehabilitation programs are not as effective as we might like. Looking at 200 studies with strong research designs, these authors find an average reduction in recidivism of 12 percent, with the best programs producing 40 percent reductions. Interestingly, the best results were achieved in programs for institutionalized juveniles, who normally would be the most serious offenders.

These are far from perfect results, but it is important to point out that they are better than those obtained from transfers to the adult system. Generally speaking, these offenders commit offenses more quickly and more often than similar youth who are retained in the juvenile justice system.[1] Serious juvenile offenders, of course, are the group most likely to be the subjects of such transfers. Despite rehabilitation's limited effectiveness with serious, violent, and chronic juvenile offenders, it seems to produce better results than those obtained from transferring these offenders to criminal court.

Adapted from Mark W. Lipsey, David B. Wilson, and Lynn Cothern, "Effective Intervention for Serious Juvenile Offenders," *Juvenile Justice Bulletin.* Washington, DC: Office of Juvenile Justice and Delinquency Prevention, April 2000.

Note

1.   Jeffrey A. Butts and Daniel P. Mears, "Reviving Juvenile Justice in a Get-Tough Era," *Youth & Society* 33(2): 175–80, December 2001.

✦ ✦ ✦

Effective intervention plays an essential role in any strategy designed to diminish the rates of juvenile delinquency. Individuals who are employed in the juvenile justice system use intervention as an important component of dispositional sanctions imposed in juvenile cases. This is particularly true for the treatment of serious, violent, and chronic juvenile offenders (serious offenders) who have the potential for long and harmful criminal careers and who, absent effective interventions, are likely to recidivate while at the age for peak offending.

Which interventions are most effective in dealing with the serious offender? Although recent research reviews have shown that some intervention programs result in lowered recidivism among youthful offenders, the reviews have only asked whether intervention is *generally* effective (Andrews et al., 1990; Cullen and Gilbert, 1982; Garrett, 1985; Gendreau and Ross, 1987; Lipsey, 1992; Palmer, 1994). Little systematic attention has been given to the effectiveness of interventions with distinct types of offenders, and little intervention research has looked specifically at serious offenders.

This Bulletin presents the results of a meta-analysis (a systematic synthesis of quantitative research results) that posed two questions:

- Can intervention programs reduce recidivism rates among serious delinquents?

- If so, what types of programs are most effective?

The Bulletin describes the procedures used to select studies for the meta-analysis, presents the methods of analysis used to answer the above questions, and then discusses effective interventions for noninstitutionalized and institutionalized offenders.

Selection Procedures

The results reported here were derived by updating a previously conducted meta-analysis of the effects of intervention on delinquency (Lipsey, 1992, 1995) with more recent studies. A subset of studies on serious offenders was selected from that meta-analysis, yielding 200 experimental or quasi-experimental studies of interventions for both noninstitutionalized and institutionalized serious offenders. The studies selected for the new database had the following characteristics:

- The great majority, or all, of the juveniles were reported to be adjudicated delinquents. Most had records of prior offenses that involved person or property crimes or other, more serious, acts of delinquency (but not primarily substance abuse, status offenses, or traffic offenses).

- The referral to the intervention program was made by someone within the juvenile justice system, or the juveniles were recruited directly by the researcher.

Other studies included were those in which most or all of the juveniles in the study had aggressive histories or those whose specific purpose was to change aggressive juvenile behavior.

Methods of Analysis and Findings

Profile of Studies in the Database

The pool of studies selected for the meta-analytic database shared the following features:

- They were conducted in the United States by psychologists, criminologists, or sociologists and were published after 1970.

- The sample populations were largely male, mostly white or of mixed ethnicity, with an average age of 14 to 17 years. Most of the juveniles had prior offenses. In two-thirds of the samples, some or all of the juveniles had a history of aggressive behavior.

- In most of the samples, juveniles were under the supervision of the juvenile justice system and were receiving court-ordered intervention. In one-third of the sample groups, juvenile justice personnel administered treatment. In one-fifth of the groups, treatment was administered by mental health personnel in public or private agencies. In the remainder of the groups, it was administered by other counselors, laypersons, or researchers.

- For noninstitutionalized juveniles, the interventions studied included counseling, skill-oriented programs, and multiple services (combinations of services or treatments that involved several different approaches). For institutionalized juveniles, they included counseling, skill-oriented programs, and community residential programs. Treatments usually lasted 1 to 30 weeks and involved continuous contact or sessions that ranged from once or twice per week to daily, for 1/2 hour to 10 hours per week.

- Almost half of the studies used random assignment to experimental conditions; many of the others used some form of matching. Control groups typically received the usual treatment (e.g., regular probation or institutional programs). The recidivism outcome variables that were measured most frequently were police contact or arrest, court contact, or parole violations.

Recidivism Effect Size

Only one recidivism outcome measure was selected from each study. Police contact or arrest was selected if it was available; otherwise, officially recorded contact with juvenile court or offense-based probation violations were used because they are the most comparable to police arrest. The difference between the treatment and control groups on the selected recidivism measure was calculated for each study and standardized so that different measures could be compared.

Overall, juveniles who received treatment showed an average 12-percent decrease in recidivism. This result, while not enormous, was positive, statistically significant, and large enough to be meaningful. More important, however, was the large variability in effects across studies. The remainder of this Bulletin explores the characteristics of the interventions that produced the largest effects on recidivism.

Variation in Study Methods and Procedures

The differences in methods and procedures used in the studies are the first source of variability in effect size. The use of a multiple regression equation made it possible to estimate what the mean effect size over the 200 studies would be if all the studies were uniform in method and procedure. The method-adjusted effect sizes were then analyzed in terms of various treatment variables to identify those producing larger effects.

Interventions for Noninstitutionalized Juveniles

The database was divided into studies of interventions with noninstitutionalized juveniles and studies of interventions with institutionalized juveniles because the circumstances of treatment are different and because the nature and response of the juveniles receiving treatment may differ. This section examines the effects of noninstitutional treatment using the method-adjusted effect size values (discussed previously) in relationship to four clusters of variables. These clusters, which were associated with more than half of the variation among effect sizes across the studies, are listed in decreasing order of magnitude:

- Juvenile offender characteristics.

- Treatment types.

- Treatment amount delivered (e.g., total number of weeks and frequency of treatment, and other ratings of treatment effectiveness).

- General program characteristics.

This model was further reduced to include only the variables in each category that were most closely related to intervention effects on recidivism among noninstitutionalized serious juvenile offenders. Intervention effectiveness was associated with the characteristics of the juveniles who received treatment. The effects were larger for more serious offenders (indicated by the types of prior offenses that included both person and property offenses) than for less serious offenders. Type of treatment was important and is discussed in the next section. Longer treatment was positively associated with effectiveness, whereas the mean number of hours per week was negatively correlated due to the small effects realized for low-intensity programs that operate continuously or meet frequently, such as wilderness/challenge and group counseling programs. Among general program characteristics, only the level and nature of the researcher's participation made a significant, independent contribution to effect size. Effects were larger when the researcher was more involved in the design and delivery of treatment.

Type of Treatment and Effects on Recidivism

To compare differences in treatment, observed effect sizes (the original effect size computed in each study), equated effect sizes (the effectiveness after controlling for all common variables), and method-adjusted effect sizes (the effectiveness after controlling for differences in study methods and procedures) were examined to consider the magnitude of the mean effect, the variance around each of those means, and the extent of agreement across the three different effect size estimates. Three types of treatment showed the strongest and most consistent evidence of reducing recidivism in noninstitutionalized serious offenders:

- Interpersonal skills training (based on three studies).

- Individual counseling (based on eight studies).

- Behavioral programs (based on seven studies).

It should be noted that there are only a small number of studies for each type of treatment because these treatments have not often been studied in reference to serious noninstitutionalized offenders. Following these treatment types in effectiveness were multiple services and restitution programs for juveniles on probation or parole.

The types of treatment that showed the clearest evidence that they were not effective included wilderness/challenge programs, early release from probation or parole (based on only two programs), deterrence programs, and vocational programs.

One group of treatment types, including employment-related programs; academic programs; and advocacy/social casework, group counseling, and family counseling programs, presented mixed or ambiguous evidence. This group showed inconsistent effect size estimates. On the other hand, their equated effect sizes (which account for method and procedure, juvenile characteristics, and other differences) were favorable. However, without understanding the variables contributing to these differences, it is difficult to know whether the effectiveness calculated for this group of treatments was due to the treatment or to another variable.

Interventions for Institutionalized Juveniles

Of the 200 studies analyzed, 83 dealt with programs for institutionalized youth; of these programs, 74 were in juvenile justice institutions and 9 were in residential facilities under private or mental health administration. Using the same method of regression analysis, researchers examined the same four clusters of variables as in the sample of studies with noninstitutionalized offenders. The clusters associated with the largest variation in method-adjusted effect size were, in decreasing order of magnitude:

- General program characteristics.

- Treatment types.

- Treatment amount delivered (e.g., total number of weeks and frequency of treatment, and other ratings of treatment effectiveness).

- Juvenile offender characteristics.

This model was further reduced (using the same procedure described earlier) to weed out the weakest variables. This process indicated that the characteristics of institutionalized juveniles accounted for the smallest proportion of effect size variation. This was in contrast to noninstitutionalized juveniles, for whom juvenile characteristics were most important. This means that the conclusions yielded by this model need not be differentiated by juvenile characteristics such as age, gender, ethnic mix, or prior offense history.

Two variables emerged that were important in terms of the amount of treatment provided. First, monitoring to ensure that all juveniles received the intended treatment was essential. Second, the length of treatment was related to the size of treatment effect; that is, the longer the treatment (the average in this sample was 25 weeks), the larger the effects. The type of treatment also was important and is discussed in the next section.

General program characteristics (i.e., the way in which a program is organized, staffed, and administered) were more related to the size of recidivism effects than the type or amount of treatment. The largest treatment effects were found for well-established programs (2 years or older). However, the variable most strongly related to effect size was administration by mental health personnel, in contrast to juvenile justice personnel.

Type of Treatment and Effects on Recidivism

The different types of treatment for institutionalized juveniles were grouped according to the magnitude of mean effect sizes and the consistency of effect sizes. Again, it is important to note that the small number of studies forming the basis of these estimates limits the ability to draw strong conclusions. Two types of treatment showed relatively large, statistically significant mean effect sizes for institutionalized offenders across all estimation procedures: interpersonal skills programs (involving training in social skills and anger control) and teaching family homes (community-based, family-style group homes). Interpersonal skills training was also one of the treatments that had a stronger effect on noninstitutionalized juveniles. Strong, but less consistent, results appeared for multiple service programs, community residential programs (mostly other than juvenile justice programs), and other miscellaneous treatments.

Milieu therapy (in which the total environment, including peers, is structured to support the goals of treatment) showed consistent null results. Drug abstinence programs, wilderness/challenge programs, and employment-related programs did not show statistically significant or consistent mean effects.

The middle tier consisted of behavioral programs and individual, group, and guided group counseling (involving a facilitated group in which members develop norms, give feedback, and make decisions that regulate behavior). Some were statistically significant and some were consistent across the three estimation procedures, but none met all the criteria. In the case of behavioral programs, this may have been because only two studies were included. For the three varieties of counseling, the effect size estimates were inconsistent. Observed effects were confounded with other study characteristics, making it difficult to determine actual treatment effects.

Effectiveness of Treatment Types

The question asked at the beginning of this Bulletin, "Can intervention programs reduce recidivism rates among serious delinquents?" has been answered. A review of the statistical findings of 200 studies found that the average intervention effect for these studies was positive, statistically significant, and equivalent to a recidivism reduction of about 6 percentage points from a 50-percent baseline, but variation in effects across studies was considerable.

Because there were relatively few studies of any one type of treatment and a range of influential variables, only tentative conclusions can be drawn from this meta-analysis. The first and most important finding is that sufficient research has yet to be conducted on the effects of intervention with serious offenders. Keeping this in mind, then, the question arises, "What types of programs are most effective for reducing recidivism?"

Again, the differences between interventions with institutionalized and noninstitutionalized offenders should be noted. For noninstitutional interventions, effects were most strongly related to the characteristics of the juveniles, especially those with a history of prior offenses. The influence of treatment type and amount was intermediate, and program characteristics were weakly related to effect size. This order was reversed for interventions with institutionalized juveniles. Program characteristics were most strongly related to the size of intervention effects; the type and amount of treatment were moderately related, and the characteristics of the juveniles were not especially important.

The specific program characteristics most closely connected with the reduction of reoffense rates of serious offenders were different for institutional programs for incarcerated offenders than for noninstitutional programs for offenders on probation or parole in the community. These characteristics did not necessarily have to do with the type of intervention; some were part of the administrative context or due to the characteristics of the juveniles treated. Therefore, a good match between program concept, host organization, and the targeted juvenile is essential.

Effective Interventions for Noninstitutionalized Offenders

The selection criteria for the 117 studies of noninstitutionalized offenders included in this meta-analysis were not highly restrictive, resulting in a range of programs in the study. The samples also varied considerably in terms of the severity of the juveniles' offense records. This allowed for some analysis of whether the interventions generally used with noninstitutionalized offenders would also be effective in reducing the recidivism of more serious offenders. The research directly addressing this question is limited, so there is no assurance that these interventions would be effective. However, this meta-analysis indicated that the intervention effects were larger for samples having greater numbers of serious offenders (with prior offenses). Also, there was little difference in the effects of interventions with respect to other characteristics of the samples (extent of aggressive history, gender, age, and ethnic mix). These two factors provide reason to believe that the interventions that are generally effective for noninstitutionalized delinquents would be equally effective with more serious offenders. Table 1 compares the effectiveness of different types of treatments for noninstitutionalized and institutionalized offenders. Treatment types are given in descending order of effectiveness.

In this meta-analysis, the types of treatment that were the most effective for noninstitutionalized offenders—individual counseling, interpersonal skills, and behavioral programs—were shown to reduce recidivism by about 40 percent, a significant decrease. It is interesting to note that individual counseling appears to be an effective form of treatment for noninstitutionalized serious offenders but not for institutionalized offenders. Further examination of this discrepancy is warranted but was beyond the scope of the meta-analysis.

Following is a description of the most effective intervention programs for noninstitutionalized offenders, as represented in table 1.

Individual Counseling.

* Juvenile probationers received one-to-one counseling from citizen volunteers in addition to regular probationary supervision (Moore, 1987).

* Reality therapy counseling, in which clients practiced eight steps until they were able to take charge of their lives, was given in weekly hour-long sessions for 12 weeks by two students enrolled in graduate-level counseling courses (Bean, 1988).

* Juvenile sexual offenders were treated with multisystemic therapy (Borduin et al., 1990).

Interpersonal Skills.

* An experimental training program used drama and the production of videos to help delinquent juveniles see themselves from the perspective of others and to provide remedial training in role-taking skills (Chandler, 1973).

* An intensive 10-day course in a large camp or church retreat facility for juveniles included followup that involved commitment to one or more personal or community projects (Delinquency Research Group, 1986).

Table 1.   A Comparison of Treatment Types in Order of Effectiveness

Types of Treatment Used With Noninstitutionalized Offenders	Types of Treatment Used With Institutionalized Offenders
Positive effects, consistent evidence	
Individual counseling Interpersonal skills Behavioral programs	Interpersonal skills Teaching family homes
Positive effects, less consistent evidence	
Multiple services Restitution, probation/parole	Behavioral programs Community residential Multiple services
Mixed but generally positive effects, inconsistent evidence	
Employment related Academic programs Advocacy/casework Family counseling Group counseling	Individual counseling Guided group counseling Group counseling
Weak or no effects, inconsistent evidence	
Reduced caseload, probation/parole	Employment related Drug abstinence Wilderness/challenge
Weak or no effects, consistent evidence	
Wilderness/challenge Early release, probation/parole Deterrence programs Vocational programs	Milieu therapy

Behavioral Programs.

- Adjudicated delinquents were ordered by the court to a family counseling program as a condition of probation (Gordon, Graves, and Arbuthnot, 1987).

- Probationers were included in a contingency contracting program as a method of behavior therapy (Jessness et al., 1975).

Multiple Services.

- A probation program offered 24 different treatment techniques, with no juvenile receiving more than 12 or fewer than 4 techniques (Morris, 1970).

- A project provided 3 months of intensive services to youth on probation, followed by approximately 9 months of followup services (Browne, 1975).

- Youth were placed under intensive case management and received an array of services to meet their specific needs (Weisz et al., 1990).

Effective Interventions for Institutionalized Offenders

Of the 83 studies on interventions with institutionalized offenders examined in the meta-analysis, 74 involved juveniles in the custody of juvenile justice institutions and 9 involved residential institutions administered by mental health or private agencies. All juveniles had committed serious offenses warranting confinement or close supervision in an institutional facility.

Recidivism effect sizes for the different treatment types were most consistently positive for interpersonal skills interventions and teaching family homes. Recidivism effects for behavioral, community residential, and multiple service programs were somewhat less consistently positive. However, the small number of studies in each category makes it difficult to draw strong conclusions about the relative effectiveness of treatment types for institutionalized offenders. Using control group results from the available studies, the researchers estimated that the recidivism rate for these juveniles would be approximately 50 percent without treatment. Relative to that, the most effective treatments would reduce recidivism by 30–35 percent, a significant decrease considering the seriousness of these juveniles' delinquency.

The following describes the most effective intervention programs for institutionalized offenders. . . .

Interpersonal Skills.

- Adolescent boys living in a community home school participated in twelve 1-hour sessions in social skills training over 6 weeks (Spence and Marzillier, 1981).

- Adolescent boys at a youth center participated in aggression replacement training, which took place in 30 sessions over 10 weeks (Glick and Goldstein, 1987).

- The Social Interactional Skills Program was a structured didactic program that encouraged youth to recall problematic past experiences and identify negative social stimuli that affected their social interactions (Shivrattan, 1988).

Teaching Family Homes.

- In a community-based, family-style group home, supervising adults (called teaching parents) used behavior modification with six to eight delinquent juveniles (Kirigan et al., 1982).

- Adjudicated delinquents were in a community-based, family-style, behavior modification group home where teaching parents used a token economy to help youth progress behaviorally and academically (Wolf, Phillips, and Fixson, 1974).

Behavioral Programs.

- Incarcerated male and female adolescents participated in a 12-week cognitive mediation training program involving small discussion groups ranging in size from 10 to 14 youth (Guerra and Slaby, 1990).

- Institutionalized male delinquents participated in a stress inoculation training program that included defining anger, analyzing recent anger episodes, reviewing self-monitoring data, and constructing an individualized six-item anger hierarchy (Schlicter and Horan, 1981).

- Girls in a correctional institution were trained in reinforcement therapy principles and acted as peer counselors for incoming wards (Ross and McKay, 1976).

Community Residential Programs.

- A community-based group home for girls offered advocacy, counseling, educational support, and vocational support (Minnesota Governor's Commission on Crime Prevention and Control, 1973).

- Institutionalized youth placed in a 32-bed therapeutic community setting in an inner-city neighborhood received counseling, remedial education, vocational assessment and training, and other services (Auerbach, 1978).

- A community-based residential treatment center for adjudicated youth used extensive group discussion as therapy and emphasized progressive assumption of self-responsibility (Allen-Hagen, 1975).

Multiple Services.

- A probation department used a camp as an experimental program. The camp provided supportive services such as vocational training, skill-oriented education, job placement, and cottage living (Kawaguchi, 1975).

- Institutionalized boys were treated in a multifaceted program to overcome academic, vocational, and psychological deficits (Thambidurai, 1980).

- A planned reentry program used a short-term, 52-bed living unit that included cottage living, counseling, education, and recreation activities (Seckel and Turner, 1985).

The Challenge of Providing Effective Interventions for Serious Juvenile Offenders

Two views are often expressed about the effectiveness of intervention with serious offenders. According to the risk principle (Andrews et al., 1990), treatment for delinquent behavior is most effective when provided to juveniles who are at highest risk for reoffending. The opposite view is that serious juvenile delinquents are the most hardened and least likely to respond to treatment. The results of this meta-analysis support the first view—that is, serious delinquents can be helped.

On average, the 200 intervention programs studied produced positive, statistically significant effects equivalent to a 12-percent reduction in recidivism. Intervention, therefore, can reduce recidivism. However, it is difficult to know which types of programs to use. The best programs reduced recidivism by as much as 40 percent, whereas others had negligible effects on recidivism. By determining the characteristics of effective intervention, new and better programs can be designed, tested, implemented, and evaluated.

References

Allen-Hagen, B. 1975. *Youth Crime Control Project: A Final Report on an Experimental Alternative to Incarceration of Young Adult Offenders*. Research Report No. 75-1. Washington, DC: Washington, DC Department of Corrections.

Andrews, D.A., Zinger, I., Hoge, R.D., Bonta, J., Gendreau, P., and Cullen, F.T. 1990. Does correctional treatment work? A clinically relevant and psychologically informed meta-analysis. *Criminology* 28(3):369–404.

Auerbach, A.W. 1978. The role of the therapeutic community "Street Prison" in the rehabilitation of youthful offenders. Doctoral dissertation. Washington, DC: George Washington University. University Microfilms No. 78-01086.

Bean, J.S. 1988. The effect of individualized reality therapy on the recidivism rates and locus of control orientation of male juvenile offenders. Doctoral dissertation. Oxford, MS: University of Mississippi. *Dissertation Abstracts International* 49, 2370B. University Microfilms No. 88-18138.

Borduin, C.M., Henggeler, S.W., Blaske, D.M., and Stein, R.J. 1990. Multisystemic treatment of adolescent sexual offenders. *International Journal of Offender Therapy and Comparative Criminology* 34:105–113.

Browne, S.F. 1975. *Denver High Impact Anti-crime Program: Evaluation Report*. Denver, CO: Denver Manpower Administration.

Chandler, M.J. 1973. Egocentrism and antisocial behavior: The assessment and training of social perspective-taking skills. *Developmental Psychology* 9:326–333.

Cullen, F.T., and Gilbert, K.E. 1982. *Reaffirming Rehabilitation*. Cincinnati, OH: Anderson.

Delinquency Research Group. 1986. *An Evaluation of the Delinquency of Participants in the Youth at Risk Program*. Claremont, CA: Claremont Graduate School, Center for Applied Social Research.

Garrett, C.J. 1985. Effects of residential treatment on adjudicated delinquents: A meta-analysis. *Journal of Research in Crime and Delinquency* 22(4):287–308.

Gendreau, P., and Ross, R.R. 1987. Revivification of rehabilitation: Evidence from the 1980s. *Justice Quarterly* 4(3):349–407.

Glick, B., and Goldstein, A.P. 1987. Aggression replacement training. *Journal of Counseling and Development* 65(7):356–362.

Gordon, D.A., Graves, K., and Arbuthnot, J. 1987. Prevention of adult criminal behavior using family therapy for disadvantaged juvenile delinquents. Unpublished manuscript. Athens, OH: Ohio University.

Guerra, N.G., and Slaby, R.G. 1990. Cognitive mediators of aggression in adolescent offenders: 2. Intervention. *Developmental Psychology* 26(2):269–277.

Jessness, C.F., Allison, F.S., McCormic, P.M., Wedge, R.F., and Young, M.L. 1975. *Evaluation of the Effectiveness of Contingency Contracting with Delinquents*. Sacramento, CA: California Youth Authority.

Kawaguchi, R.M. 1975. *Camp Fenner Canyon Evaluation: Final Report*. Los Angeles, CA: Los Angeles County Probation Department.

Kirigan, K.A., Braukmann, C.J., Atwater, J.D., and Worl, M.M. 1982. An evaluation of teaching family (Achievement Place) group homes for juvenile offenders. *Journal of Applied Behavior Analysis* 15(1):1–16.

Lipsey, M.W. 1992. Juvenile delinquency treatment: A meta-analysis inquiry into the variability of effects. In *Meta-analysis for Explanation. A Casebook*, edited by T.D. Cook, H. Cooper, D.S. Cordray, H. Hartmann, L.V. Hedges, R.J. Light, T.A. Louis, and F. Mosteller. New York, NY: Russell Sage, pp. 83–127.

———. 1995. What do we learn from 400 research studies on the effectiveness of treatment with juvenile delinquents? In *What Works? Reducing Reoffending*, edited by J. McGuire. New York, NY: John Wiley, pp. 63–78.

Minnesota Governor's Commission on Crime Prevention and Control. 1973. *An Evaluation of the Group Residence Program for Juvenile Girls: June 1972 through April 1973*. St. Paul, MN: Minnesota Department of Corrections.

Moore, R.H. 1987. Effectiveness of citizen volunteers functioning as counselors for high-risk young male offenders. *Psychological Reports* 61(3):823–830.

Morris, J.A. 1970. *First Offender: A Volunteer Program for Youth in Trouble with the Law*. New York, NY: Funk and Wagnalls.

Palmer, T. 1994. *A Profile of Correctional Effectiveness and New Directions for Research*. Albany, NY: State University of New York Press.

Ross, R.R., and McKay, B. 1976. A study of institutional treatment programs. *International Journal of Offender Therapy and Comparative Criminology: An Interdisciplinary Journal* 20(2):167–173.

Schlicter, K.J., and Horan, J.J. 1981. Effects of stress inoculation on the anger and aggression management skills of institutionalized juvenile delinquents. *Cognitive Therapy and Research* 5(4):359–365.

Seckel, J.P., and Turner, J.K. 1985. *Assessment of Planned Re-Entry Programs (PREP)*. Sacramento, CA: California Youth Authority.

Shivrattan, J.L. 1988. Social interactional training and incarcerated juvenile delinquents. *Canadian Journal of Criminology* 30(1):145–163.

Spence, S.H., and Marzillier, J.S. 1981. Social skills training with adolescent male offenders: II. Short-term, long-term and generalized effects. *Behavior Research and Therapy* 19:349–368.

Thambidurai, G.A. 1980. A comparative outcome study of a contract parole program for individuals committed to the youth correctional complex in the state of New Jersey. Doctoral dissertation. New Brunswick, NJ: Rutgers University. *Dissertation Abstracts International* 41, 371B. University Microfilms No. 80-16503.

Weisz, J.R., Walter, B.R., Weiss, B., Fernandez, G.A., and Mikow, V.A. 1990. Arrests among emotionally disturbed violent and assaultive individuals following minimal versus lengthy intervention through North Carolina's Willie M Program. *Journal of Consulting and Clinical Psychology* 58:720–728.

Wolf, M.M., Phillips, E.L., and Fixson, D.L. 1974. *Achievement Place: Phase II* (Vol. 1). Rockville, MD: National Institute of Mental Health, Center for Studies of Crime and Delinquency. ✦

Part IX

Juvenile Justice and Specific Groups

In the past, both the rates of offending and the patterns of official processing by the juvenile justice officials kept girls' delinquency rates low—girls did not commit as serious or frequent offenses as boys, and when they did, they tended to be processed in more lenient ways than boys were. Both of those patterns have been changing recently. As a result, female delinquents are presently the fastest growing and least visible group of juvenile offenders.

The opposite situation has more or less occurred with minorities. Especially in the past, both the rates of offending and the patterns of official processing resulted in these groups having very high rates of official delinquency. More recently, the "over-representation" of minorities in the juvenile justice system has become a concern. It is clear that, even controlling for the frequency and seriousness of offending, minorities receive greater punishments than majority youths who commit similar offenses and have similar prior records.

The two chapters in this part examine these handling of these two groups in the juvenile justice system. ✦

Chapter 17

Minorities in the Juvenile Justice System

Office of Juvenile Justice and Delinquency Prevention

Editor's Introduction

Racial discrimination used to be a very important source of differential processing in juvenile justice. While it is unclear whether that remains true today, it is undoubtedly true that there are very large differences in the way youths from majority and minority groups are processed by the juvenile justice system. Chapter 17 states: "There is substantial evidence of widespread disparity in juvenile case processing" for minority youth, especially black youth.

"Disparity" means that cases involving minority and majority youth are processed differently even though the cases themselves are similar. Basically, minority youth receive harsher outcomes than majority youth who commit similar offenses, especially when the outcomes involve confinement. There may be several reasons for this, including but not limited to racial discrimination.[1] Whatever the reason, it is a very serious problem that merits close examination.

The Juvenile Justice and Delinquency Prevention Act of 2002 required states to address disproportionate minority contact at all decision points in the juvenile justice system.[2] Chapter 17 provides an overview of the problem that both the states and the federal government are attempting to deal with at the present time.

Notes

1. For example, Thomas J. Bernard, Jennifer Calnon, Robin Engel, and Zachery Hays, "Efficiency and Differential Processing," *Journal of Crime and Justice* 28(1), 2005, argue that the search for efficiency in processing leads to the concentration of resources on high crime rate groups. This results in harsher outcomes that are associated with the individuals' minority status but not with their actual behavior.

Adapted from Office of Juvenile Justice and Delinquency Prevention, "Minorities in the Juvenile Justice System," *1999 National Report Series, Juvenile Justice Bulletin.* Washington, DC: U.S. Department of Justice, 1999. Copyright is not claimed in this article, a publication of the United States government.

2.   For a report on state efforts to comply with this law, see Heidi M. Hsia, George S.
     Bridges, and Rosalie McHale, *Disproportionate Minority Confinement: 2002 Update.*
     Washington, DC: U.S. Office of Juvenile Justice and Delinquency Prevention, Sep-
     tember, 2004. See also Michael J. Leiber, "Disproportionate Minority Confinement
     (DMC) of Youth: An Analysis of State and Federal Efforts to Address the Issue,"
     Crime and Delinquency 48(1): 3–45, 2002. A review of 34 recent studies on minor-
     ity processing in juvenile justice can be found in Carl E. Pope, Rick Lovell, and
     Heide M. Hsia, "Disproportionate Minortity Confinement: A Review of the Re-
     search Literature from 1989 Through 2001," *Juvenile Justice Bulletin.* Washington,
     DC: OJJDP, 2002.

✦ ✦ ✦

Overrepresentation, Disparity, and Discrimination Have Different Meanings

Overrepresentation refers to a situation in which a larger proportion of a particular group is present at various stages within
the juvenile justice system (such as intake, detention, adjudication,
and disposition) than would be expected based on their proportion in
the general population.

Disparity means that the probability of receiving a particular outcome (for example, being detained in a short-term facility vs. not
being detained) differs for different groups. Disparity may in turn
lead to overrepresentation.

Discrimination occurs if and when juvenile justice system decision-
makers treat one group of juveniles differently from another group of
juveniles based wholly, or in part, on their gender, racial, and/or ethnic status.

Neither Overrepresentation nor Disparity Necessarily Implies Discrimination

One possible explanation for disparity and overrepresentation is,
of course, discrimination. This line of reasoning suggests that because of discrimination on the part of justice system decision-
makers, minority youth face higher probabilities of being arrested by
the police, referred to court intake, held in short-term detention, peti-
tioned for formal processing, adjudicated delinquent, and confined in
a secure juvenile facility. Thus, differential actions throughout the
justice system may account for minority overrepresentation.

Disparity and overrepresentation, however, can result from factors
other than discrimination. Factors relating to the nature and volume
of crime committed by minority youth may explain disproportionate
minority confinement. This line of reasoning suggests that if minority

youth commit proportionately more crime than white youth, are involved in more serious incidents, and have more extensive criminal histories, they will be overrepresented in secure facilities, even if no discrimination by system decision-makers occurred. Thus, minority youth may be overrepresented within the juvenile justice system because of behavioral and legal factors.

In any given jurisdiction, either or both of these causes of disparity may be operating. Detailed data analysis is necessary to build a strong case for one or the other causal scenario. On a national level, such detailed analysis is not possible with the data that are available. For example, national data use broad offense categories—such as robbery, which includes both felony and non-felony robberies. More severe outcomes would be expected for juveniles charged with felony robbery. Disparity in decisions regarding transfer to criminal court would result if one group of offenders had a higher proportion of felony robberies than another group (since transfer provisions are often limited to felony offenses). The national data, however, do not support analysis that controls for offense at the felony/non-felony level of detail. Similarly, although prior criminal record is the basis for many justice system decisions, criminal history data are not available nationally.

Thus, at the national level, questions regarding the causes of observed disparity and overrepresentation remain unanswered.

There Is Substantial Evidence of Widespread Disparity in Juvenile Case Processing

While research findings are not completely consistent, data available for most jurisdictions across the country show that minority (especially black) youth are overrepresented within the juvenile justice system, particularly in secure facilities. These data further suggest that minority youth are more likely to be placed in public secure facilities, while white youth are more likely to be housed in private facilities or diverted from the juvenile justice system. Some research also suggests that differences in the offending rates of white and minority youth cannot explain the minority overrepresentation in arrest, conviction, and incarceration counts. . . .

Self-Reported Delinquent and Deviant Behaviors of Youth Varied by Race and Ethnicity

A New Self-Report Survey Documents Delinquent and Deviant Behaviors of Youth

The first wave of the 1997 National Longitudinal Survey of Youth (NLSY97) interviewed a nationally representative sample of 9,000 youth who were between the ages of 12 and 16 at year-end 1996. The survey asked youth to report whether they had engaged in a variety of deviant and delinquent behaviors. Plans are to interview members of this cohort every 2 years to track changes in delinquent and criminal activity over the life course.

Less Than One-Tenth (8%) of Youth Ages 12–16 Said They Had Ever Been Arrested

Of the 8% of youth who had ever been arrested, a substantial proportion (40%, or 3% of all youth) reported two or more arrests.

The Proportion of Youth Ever Arrested Varied Significantly by Race and Ethnicity for Males but Not for Females

White males (9%) were less likely to have ever been arrested than black males (13%) or Hispanic males (12%). Further, a greater proportion of black males (7%) and Hispanic males (6%) than white males (4%) were arrested more than once.

Equal proportions of white (5%), black (6%), and Hispanic (7%) females had ever been arrested. In addition, white (2%), black (2%), and Hispanic (3%) females were equally likely to have been arrested more than once. . . .

In 1996, Black Juveniles Were Referred to Juvenile Court at a Rate More Than Double That for Whites

The Offense Profiles of White Caseloads and Black Caseloads Differ

Caseloads of black juveniles contained a greater proportion of person offenses than did caseloads of white juveniles and those of other races. Property offense cases accounted for the largest proportion of cases for all racial groups, although among black juveniles, property cases accounted for fewer than half of the cases processed in 1996. For all races, drug offense cases accounted for the smallest proportion of the 1996 caseload. . . .

Caseload offense profiles for 1996 differed from offense profiles for 1987 for all racial groups. Regardless of race, the proportion of cases involving person offenses was greater in 1996 than in 1987. Among black juveniles, person offenses increased 3 percentage points. Among white juveniles and those of other races, person offenses increased 6 percentage points. . . .

White Juveniles Were Less Likely to Be Detained Than Black Juveniles and Juveniles of Other Races

White Youth Were Least Likely to Be Detained

Secure detention was nearly twice as likely in 1996 for cases involving black youth as for cases involving whites, even after controlling for offense. Detention was least likely for cases involving white youth charged with property crimes. Detention was most likely for cases involving black youth charged with drug offenses. . . .

For Blacks, Growth in Detained Cases Outpaced Growth in Delinquency Cases Overall

For black youth, the relative increase in the number of delinquency cases involving detention was greater than the relative increase in delinquency cases overall. For white juveniles and juveniles of other races, growth in the overall delinquency caseload was greater than growth in the detention caseload. . . .

Black Youth Were Overrepresented in Detention Caseloads in 1996

As a result of their greater probability of detention in 1996, black youth were overrepresented in the detention caseload, compared with their proportions in the overall delinquency caseload. While black youth made up 30% of all delinquency cases processed in 1996, they were involved in 45% of detained cases. This overrepresentation was greatest for drug offenses: blacks accounted for 33% of all drug cases processed, but 59% of drug cases detained. . . .

In all offense categories, youth of other races made up less than 5% of all cases processed and of those involving detention. . . .

Minorities Accounted for 7 in 10 Youth Held in Custody for A Violent Offense

More Than 6 in 10 Juveniles in Residential Placement Were Minority Youth

In 1997, two-thirds of all juveniles in custody in public facilities were minorities as were just over half of all juveniles in private facilities. . . .

The Racial/Ethnic Profile of Juveniles Held in 1997 Is Similar to the Profile of Those Held in 1995

Data from the 1995 Children in Custody census show race proportions similar to those derived from the CJRP data. . . .

In 1995, more than two-thirds of all juveniles in custody in public facilities were minorities as were just under half of all juveniles in private facilities. . . .

Half of Females in Residential Placement Were Minorities

Minorities were somewhat less disproportionate in the female custody population than in the male custody population. . . .

Females Accounted for a Slightly Greater Proportion of White Than Minority Youth in Custody

The female proportion of juveniles in residential placement varied by race and ethnicity. Females accounted for 18% of non-minority white juveniles in residential placement. Among minorities overall, females accounted for 11% of juveniles in residential placement; however, the female proportion was 21% for American Indians and only 9% for Hispanics and Asians. . . .

On the 1997 Census Day, Minority Offenders Had Been in Residential Placement Longer Than Other Juveniles

Juveniles in Residential Placement

Information on length of stay is key to understanding the justice system's handling of juveniles in residential placement. The Census of Juveniles in Residential Placement (CJRP), first conducted in October 1997, captures information on the number of days since admission for each juvenile in residential placement up until the date of the census. The CJRP looks both at juveniles detained while awaiting adjudication or disposition and committed juveniles (those adjudicated, disposed, and placed in the facility). While the data cannot determine complete length of stay, the CJRP does provide an overall profile of the time juveniles had been in the facility at the time of the census—a 1-day snapshot of time in the facility. The CJRP also collects individual-level data regarding juveniles in facilities, providing juvenile justice policymakers with a more complete look at who is in the facilities and how long they have been detained or committed.

Minorities Had Been in Facilities Longer Than Non-Minority Whites

Among committed juveniles, minorities had been in the facility an average of 193 days. In comparison, committed non-minority whites had been in the facility an average of 174 days—2 weeks less. A similar pattern was found among detained juveniles. Detained minority juveniles had been in the facility an average of 1 week longer than non-minority whites (43 days vs. 36 days).

Demographic Differences in Time in the Facility Reflect Differences in Offense Profiles

Juveniles held for violent offenses had been in placement longer on average than other juveniles. Overall, committed delinquents had been in the facility an average of just over 6 months (186 days). Juveniles committed for Violent Crime Index offenses, in comparison, had been in the facility an average of nearly 9 months (266 days). Findings were similar for detained juveniles.

A closer look at the 1997 CJRP finding that minority youth had been in placement longer than their non-minority white counterparts indicates this finding is attributable to differences in offense profiles: minorities had larger proportions of person offenders, particularly violent person offenders, in their population. Within individual offense categories, demographic differences in time in the facility were negligible. . . .

Nationally, Custody Rates for Black Juveniles Were Substantially Higher Than Rates for Other Groups

For every 100,000 non-Hispanic black juveniles in the population, 1,018 were in a residential placement facility on October 29, 1997—for Hispanics the rate was 515, and for non-Hispanic whites it was 204. . . .

Males, 17-Year-Olds, Minorities, and Person Offenders Predominate Among Youth Sent to Adult Prisons

Youth Under Age 18 Accounted for 2% of New Court Commitments to State Adult Prisons

Thirty-six States (containing 81% of the 1996 U.S. population ages 10–17) contributed data for 1992–1996 to the National Corrections

Reporting Program (NCRP). These States reported approximately 5,600 new court commitments to their adult prison systems involving youth under 18.

These youth accounted for nearly 2% of all new court commitments. Nearly 3 in 4 of these youth were 17 years old at admission. States with an upper age of juvenile jurisdiction below 17 accounted for half of all under-18 admissions.

The Under-18 Proportion of New Admissions Varied by Offense

Under-18 youth accounted for 4% of new admissions for person offenses, 7% of new admissions for robbery, 5% of those for murder, and 3% of those for aggravated assault and weapons offenses. For all other offense categories, the under-18 proportion was 2% or less.

More Than Three-Quarters of Youth Newly Admitted to State Prison Were Minorities

Minorities made up a greater proportion of new court commitments involving youth under age 18 than of those involving older offenders. Blacks accounted for the largest proportion of new prison admissions for both age groups.

The minority proportion of new admissions varied by offense category. Drug offenses had the greatest proportion of minority admissions for both age groups. ✦

Chapter 18

Investing in Girls

A 21st Century Strategy

Leslie Acoca

Editor's Introduction

In 2002, Congress required the states to address disproportionate minority contact (DMC) at all decision points in the juvenile justice system. A decade earlier, in 1992, Congress had done something similar when it required that states examine their services for girls as a condition of receiving federal funds. This resulted in "challenge grants" by which the federal government induced the states to offer "gender-specific" services for girls in juvenile corrections.[1]

Where minorities are overrepresented in juvenile justice (i.e., there are a greater proportion of minorities in juvenile justice than in the general population), girls are underrepresented. But despite the fact that girls have been a small group in juvenile justice in the past, at present they are its fastest growing group.

Chapter 18 reviews recent official statistics related to girls' offending and their increasing presence in the juvenile justice system. It also states that the meaning of these statistics is "hotly disputed by researchers and policymakers." The question is whether girls are "catching up" to boys in their offending behavior. An alternate explanation of these statistics would focus on changes in the official processing of girls by juvenile justice officials. Thus, the situation with girls raises a similar issue as was raised with minorities: do the statistics reflect differences in offending or differences in case processing?

Whether or not girls are "catching up" with boys in their offending behavior, official statistics still indicate that boys commit the vast majority of juvenile offenses, particularly more serious offenses. According to the FBI Uniform Crime Reports, boys in 2004 accounted for 70 percent of all arrests of those who were under the age of 18.[2] This included 88 percent of arrests for murder and

---

Adapted from Leslie Acoca, "Investing in Girls: A 21st Century Strategy," *Juvenile Justice* 6(1): 3–13, 1999. Copyright is not claimed in this article, a publication of the United States government.

for burglary, 76 percent of arrests for aggravated assault, 90 percent of arrests for robbery, 86 percent of arrests for arson, and 83 percent of arrests for drug offenses. And as might be expected, boys also accounted for over 97 percent of the arrests for rape of those under the age of 18. The only offenses for which girls were a majority of those arrested were prostitution (72 percent) and runaway (60 percent).

Regardless of whether girls are "catching up" with boys in their offending behavior, they are a rapidly increasing presence in our juvenile corrections systems. Therefore, much more than in the past, it is imperative to examine their problems and needs in order to determine how best to respond to their offending behavior. Chapter 18 presents a broad examination of this issue.

Notes

1. See Kimberly Kempf-Leonard and Lisa L. Sample, "Disparity based on sex: Is gender-specific treatment warranted?" *Justice Quarterly* 17(1): 89–138, March 2000. This article presents a good review of research on differential case processing by gender.

2. *Crime in the United States, 2004*, Federal Bureau of Investigation, U.S. Department of Justice, Washington, DC: U.S. Government Printing Office, 2005, data compiled from Tables 38 and 39.

◆ ◆ ◆

Introduction

As Americans look back over the 20th century, the increasing criminalization of girls and women and the realization that they now make up the fastest growing segments of the juvenile and criminal justice systems must spark a major public response. Further, as a comprehensive national strategy to promote public safety into the 21st century is developed, the youngest and least visible female offenders—adolescent girls—and their children must be a core focus. Given the developmental and childbearing potential of these young women and the generally low risk they pose to their communities, addressing their needs offers the Nation its best hope of halting the intergenerational cycle of family fragmentation and crime.

Any effort to understand and develop strategies to reverse the accelerating entry of girls into the juvenile justice system must begin with an examination of the current statistical picture. Between 1993 and 1997, increases in arrests were greater (or decreases smaller) for girls than for boys in almost every offense category (Snyder, in press). The 748,000 arrests of girls younger than 18 years old in 1997 represent 26 percent of all juvenile arrests made that year. This proportion has been climbing slowly since 1986 when girls constituted 22 percent of all juvenile arrests (Chesney-Lind and Shelden, 1998).

Buttressing claims that girls are beginning to catch up with boys in terms of their involvement with more serious and violent crimes, the Violent Crime Index arrest rate for girls rose 103 percent between 1981 and 1997, compared with a 27 percent increase for boys during the same time period. In assessing this disproportionate rise, however, one should keep in mind that the arrest rate for juvenile males for these crimes remains five times that for females (Snyder, in press).

It should also be noted that the greatest increases in arrests of girls between 1993 and 1997 were for drug abuse and curfew violations (Snyder, in press). The escalating number of girls arrested for drug-related offenses should be of particular concern as should the results of a 1998 survey indicating that substance use and abuse among adolescent girls in the general population are rising (Drug Strategies, 1998). Other studies indicate that the unprecedented increase in the number of incarcerated adult women since the early 1980's has largely been due to drug-related offending (Mauer and Huling, 1995).

There have also been greater increases in the number of delinquency cases involving young women handled by juvenile courts than in those pertaining to young men. Between 1986 and 1995, the number of delinquency cases involving girls increased 68 percent, compared with a 40-percent increase in those involving boys (Sickmund, 1997). Further, paralleling the changes evident in arrest statistics, "the relatively greater increase in cases involving females was due to changes in person offense cases (up 146% for females versus 87% for males) and property offense cases (up 50% among females compared with 17% among males)" (Sickmund, 1997:3). . . .

On the surface, these broad national data seem to indicate dramatic increases in the proportion and seriousness of delinquent acts committed by girls. However, the reality underlying the statistics is hotly disputed by researchers and policymakers. Are girls becoming more violent, or are recent trends partially an artifact of girls' lower base rate of arrests and delinquency cases since the 1970's (Chesney-Lind and Shelden, 1998)? What influences do changing and often less tolerant family and societal attitudes toward girls, shifts in law enforcement practices (particularly toward gangs), and the increasing availability of weaponry exert on girls' offending? And finally, are girls traditionally drawn into the juvenile justice system for less serious crimes than their male counterparts?

What is beyond dispute is the need to construct a blueprint for a comprehensive continuum of gender-responsive prevention, intervention, and graduated sanctions services that can be tailored to meet the needs of diverse jurisdictions. Equally clear is the requirement that any such blueprint have as its foundation a research-based pro-file of the characteristics, needs, and life circumstances of girls at risk of entering the juvenile justice system and those already involved with the system. External barriers such as the paucity of programs specifically designed for girls and the anticipated impact of new Fed-eral welfare and adoption legislation on adolescent mothers and their children should also be taken into account. Addressing these issues can no longer be an afterthought. Specific Federal, State, and local legislative and organizational remedies must be sought.

Characteristics of Girls at Risk of Entering or Involved With the Juvenile Justice System

To address many of the challenges noted above, in 1998, the Na-tional Council on Crime and Delinquency (NCCD) conducted a multi-dimensional study of girls in the California juvenile justice system (Acoca and Dedel, 1998). To obtain an official perspective on female offenders, NCCD accessed juvenile justice system databases and con-ducted an in-depth review of nearly 1,000 case files from multiple points within the probation systems of four California counties. In an effort to delve beneath the surface of statistical and official profiles and obtain the girls' description of their characteristics and needs, NCCD interviewed nearly 200 girls in county juvenile halls. The fol-lowing study findings confirm the results from much of the research that has been conducted over the past 25 years by pioneers such as professors Meda Chesney-Lind, Joanne Belknap, and others. The findings also offer additional information that supports the need to reach girls early with intensive intervention and services before they reach the breaking point—that point in early adolescence when so much can go wrong in the lives of girls.

Victimization and Girls' Pathways to Offending

Leading academics who have examined the constellation of life cir-cumstances typically shared by adult and juvenile female offenders have posited that they follow a unique route into the justice system. According to Belknap and Holsinger, "The most significantly and po-tentially useful criminological research in recent years has been the recognition of girls' and women's pathways to offending" (Belknap and Holsinger, 1998:1). These and other scholars have consistently identified victimization—physical, sexual, and emotional—as the first step along females' pathways into the juvenile and criminal jus-tice systems and as a primary determinant of the types and patterns of offenses typically committed by girls and women.

Key findings of the 1998 NCCD study of girls in the California juvenile justice system confirm the pathways approach and closely parallel the findings of a 1995 survey of 151 adult female State prisoners; this survey revealed that one of the most universally shared attributes of adult female prisoners was a history of violent victimization (Acoca and Austin, 1996). Ninety-two percent of the juvenile female offenders interviewed in 1998 reported that they had been subjected to some form of emotional, physical, and/or sexual abuse (Acoca and Dedel, 1998). Despite their age, however, a higher number of the younger women interviewed reported that they had been physically abused, including 25 percent who reported that they had been shot or stabbed one or more times (Acoca and Dedel, 1998). Of critical importance to understanding why many women and girls begin to commit offenses are the early age at which they suffer abuse and the negative repercussions of this abuse on their lives.

Victimization—Physical, Sexual, and Emotional—Is the First Stop Along Females' Pathways Into the Juvenile Justice System. The ages at which adolescent girls interviewed were reportedly most likely to be beaten, stabbed, shot, or raped were 13 and 14 (Acoca and Dedel, 1998). Not surprisingly, a high proportion of girls first enter the juvenile justice system as runaways, who often were seeking to escape abuse at home (Chesney-Lind and Shelden, 1998). In addition, 75 percent of young women interviewed reported regular use of drugs, including alcohol, which typically began at about age 14 (Acoca and Dedel, 1998:91).

Many academics and practitioners agree (Covington, 1998) and NCCD data reveal that clear correlations exist between the victimization of women and girls and specific high-risk behaviors such as serious drug abuse (Acoca and Dedel, 1998). One reason for this close connection is the capacity of mood-altering chemicals to temporarily dull the psychological devastation wrought by experiences of physical and sexual violation. Tragically, statistical analysis of interview data revealed that both the experience of victimization and substance abuse correlated with multiple risky behaviors including truancy, unsafe sexual activity, and gang involvement (Acoca and Dedel, 1998).

Certain Abuses Follow Girls Into the Juvenile Justice System. Many girls report and, in some instances, NCCD field researchers have observed that certain abuses follow girls into the juvenile justice system. Specific forms of abuse reportedly experienced by girls from the point of arrest through detention include the consistent use by staff of foul and demeaning language, inappropriate touching, pushing and hitting, isolation, and deprivation of clean clothing. Some strip searches of girls were conducted in the presence of male officers, underscoring the inherent problem of adult male staff supervising adolescent female detainees. Of special concern were the routine

nature of these acts and the pervasive atmosphere of disrespect toward the girls that they reported permeates not just juvenile justice
settings, but also other community institutions.

Family Fragmentation

The data reveal that the families and caretakers of these girls were
subject to a wide range of stressors, including poverty, death, and an
intergenerational pattern of arrest and incarceration.

According to their case files, more than 95 percent of the girls were
assessed as lacking a stable home environment, and 11 percent had
experienced or witnessed the death of one or both parents or a sibling. Many of the girls interviewed recalled moving back and forth between relatives while they were growing up or being placed in a foster
or group home, typically between the ages of 12 and 14, through the
child welfare or juvenile justice system.

More than one-half (54 percent) of the girls interviewed reported
having mothers who had been arrested or incarcerated. By contrast,
46 percent of the girls' fathers had reportedly been locked up at some
point, and 15 percent of the fathers were reportedly incarcerated at
the time of the interview. Interviews with the girls indicated that
some girls had little or no contact with their fathers, which could account for the lower reported percentage of incarcerated fathers.

Extending the theme of family fragmentation into the next generation, "an alarming 83 percent of the young women interviewed who
were mothers reported that they had been separated from their infants within the first three months of their children's lives, a pivotal
developmental stage" (Acoca and Dedel, 1998:11). Further, 54 percent
of girls who were mothers had not had a single visit with their child
or children while in detention or placement (Acoca and Dedel, 1998).

Academic Failure and Schools as a Battleground

Failing in school was almost as universal an experience as victimization in the lives of the girls interviewed. Ninety-one percent of girls
reported that they had experienced one or more of the following:
being suspended or expelled, repeating one or more grades, and/or
being placed in a special classroom. Eighty-five percent of girls had
been expelled or suspended, and the median age for the first of these
experiences was 13. Of girls placed in special classrooms, only 1 percent said that the placement helped them stay out of trouble. Finally,
many girls described school as a battleground in which sexual harass-
ment, racism, interpersonal rivalries with peers, and inattention from
adult professionals made dropping out appear to be a necessary
means of escape.

Health and Mental Health Issues

Eighty-eight percent of the girls interviewed for this study reported that they had experienced one or more serious physical health problems and more than half (53 percent) stated that they needed psychological services. Twenty-four percent said that they had seriously considered suicide, and 21 percent had been hospitalized in a psychiatric facility on at least one occasion.

Twenty-nine percent of the girls interviewed had been pregnant one or more times and 16 percent had been pregnant while in custody. Of those girls who had been pregnant in custody, 23 percent had miscarried and 29 percent had been placed in physical restraints at some point, usually during transport.

Nonserious, Nonviolent Offense Patterns

Consistent with studies of the offense patterns of girls conducted since the 1970's, the majority of girls surveyed were charged with less serious offenses (e.g., property, drug, and status offenses) than violent offenses (e.g., murder, assault). The highest percentage (36 percent) of these girls were probation violators, many of whom reported that their first offense was running away, truancy, curfew violation, or some other status offense. Girls in Southern California reported that having a tattoo or wearing baggy clothes that could be perceived as markers of gang affiliation were sufficient to bring them into contact with law enforcement. Once they were placed on probation, any subsequent offense, even another status offense, became a violation of a valid court order and a vector for their greater involvement in the juvenile justice system.

Case Files of Girls Revealed Most Assault Charges to Be the Result of Nonserious, Mutual Combat Situations With Parents. Qualitative analysis of the circumstances surrounding the offenses of the relatively high percentage (34 percent) of girls reporting person offenses (including assault, robbery, homicide, and weapons offenses) revealed a disturbing picture. A majority of the girls' more serious charges fell into the assault category. A close reading of the case files of girls charged with assault revealed that most of these charges were the result of nonserious, mutual combat situations with parents. In many cases, the aggression was initiated by the adults. The following descriptions excerpted from case files are typical and telling: "Father lunged at her while she was calling the police about a domestic dispute. She (girl) hit him." "She (girl) was trying to sneak out of the house at night, but mom caught her and pushed her against the wall." In some instances, the probation reports describing the assaults indicate the incongruous nature of many of these incidents. In one case, a girl was arrested for throwing cookies at her mother.

The Disparate Treatment of Minorities Appears to Be an Important Factor. The small number of girls arrested for the most serious offenses—robbery, homicide, and weapons offenses—reportedly committed these crimes almost exclusively within the context of their relationships with codefendants. These relationships fell into two distinct categories: dependent or equal. The first group included girls who were following the lead of male offenders (often adults) who were typically the primary perpetrators of the crime. The second group included girls functioning in female-only groups or mixed-gender groups (including gangs) as equal partners in the commission of their offenses.

Finally, the availability of weapons and an increased willingness to use them appeared to be factors in girls' involvement with serious and violent crime. Although the exact relationship between gang membership and more serious offenses committed by girls was not determined, nearly half of the girls interviewed (47 percent) reported gang affiliation, and 71 percent of these girls stated that they had been "very involved."

The disparate treatment of minorities appears to be an important factor in the processing of girls' cases. Nationally and in the NCCD sample, approximately two-thirds of the girls in the juvenile justice system are minorities, primarily African American and Hispanic. Statistical analysis of the NCCD interview data revealed a significant relationship between the girls' racial status and their drug use, history, and offense type. In summary, although whites reported the most drug use, compared with other racial groups, they were significantly more likely to also report that their most recent charge was a probation violation. By contrast, African Americans and Hispanics, despite significantly less drug involvement, were equally likely to report that their most recent charge was for a drug/property or person offense as they were to report a current probation violation.

The Breaking Point

NCCD interviews with girls in the juvenile justice system revealed a remarkable convergence of traumatic experiences and risky behaviors between the ages of 12 and 14. To recapitulate a few of these, the median age at which girls reported first becoming victims of sexual assault was 13 and the median age at which they were first shot or stabbed was 14. Thirteen was the age at which girls were most likely to report becoming sexually active and 14 was the median age at which they delivered their first child. In terms of risky behaviors, girls were most likely to begin using alcohol and other drugs, experience their first suspension or expulsion from school, run away from home, and not surprisingly, experience their first arrest at ages 13 and 14. All these events generally occur in communities in which virtually all institutions—families, schools, and public agencies, including juvenile justice—are failing girls. . . .

References

Acoca, L., and Austin, J. 1996. *The Hidden Crisis: The Women Offenders Sentencing Study and Alternative Sentencing Recommendations Project*. San Francisco, CA: National Council on Crime and Delinquency.

Acoca, L., and Dedel, K. 1998. *No Place to Hide: Understanding and Meeting the Needs of Girls in the California Juvenile Justice System*. San Francisco, CA: National Council on Crime and Delinquency.

Belknap, J., and Holsinger, K. 1998. An overview of delinquent girls: How theory and practice failed and the need for innovative changes. In *Female Offenders: Critical Perspectives and Effective Interventions*, edited by R.T. Zaplin. Gaithersburg, MD: Aspen Publishers.

Chesney-Lind, M., and Shelden, R.G. 1998. *Girls, Delinquency, and Juvenile Justice*. Belmont, CA: West/Wadsworth.

Covington, S. 1998. The relational theory of women's psychological development: Implications for the criminal justice system. In *Female Offenders: Critical Perspectives and Effective Interventions*, edited by R.T. Zaplin. Gaithersburg, MD: Aspen Publishers.

Drug Strategies. 1998. *Keeping Score, Women and Drugs: Looking at the Federal Drug Control Budget*. Washington, DC: Drug Strategies.

Mauer, M., and Huling, T. 1995. *Young Black Americans and the Criminal Justice System: Five Years Later*. Washington, DC: The Sentencing Project.

Sickmund, M. 1997. *Offenders in Juvenile Court, 1995*. Bulletin. Washington, DC: U.S. Department of Justice, Office of Justice Programs, Office of Juvenile Justice and Delinquency Prevention.

Snyder, H.K. In press. *Juvenile Arrests 1998*. Bulletin. Washington, DC: U.S. Department of Justice, Office of Justice Programs, Office of Juvenile Justice and Delinquency Prevention. ✦

Part X

Juvenile Justice in the Future

An issue that has repeatedly appeared throughout this book is whether juvenile justice in general, and the juvenile court in particular, will survive. The question first appeared in Chapter 1, which discussed the many ways in which the "get tough" movement has transformed juvenile justice. One of the conclusions of Chapter 9 was that juveniles were being transferred out of the juvenile court in two directions. Less serious offenders were being transferred to new specialized courts such as the teen courts, which then were explored in Chapter 10. More serious offenders were being transferred to the criminal courts, as discussed in Chapters 11 and 12.

The two chapters in this final part of the book take very different approaches to the future of juvenile justice. The first chapter argues that the trends toward the criminal court should continue, and that the juvenile justice system essentially should be eliminated. The second chapter argues that juvenile justice is presently being "re-invented" from within, as practitioners within the system return to the original ideals of the court despite the overwhelming rhetoric of opposition from politicians. ✦

Chapter 19

The Honest Politician's Guide to Juvenile Justice in the Twenty-First Century

Barry C. Feld

Editor's Introduction

Chapter 19 recommends that the trend toward the criminalization of the juvenile court be taken to its logical conclusion and that the juvenile court be eliminated. The chapter argues that the fundamental flaw in the original juvenile court is that it attempts to combine social welfare with criminal justice, and that this combination is fundamentally untenable. It recommends instead a return to the basic situation that existed prior to the founding of the juvenile court in 1899—youth are tried in the same courts as adults, but receive less punishment for similar offenses. Mitigation would not be discretionary but would result from a formula for a "youth discount" contained in sentencing guidelines. This discount would be larger for younger juveniles and smaller for older juveniles—"a 14-year-old offender might receive, for example, 25–33 percent of the adult penalty; a 16-year-old defendant, 50–66 percent; and an 18-year-old adult, the full penalty."

✦ ✦ ✦

In this article, I briefly describe the transformation of the juvenile court from a social welfare agency into a deficient criminal court. Second, I argue that juvenile courts' underlying idea is fundamentally flawed because in it the courts attempt to combine social welfare and

Adapted from Barry C. Feld, "The Honest Politician's Guide to Juvenile Justice," *The Annals of the American Academy of Political and Social Sciences* 564:10–27, copyright © 1999 by Sage Publications, Inc. Reprinted by permission of Sage Publications, Inc.

penal social control in one agency. Because welfare and control functions embody inherent and irreconcilable contradictions, juvenile courts inevitably do both badly. If a state separates social welfare goals from criminal social control functions, then no need remains for a separate juvenile court. Rather, a state could try all offenders in one integrated criminal justice system. But children do not possess the same degree of criminal responsibility as adults. Adolescent developmental psychology, criminal law jurisprudence, and sentencing policy provide a rationale to formally recognize youthfulness as a mitigating factor when judges sentence younger offenders. A "youth discount" provides a sliding scale of criminal responsibility for younger offenders who have not quite learned to be responsible or developed fully their capacity for self-control. Combining enhanced procedural safeguards with formal mitigation of sentences provides youths with greater protections and justice than they currently receive in either the juvenile or criminal justice systems. . . .

The Inherent Contradictions of the Juvenile Court

Juvenile courts punish rather than treat young offenders and use a procedural regime under which no adult would consent to be tried. The fundamental shortcoming of the juvenile court's welfare idea reflects a failure of conception and not simply a century-long failure of implementation. The juvenile court's creators envisioned a social service agency in a judicial setting and attempted to fuse its welfare mission with the power of state coercion. Combining social welfare and penal social control functions in one agency ensures that juvenile courts do both badly. Providing for child welfare represents a societal responsibility rather than a judicial one. Juvenile courts lack control over the resources necessary to meet child welfare needs exactly because of the social class and racial characteristics of their clients and because of the public's fear of "other people's children." In practice, juvenile courts almost inevitably subordinate welfare concerns to crime control considerations.

If we formulated child welfare programs ab initio, would we choose a juvenile court as the most appropriate agency through which to deliver social services, and would we make criminality a condition precedent to the receipt of services? If we would not initially choose a court to deliver social services, then does the fact of a youth's criminality confer upon the court any special competency as a welfare agency? Many young people who do not commit crimes desperately need social services, and many youths who commit crimes do not require or will not respond to social services. In short, criminality represents an inaccurate and haphazard criterion upon which to allocate social services. Because our society denies adequate help and assistance to meet the social welfare needs of all young people, juvenile courts' treatment ideology serves primarily to legitimate judicial coercion of some youths because of their criminality.

The attempt to combine social welfare and criminal social control in one agency constitutes the fundamental flaw of the juvenile court. The juvenile court subordinates social welfare concerns to criminal social control functions because of its inherently penal focus. Legislatures do not define juvenile courts' jurisdiction on the basis of characteristics of children for which the children are not responsible and for which effective intervention could improve their lives. For example, juvenile court law does not define eligibility for welfare services or create an enforceable right or entitlement based upon young people's lack of access to quality education, lack of adequate housing or nutrition, unmet health needs, or impoverished families—none of which are their fault. In all of these instances, children bear the burdens of their parents' circumstances literally as innocent bystanders. Instead, states' juvenile codes define juvenile court jurisdiction based upon a youth's committing a crime, a prerequisite that detracts from a compassionate response. Unlike disadvantaged social conditions that are not their fault, criminal behavior represents the one characteristic for which adolescent offenders do bear at least partial responsibility. In short, juvenile courts define eligibility for services on the basis of the feature least likely to elicit sympathy and compassion, and they ignore the social structural conditions or personal circumstances more likely to evoke a greater desire to help. Juvenile courts' defining characteristic strengthens public antipathy to "other people's children" by emphasizing primarily that they are law violators. The recent criminological triage policies that stress punishment, accountability, and personal responsibility further reinforce juvenile courts' penal foundations and reduce the legitimacy of youths' claims to humanitarian assistance.

The Kid Is a Criminal, and the Criminal Is a Kid

States should uncouple social welfare from social control, try all offenders in one integrated criminal justice system, and make appropriate substantive and procedural modifications to accommodate the youthfulness of some defendants. Substantive justice requires a rationale to sentence younger offenders differently from and more leniently than older defendants, a formal recognition of youthfulness as a mitigating factor. Procedural justice requires providing youths with full procedural parity with adult defendants and additional safeguards to account for the disadvantage of youth in the justice system. These substantive and procedural modifications can avoid the worst of both worlds, provide youths with protections functionally equivalent to those accorded adults, and do justice in sentencing.

My proposal to abolish juvenile courts constitutes neither an unqualified endorsement of punishment nor a primitive throwback to earlier centuries' vision of children as miniature adults. Rather, it honestly acknowledges that juvenile courts currently engage in criminal social control, asserts that younger offenders in a criminal justice system deserve less severe penalties for their misdeeds than do more mature offenders simply because they are young, and addresses many problems created by trying to maintain dichotomous and contradictory criminal justice systems based on an arbitrary age classification of a youth as a child or as an adult (Feld 1997).

Formulating a sentencing policy when the kid is a criminal and the criminal is a kid entails two tasks. First, I will provide a rationale for sentencing younger offenders differently from and more leniently than adult offenders. Explicitly punishing younger offenders rests on the premise that adolescents possess sufficient moral reasoning, cognitive capacity, and volitional control to hold them partially responsible for their behavior, albeit not to the same degree as adults. Developmental psychological research, jurisprudence, and criminal sentencing policy provide the rationale for why young offenders deserve less severe consequences for their misdeeds than do older offenders and justify formal recognition of youthfulness as a mitigating factor. Second, I will propose a youth discount—shorter sentences for reduced responsibility—as a practical administrative mechanism to implement youthfulness as a mitigating factor in sentencing.

The idea of deserved punishment entails censure and condemnation for making blameworthy choices and imposes sanctions proportional to the seriousness of a crime (von Hirsch 1976, 1993). Two elements—harm and culpability—define the seriousness of a crime. A perpetrator's age has relatively little bearing on assessments of harm—the nature of the injury inflicted, risk created, or value taken. But evaluations of seriousness also entail the quality of the actor's choice to engage in the criminal conduct that produced the harm. Youthfulness is a very important factor with respect to the culpability of a criminal actor because it directly affects the quality of choices. Responsibility for choices hinges on cognitive and volitional competence. Youths differ socially, physically, and psychologically from adults: they have not yet fully internalized moral norms, developed sufficient empathic identification with others, acquired adequate moral comprehension, or had sufficient opportunity to develop the ability to restrain their actions. They possess neither the rationality (cognitive capacity) nor the self-control (volitional capacity) for their criminal responsibility to be equated fully with that of adults. In short, their immaturity affects the quality of their judgments in ways that are relevant to criminal sentencing policy. Ultimately, a youth sentencing policy should enable young offenders to survive the mistakes of adolescence with their life chances intact.

Adolescence as a Form of Reduced Culpability

Certain characteristic developmental differences distinguish the quality of decisions that young people make from the quality of decisions by adults, and justify a somewhat more protective stance when states sentence younger offenders. Psychosocial maturity, judgment, and temperance provide conceptual prisms through which to view adolescents' decision-making competencies and to assess the quality of their choices (Cauffman and Steinberg 1995; Steinberg and Cauffman 1996; Scott 1992; Scott and Grisso 1997). Adolescents and adults differ in the quality of judgment and self-control they exercise because of relative differences in breadth of experience, short-term versus long-term temporal perspectives, attitudes toward risk, impulsivity, and the importance they attach to peer influences. These developmentally unique attributes affect youths' degree of criminal responsibility. Young people are more impulsive, exercise less self-control, fail adequately to calculate long-term consequences, and engage in more risky behavior than do adults. Adolescents may estimate the magnitude or probability of risks, may use a shorter time frame, or may focus on opportunities for gains rather than possibilities of losses differently from adults (Furby and Beyth-Marom 1992). Young people may discount the negative value of future consequences because they have more difficulty than adults in integrating a future consequence into their more limited experiential baseline (Gardner and Herman 1990). Adolescents' judgments may differ from those of adults because of their disposition toward sensation seeking, impulsivity related to hormonal or physiological changes, and mood volatility (Steinberg and Cauffman 1996; Cauffman and Steinberg 1995). Adolescents respond to peer group influences more readily than do adults because of the crucial role that peer relationships play in identity formation (Scott 1992; Zimring 1981). Most adolescent crime occurs in a group context, and having delinquent friends precedes an adolescent's own criminal involvement (Elliott and Menard 1996). Group offending places normally law-abiding youths at greater risk of involvement and reduces their ability publicly to withdraw. Because of the social context of adolescent crime, young people require time, experience, and opportunities to develop the capacity for autonomous judgments and to resist peer influence.

Developmental processes affect adolescents' quality of judgment and self-control, directly influence their degree of criminal responsibility and deserved punishment, and justify a different criminal sentencing policy. While young offenders possess sufficient understanding and culpability to hold them accountable for their acts, their crimes are less blameworthy than adults' because of reduced culpability and limited appreciation of consequences and also because their life circumstances understandably limit their capacity to learn to make fully responsible choices.

When youths offend, the families, schools, and communities that socialize them bear some responsibility for the failures of those socializing institutions. Human beings depend upon others to nurture them and to enable them to develop and exercise the moral capacity for constructive behavior. The capacity for self-control and self-direction is not simply a matter of moral luck or good fortune but a socially constructed developmental process that provides young people with the opportunity to develop a moral character. Community structures affect social conditions and the contexts within which adolescents grow and interact with peers. Unlike presumptively mobile adults, juveniles, because of their dependency, lack the means or ability to escape from their criminogenic environments.

Zimring (1982) describes the "semi-autonomy" of adolescence as a "learner's permit" that gives youths the opportunity to make choices and to learn to be responsible but without suffering fully the long-term consequences of their mistakes. The ability to make responsible choices is learned, and the dependent status of youth systematically deprives adolescents of chances to learn to be responsible. Young people's socially constructed life situation understandably limits their capacity to develop self-control, restricts their opportunities to learn and exercise responsibility, and supports a partial reduction of criminal responsibility. A youth sentencing policy would entail both shorter sentences and a higher offense-seriousness threshold before a state incarcerates youths than for older offenders.

Youth Discount

The binary distinctions between children and adults that provide the basis for states' legal age of majority and the jurisprudential foundation of the juvenile court ignore the reality that adolescents develop along a continuum, and create an unfortunate either-or forced choice in sentencing. By contrast, shorter sentences for reduced responsibility represent a more modest and readily attainable reason to treat young offenders differently from adults than the rehabilitative justifications advanced by Progressive child savers. Protecting young people from the full penal consequences of their poor decisions reflects a policy to preserve their life chances for the future, when they presumably will make more mature and responsible choices. Such a policy both holds young offenders accountable for their acts because they possess sufficient culpability and mitigates the severity of consequences because their choices entail less blame than those of adults.

Sentencing policy that integrates youthfulness, reduced culpability, and restricted opportunities to learn self-control with penal principles of proportionality would provide younger offenders with categorical fractional reductions of adult sentences. If adolescents as a class characteristically make poorer choices than adults, then sentencing policies should protect young people from the full penal consequences of their bad decisions. Because youthfulness constitutes a universal form of reduced culpability or diminished responsibility, states should treat it categorically as a mitigating factor, without regard to nuances of individual developmental differences. Youth development is a highly variable process, and chronological age is a crude, imprecise measure of criminal maturity and the opportunity to develop the capacity for self-control. Despite the variability of adolescence, however, a categorical youth discount that uses age as a conclusive proxy for reduced culpability and shorter sentences remains preferable to any individualized inquiry into the criminal responsibility of each young offender. Developmental psychology does not possess reliable clinical indicators of moral development that equate readily with criminal responsibility and accountability. For young criminal actors who are responsible, to some degree, clinical testimony to precisely tailor sanctions to culpability is not worth the burden or diversion of resources that the effort would entail. Because youthful mitigated criminal responsibility is a legal concept, there simply is no psychiatric analogue to which clinical testimony would correspond. Rather, a youth discount categorically recognizes that criminal choices by young people are to some degree qualitatively different from those of adults and constitute a form of partial responsibility without any additional clinical indicators.

This categorical approach would take the form of an explicit youth discount at sentencing, a sliding scale of criminal responsibility. A 14-year-old offender might receive, for example, 25–33 percent of the adult penalty; a 16-year-old defendant, 50–66 percent; and an 18-year-old adult, the full penalty, as currently occurs (Feld 1997). The deeper discounts for younger offenders correspond to the developmental continuum and their more limited opportunities to learn to be responsible and to exercise self-control. Because reduced culpability provides the rationale for youthful mitigation, younger adolescents bear less responsibility and deserve proportionally shorter sentences than older youths. With the passage of time, increased age, and more

numerous opportunities to develop the capacity for self-control, social tolerance of criminal deviance and claims for youthful mitigation
decline. Discounted sentences that preserve younger offenders' life
chances require that the maximum sentences they receive remain
very substantially lower than those imposed on adults. Capital sentences and draconian mandatory minimum sentences—for example,
life without parole—have no place in sentencing presumptively less
blameworthy adolescents. Because of the rapidity of adolescent development and the life-course-disruptive consequences of incarceration, the rationale for a youth discount also supports requiring a
higher in/out threshold of offense seriousness and culpability as a
prerequisite for imprisonment.

Only states whose criminal sentencing laws provide realistic, hu-
mane, and determinate sentences that enable a judge actually to determine real-time sentences can readily implement a proposal for
explicit fractional reductions of youths' sentences. One can know the
value of a youth discount only in a sentencing system in which courts
know in advance the standard, or going rate, for adults. In many jurisdictions, implementing a youth discount would require significant
modification of the current sentencing laws, including adoption of
presumptive sentencing guidelines with strong upper limits on punishment severity, elimination of all mandatory minimum sentences,
and introduction of some structured judicial discretion to mitigate
penalties based on individual circumstances. Attempts to apply youth
discounts idiosyncratically within the flawed indeterminate or
mandatory-minimum sentencing regimes that currently prevail in
many jurisdictions runs the risk of simply reproducing all of their ex-
isting inequalities and injustices.

Virtues of an Integrated Criminal Justice System

A graduated age-culpability sentencing scheme in an integrated
criminal justice system avoids the inconsistencies associated with the
binary either-juvenile-or-adult drama currently played out in judicial
waiver proceedings and in prosecutorial charging decisions, and it in-
troduces proportionality to the sentences imposed on the many
youths currently tried as adults. It also avoids the punishment gap
when youths make the transition from one justice system to the other,
and it ensures similar consequences for similarly situated offenders.
Adolescence and criminal careers develop along a continuum; the
current bifurcation between the two justice systems confounds efforts to respond consistently to young career offenders. A sliding
scale of criminal sentences based on an offender's age as a proxy
for culpability accomplishes simply and directly what the various

blended jurisdiction statutes attempt to achieve indirectly (Feld 1995). A formal policy of youthfulness as a mitigating factor avoids the undesirable forced choice between inflicting undeservedly harsh penalties on less culpable actors and doing nothing about the manifestly guilty.

An integrated justice system also allows for integrated record keeping and enables officials to identify and respond to career offenders more readily than the current jurisdictional bifurcation permits. Even adolescent career offenders deserve enhanced sentences based on an extensive record of prior offending. But an integrated justice system does not require integrated prisons. The question of how long differs from questions of where and what. States should maintain age-segregated youth correctional facilities both to protect younger offenders from adults and to protect geriatric prisoners from younger inmates. Virtually all young offenders will return to society, and the state should provide them with resources for self-improvement because of its basic responsibility to its citizens and its own self-interest. A sentencing and correctional policy must offer youths room to reform and provide opportunities and resources to facilitate young offenders' constructive use of their time.

Finally, affirming partial responsibility for youth constitutes a virtue. The idea of personal responsibility and accountability for behavior provides an important cultural counterweight to a popular culture that endorses the idea that everyone is a victim, that all behavior is determined, and that no one is responsible. The juvenile court elevated determinism over free will, characterized delinquents as victims rather than perpetrators, and subjected them to an indeterminate quasi-civil commitment process. The juvenile court's treatment ideology denied youths' personal responsibility, reduced offenders' duty to exercise self-control, and eroded their obligations to change. If there is any silver lining in the current cloud of get-tough policies, it is the affirmation of responsibility. A culture that values autonomous individuals must emphasize both freedom and responsibility. A criminal law that bases sentences on blameworthiness and responsibility must recognize the physical, psychological, and socially constructed differences between youths and adults. Affirming responsibility forces politicians to be honest when the kid is a criminal and the criminal is a kid. The real reason states bring young offenders to juvenile courts is not to deliver social services but because the offenders committed a crime. Once politicians recognize that simple truth, then justice can follow.

References

Cauffman, Elizabeth and Laurence Steinberg. 1995. The Cognitive and Affective Influences on Adolescent Decision-Making. *Temple Law Review* 68:1763–89.

Elliott, Delbert and Scott Menard. 1996. Delinquent Friends and Delinquent Behavior: Temporal and Developmental Patterns. In *Delinquency and Crime: Current Theories,* ed. J. David Hawkins. New York: Cambridge University Press.

Feld, Barry C. 1995. Violent Youth and Public Policy: A Case Study of Juvenile Justice Law Reform. *Minnesota Law Review* 79:965–1128.

———. 1997. Abolish the Juvenile Court: Youthfulness, Criminal Responsibility, and Sentencing Policy. *Journal of Criminal Law & Criminology* 88:68–136.

Furby, Lita and Ruth Beyth-Marom. 1992. Risk Taking in Adolescence: A Decision-Making Perspective. *Developmental Review* 12:1–44.

Gardner, William and Janna Herman. 1990. Adolescents' AIDS Risk Taking: A Rational Choice Perspective. In *Adolescents and the AIDS Epidemic,* ed. William Gardner, Susan G. Millstein, and Bruce Leroy Cox. San Francisco: Jossey-Bass.

Scott, Elizabeth S. 1992. Judgment and Reasoning in Adolescent Decision Making. *Villanova Law Review* 37:1607–69.

Scott, Elizabeth S. and Thomas Grisso. 1997. The Evolution of Adolescence: A Developmental Perspective on Juvenile Justice Reform. *Journal of Criminal Law & Criminology* 88:137–89.

Steinberg, Laurence and Elizabeth Cauffman. 1996. Maturity of Judgment in Adolescence: Psychosocial Factors in Adolescent Decision Making. *Law and Human Behavior* 20:249–72.

von Hirsch, Andrew. 1976. *Doing Justice.* New York: Hill & Wang.

———. 1993. *Censure and Blame.* New York: Oxford University Press.

Zimring, Franklin. 1981. Kids, Groups and Crime: Some Implications of a Well-Known Secret. *Journal of Criminal Law & Criminology* 72:867–902.

———. 1982. *The Changing Legal World of Adolescence.* New York: Free Press. ✦

Chapter 20

Reviving Juvenile Justice in a Get-Tough Era

Jeffrey A. Butts and Daniel P. Mears

Editor's Introduction

Chapter 19 argued that the recent trends in juvenile justice should be extended to the point where the juvenile court itself is abolished. This recommendation more or less is based on an assumption that the original purpose of the juvenile court—reducing delinquency by treating its causes—simply cannot be achieved.

Chapter 20 takes a very different point of view. It recognizes the obvious legal and political changes that have transformed the juvenile court and made it much more similar to the adult court, but it also argues that a variety of other, less obvious changes have also been occurring. These changes are not very visible in the political and public arena, but they are much more integrated with the actual juvenile justice system as it functions on a day-to-day basis.

To a considerable extent, these changes originated with judges, attorneys, probation officers, and other professionals within juvenile justice systems across the country. To a considerable extent, these changes were based on evaluation research that provided solid information about how to reduce delinquency.

Basically, this chapter argues that juvenile justice is being transformed from within. It is being "reinvented" in a sense, but that the reinvention is a return to the original ideals of the juvenile court: individualized treatment in order to reduce youthful offending. The difference is that now, because of solid evaluation research such as that described in Part VIII, the original ideal of the juvenile court can actually be achieved.

The authors conclude: "These lesser known innovations, supported by the findings of evaluative research, helped to revive the juvenile justice system in the face of withering attacks from the political arena."

✦ ✦ ✦

Transforming Juvenile Justice

Public discussions about juvenile justice usually focus on the big issues, such as the legal ethics of criminal court transfer, the value of punishment versus rehabilitation, and the relative effectiveness of prevention. Although elected officials and the general public concentrated on these issues during recent decades, there was another, vitally important area of policy and program development undertaken by professionals inside the juvenile justice system. In many areas of the country, judges, attorneys, probation workers, and others were transforming the administration and organization of juvenile justice. These changes show great promise for creating more effective approaches to addressing juvenile crime.

For example, many parts of the juvenile justice system have begun to adopt the framework of *community justice* or *problem-solving* justice. Drawing on various program innovations, including community crime prevention, community policing, community prosecution, and community courts, the concept of community justice refocuses the nature of justice system intervention (see e.g., Connor, 2000; Karp & Clear, 2000; Rottman & Casey, 1999). Rather than simply identifying offenders, weighing the evidence against them, and imposing punishment, the community justice perspective calls on all actors in the justice system to use the processes of investigation, arrest, prosecution, and sentencing to solve problems in the community. Each incident of criminal behavior is viewed within the context of the community in which it occurs, and professionals within the justice system work to develop relationships with community leaders and other residents to understand why crime happens and to prevent future occurrences.

A community justice perspective shifts the focus of the justice system to the well-being of the entire community, and the community becomes the client for all crime-fighting agencies. Within juvenile justice, this shift in focus was suggested by the Office of Juvenile Justice and Delinquency Prevention's *Comprehensive Strategy for Serious, Violent, and Chronic Juvenile Offenders* (Wilson & Howell, 1993) and the Coordinating Council on Juvenile Justice and Delinquency Prevention's (1996) *National Juvenile Justice Action Plan*, both of which feature prominent emphases on community-based initiatives.

Another equally important shift in juvenile justice thinking is the growing emphasis on *restorative justice*. Restorative justice is an alternative framework for justice system intervention, replacing or at least counterbalancing retributive justice. Whereas retributive justice ensures that each offender suffers a punishment in proportion to the harm inflicted on the victim of the offense, restorative justice provides a means for each offender to restore that harm or at least to compensate the victim even if the victim is only the general community. There are several programs and interventions that could be called part of the restorative justice movement, but the most popular are victim-offender mediation and family group conferencing. The number of these programs increased sharply during the 1990s, and research suggests that they may offer an effective alternative to traditional court processing, especially for young offenders (Bazemore & Umbreit, 1995, 2001; McGarrell, Olivares, Crawford, & Kroovand, 2000).

Courts themselves are also being reinvented by the juvenile justice system. Many jurisdictions recently began to experiment with specialized courts for young offenders, especially teen courts and juvenile drug courts. The number of teen courts across the country increased from a few dozen programs in the 1970s to more than 600 by the end of the 1990s (Butts & Buck, 2000). In some jurisdictions, such as Anchorage, Alaska, teen courts are beginning to shoulder a majority of law enforcement referrals involving first-time delinquent offenders charged with relatively minor offenses, and early evaluations on these programs are beginning to show promise.

In addition to new program models, many states are implementing the graduated sanctioning approach (Howell, 1995; Torbet et al., 1996). Grounded in both research and common sense, graduated sanctioning ensures that there is at least some response to each instance of illegal behavior as juveniles begin to violate the law. In jurisdictions that embrace graduated sanctioning, there is a full continuum of sanctions available for responding to young offenders, including immediate sanctions for first-time offenders, intermediate and community-based sanctions for more serious offenders, and secure/residential placement for those youth who commit especially serious or violent offenses. Such approaches have the ability to introduce a greater degree of consistency in how youth within and across jurisdictions are sanctioned. More importantly, they can promote balanced and restorative sanctioning that includes victims, families, and communities; relies on the demonstrated effectiveness of rehabilitation and treatment; and emphasizes responsiveness, accountability, and responsibility as cornerstones of an effective juvenile justice system. (For more discussion of restorative justice concepts, see the articles by Bazemore, 2001, Braithwaite, 2001, and Karp & Breslin, 2001.)

Many jurisdictions are also discovering the importance of providing better and earlier screening and assessment of youth to identify those with special needs and to provide appropriate and timely interventions (Cocozza & Skowyra, 2000; Crowe, 1998; Rivers & Anwyl, 2000). Juvenile Assessment Centers (JACs), for example, are an emerging approach. JACs provide centralized, systematic, and consistent assessment of youth referred to the juvenile justice system. The underlying goal of a JAC is to provide an empirical basis for decision making for young offenders (Rivers & Anwyl, 2000). Potential benefits of the JAC model include the ability to identify and eliminate gaps and redundancies in services, better integration of case management, improved communication among agencies, greater awareness of youth needs, more appropriate interventions, and ultimately, improved outcomes for youth (Oldenettel & Wordes, 2000).

The lack of coordination and collaboration among service agencies is one of the most potent barriers to effectively preventing and reducing juvenile crime (Cocozza & Skowyra, 2000; Howell, 1995; Lipsey, 1999; Lipsey & Wilson, 1998; Rivers, Dembo, & Anwyl, 1998; Slayton, 2000). Traditionally, human services agencies were established to provide specific programs (substance use/abuse intervention, sex offender treatment, education, mental health, etc.), and each agency worked individually with its own particular client population. The result was often inefficient and ineffective interventions, and jurisdictions found it difficult to identify and work with youth who presented co-occurring disorders involving mental health problems, family problems, substance abuse, educational deficits, and other social problems (Peters & Bartoi, 1997; Peters & Hills, 1997). In response, many states have made intra- and interagency collaboration a priority in recent years (National Criminal Justice Association, 1997; Rivers & Anwyl, 2000).

Finally, in recent years, jurisdictions across the country began to recognize the need for greater investments in long-term planning as well as research and evaluation of their policies and programs (Danegger, Cohen, Hayes, & Holden, 1999). Research and evaluation in juvenile justice has been difficult in the past due to the lack of quality data. During the 1980s and 1990s, however, many states worked to enhance their data collection and analysis capacity as well as their ability to share information across agency boundaries (National Criminal Justice Association, 1997; Torbet et al., 1996). Confidentiality and privacy issues have required agencies to move carefully in this area, but the juvenile justice system has gained much from the increased availability of reliable and valid data for monitoring program operations and evaluating interventions. With sound, reliable data, agencies can assess whether a particular policy, such as a change in sentencing, has been implemented consistently (Mears, 1998). They are also more likely to identify any unintended consequences that could offset the potential benefits of a new policy (National Criminal Justice Association, 1997). With good information, agencies are beginning to finally be able to answer those all-important questions: "What works, when, and for whom?"

Conclusion

Juvenile justice policy received much attention during the 1980s and 1990s. Policy makers implemented a range of new programs designed to make the system tougher. Even as the rate of juvenile violence dropped from 1994 through 2000, policy makers continued to demand that young offenders be transferred more often to adult courts and treated with more harshness by juvenile courts. Researchers investigated the effects of these changes but were unable to detect any clear benefits. The broader use of criminal court transfer, for example, did not appear to increase public safety significantly either in terms of individual behavior by affected juveniles or in the overall rate of juvenile crime.

While the critics of juvenile justice were focusing on criminal court transfer, professionals within the juvenile justice system continued working to develop new program models and intervention strategies. Juvenile justice practitioners improved the quality and scope of prevention, broadened the range of treatment techniques for juveniles, and enhanced the community orientation of the juvenile justice system. In the past 20 years, state and local agencies have produced a steady stream of new ideas in substance abuse treatment, family-focused interventions, and community-wide crime prevention. These lesser known innovations, supported by the findings of evaluative research, helped to revive the juvenile justice system in the face of withering attacks from the political arena.

For the juvenile system to survive another century, policy makers, practitioners, and researchers will need to work together to focus on what works and to avoid polarizing debates that result in symbolic and ineffective policies. It is tempting for each new generation of policy makers to look for a silver-bullet solution to juvenile crime, but it is highly unlikely that such a strategy will generate lasting rewards. The public will benefit far more from a juvenile justice system that focuses on broad prevention efforts, early intervention with young offenders, proven rehabilitation programs, and meticulous administration. An effective system would rely on community- and restorative-based models of justice as well as greater collaboration and communication among child welfare, social service, and justice agencies. Effective juvenile justice policy will always include the use of incarceration, but lawmakers must realize that beyond the immediate benefits of incapacitation, getting tough on juvenile offenders has limited long-term value for crime prevention and public safety. Ultimately, responsible juvenile justice policy comes from being clear about who or what is the target of each intervention, focusing first on the conditions that are most susceptible to change and least costly to change, carefully implementing and monitoring interventions, and continually evaluating whether each intervention actually works. A juvenile justice system in this mold would be more efficient and effective. It would embody the principles envisioned by the founders of the juvenile court and be consistent with the theoretical foundations of community and restorative justice.

References

Bazemore, G. (2001). Young people, trouble, and crime: Restorative justice as a normative theory of informal social control and social support. *Youth & Society*, 33, 199–226.

Bazemore, G., & Umbreit, M. (1995). Rethinking the sanctioning function in juvenile court: Retributive or restorative responses to youth crime. *Crime and Delinquency*, 41, 296–316.

———. (2001). A comparison of four restorative conferencing models (Juvenile Justice Bulletin NCJ 184738). Washington, DC: Department of Justice, Office of Juvenile Justice and Delinquency Prevention.

Braithwaite, J. (2001). Restorative justice and a new criminal law of substance abuse. *Youth & Society*, 33, 227–248.

Butts, J. A., & Buck, J. (2000). *Teen courts: Focus on research* [Juvenile justice bulletin]. Washington, DC: Department of Justice, Office of Juvenile Justice and Delinquency Prevention.

Cocozza, J. J., & Skowyra, K. (2000). Youth with mental health disorders: Issues and emerging responses. *Juvenile Justice*, 7, 3–13.

Connor, R. (2000, January). Community oriented lawyering: An emerging approach to legal practice. *National Institute of Justice Journal*, 26–33.

Coordinating Council on Juvenile Justice and Delinquency Prevention. (1996). *Combating violence and delinquency: The national juvenile justice action plan*. Washington, DC: Department of Justice, Office of Juvenile Justice and Delinquency Prevention.

Crowe, A. H. (1998). *Drug identification and testing in the juvenile justice system*. Washington, DC: Department of Justice, Office of Juvenile Justice and Delinquency Prevention.

Danegger, A. E., Cohen, C. E., Hayes, C. D., & Holden, G. D. (1999). *Juvenile accountability incentive block grants: Strategic planning guide*. Washington, DC: Department of Justice, Office of Juvenile Justice and Delinquency Prevention.

Howell, J. C. (1995). *Guide for implementing the comprehensive strategy for serious, violent, and chronic juvenile offenders*. Washington, DC: Department of Justice, Office of Juvenile Justice and Delinquency Prevention.

Karp, D. R., & Breslin, B. (2001). Restorative justice in school communities. *Youth & Society*, 33, 249–272.

Karp, D. R., & Clear, T. R. (2000). Community justice: A conceptual framework. In C. M. Friel (Ed.), *Criminal justice 2000, Vol. 2: Boundary changes in criminal justice organizations* (pp. 323–368). Washington, DC: Department of Justice, National Institute of Justice.

Lipsey, M.W. (1999). Can intervention rehabilitate serious delinquents? *Annals*, 564, 142–166.

Lipsey, M.W., & Wilson, D. B. (1998). Effective interventions for serious juvenile offenders: A synthesis of research. In R. Loeber & D. P. Farrington (Eds.), *Serious and violent juvenile offenders: Risk factors and successful interventions* (pp. 313–345). Thousand Oaks, CA: Sage.

McGarrell, E. F., Olivares, K., Crawford, K., & Kroovand, N. (2000). *Returning justice to the community: The Indianapolis juvenile restorative justice experiment.* Indianapolis, IN: Hudson Institute.

Mears, D. P. (1998). Evaluation issues confronting juvenile justice sentencing reforms: A case study of Texas. *Crime and Delinquency*, 44, 443–463.

National Criminal Justice Association. (1997). *Juvenile justice reform initiatives in the states: 1994–1996.* Washington, DC: Department of Justice, Office of Juvenile Justice and Delinquency Prevention.

Oldenettel, D., & Wordes, M. (2000). *The community assessment center concept.* Washington, DC: Department of Justice, Office of Juvenile Justice and Delinquency Prevention.

Peters, R. H., & Bartoi, M. G. (1997). *Screening and assessment of co-occurring disorders in the justice system.* Delmar, NY: GAINS Center.

Peters, R. H., & Hills, H. A. (1997). *Intervention strategies for offenders with co-occurring disorders: What works?* Delmar, NY: GAINS Center.

Rivers, J. E., & Anwyl, R. S. (2000). Juvenile Assessment Centers: Strengths, weaknesses, and potential. *The Prison Journal*, 80, 96–113.

Rivers, J. E., Dembo, R., & Anwyl, R. S. (1998). The Hillsborough County, Florida, Juvenile Assessment Center. *The Prison Journal*, 78, 439–450.

Rottman, D., & Casey, P. (1999, July). Therapeutic jurisprudence and the emergence of problem solving courts. *National Institute of Justice Journal*, 12–19.

Slayton, J. (2000). *Establishing and maintaining interagency information sharing.* Washington, DC: Department of Justice, Office of Juvenile Justice and Delinquency Prevention.

Torbet, P., Gable, R., Hurst, H. IV, Montgomery, I., Szymanski, L., & Thomas, D. (1996). *State responses to serious and violent juvenile crime.* Washington, DC: Department of Justice, Office of Juvenile Justice and Delinquency Prevention.

Wilson, J. J., & Howell, J. C. (1993). *Comprehensive strategy for serious, violent, and chronic juvenile offenders: Program summary.* Washington, DC: Department of Justice, Office of Juvenile Justice and Delinquency Prevention. ✦